What For Chop Today?

Gail Haddock

What for Chop Today has been relaunched as Green Oranges on Lion Mountain under the pseudonym Emily Joy - also available as an audiobook

Edited by Joss Guttery
Published by TravellersEye

What For Chop Today?
1st Edition
Published by TravellersEye Ltd 2001

Head Office:
Colemore Farm
Colemore Green
Bridgnorth
Shropshire
WV16 4ST
United Kingdom
tel: (0044) 1746 766447   fax: (0044) 1746 766665
email: books@travellerseye.com   website: www.travellerseye.com

Set in Times
ISBN: 1903070074
Copyright 2001 Gail Haddock

Cover Photograph: 'Plassas' by kind permission of Anne Smith.

Acknowledgments

There are hundreds of people to thank for getting this book into print: the colourful cast of characters for being themselves, plus my friends and family who are probably so sick of hearing about it, that no one will want a copy!

In particular I'd like to thank Von Hondabenda for remaining my friend even after reading the draft, Alan O'Connor, for those long nights in Serabu, discussing convoluted plot lines by candle light (before we realised the truth would be complicated enough) and Pa George for the title.

Back home thanks have to go to my biological Pa George and Terry, my long-suffering husband who has taken his revenge by writing pantomime scripts. Thanks too, to James Westwood for his update on the current situation, plus Maeve Henry, Mary Brown and Hilary Johnson for their advice on early manuscripts. Also, to Sarah Masters, a neighbourly editor who helped me cut the text to publishable length, plus Joss Guttery, my editor at TravellersEye.

Finally big kisses to Craig and Paul, who should see a bit more of their mummy now.

For Eelco, Karin and Zita.

Contents

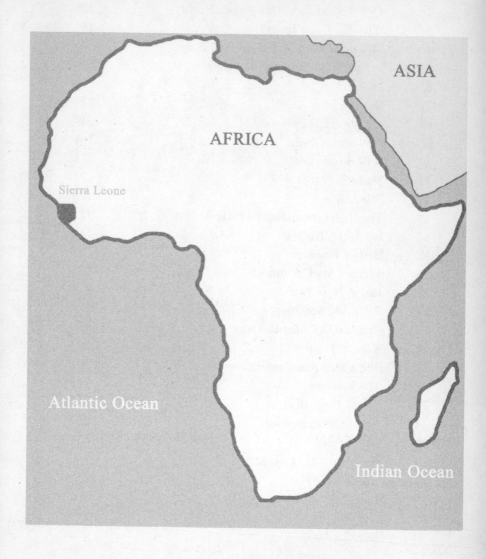

ASIA

AFRICA

Sierra Leone

Atlantic Ocean

Indian Ocean

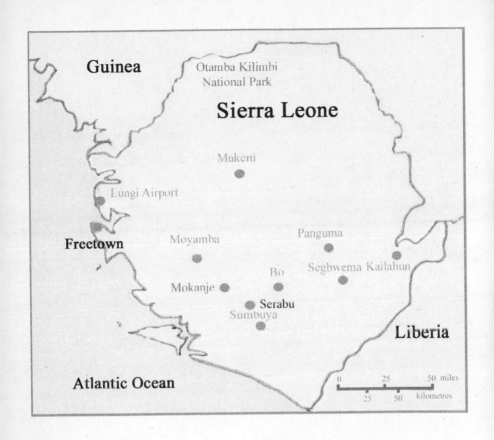

Sierra Leone, West Africa

Dr. Gail Haddock, Scotland

Population: 4 million

Marital Status: Divorced from Britain

Education: 17% literacy

Infant Mortality: 25%

Life expectancy: 42

Age: 27

Marital Status: Single

Education: Edinburgh University, MBChB

Vital statistics: 38-30-38

Life Expectancy: 84

1. Surgery For Non-Surgeons

Midnight, October 2ⁿᵈ: Serabu Hospital

I stared at the Body. It lay slumped against the wall with its head lolling forward and its arms akimbo, palms open to the black sky. Hell! Was this how it was going to be?

The hospital administrator stood by my side, waiting, no doubt, for the new doctor to spring into action. Hell, hell, hell. I took a deep breath.

"Alan." I tugged at the administrator's short sleeve.

"I...I can't." And I couldn't. Alan took a long puff of his cigarette, making the end glow hot orange in the dark. Ashamed, I looked away and focused on a raindrop clinging to the guttering of Medical Ward. Slowly it stretched until it could cling no more, then dropped onto the woolly bonnet that covered the Body's head. Alan puffed again. "Alan," I coughed. "We can't just leave it...him...there."

"Ah, no indeed." Alan stamped on his cigarette. "Stand back doctor. This is a job for an administrator."

"Huh?"

"Shhh!" Alan crept up to the Body and lifted its woolly bonnet to expose an ear. "EMERGENCY!"

"Aaah!" The Body sprang to its feet.

"Aaah!" I echoed, jumping back into a puddle.

"Kushe, kushe." Alan draped his arm round the wiry figure's shoulders. "Is Serabu Hospital's laziest nightwatchman sleeping on duty again?"

"I notto sleep, Mr. Alan," replied the Body.

"Sweet dreams, I hope, Almamy?" Alan pulled a box of matches from his pocket and lit another cigarette. I hung back in the shadows.

"No, Mr. Alan, I notto dream."

"Well if I find you asleep one more time, Almamy, it will be nightmares. Understand? Bad, bad dreams."

"No, no. I notto sleep, Mr. Alan." Almamy shook his head until his woolly bonnet fell off.

"Of course not." Alan picked up the bonnet and brushed it down. "Your hat, Almamy. Better have you looking your best for Dr. Gail." Alan pulled me forward.

"Dr. Gay!" Almamy sandwiched my pale hand in his black vice and crushed it with delight. "Kushe, kushe, Dr. Gay!"

"Aaaah, kushe, Almamy," I gasped. "How di body?" At least I could remember 'Hello, how are you?'

Almamy replied by dropping his trousers to reveal a large scrotal hernia.

"Almamy has been saving his hernia," whispered Alan. "For the new lady doctor."

"I'm sorry," I spluttered, choking back my giggle. "I'm not a surgeon." Unimpressed, Almamy tugged up his trousers, pulled his woolly bonnet back over his eyes and made himself comfortable against the wall.

April, Surgery For Non-Surgeons Course: Birmingham Accident Hospital.

"Lovely knitting, Dr. Haddock." Mr. Bewes was staring at the cat's cradle imprisoning my stubby fingers.

"Er…" I cleared my throat and followed my tutor's gaze to Fiona's beautiful line of knots. Fiona was a friend from medical school days - consistently near the top, compassionate, steady, able, hardworking, serene, professional, and if that wasn't bad enough she was slim, pretty and ever so nice too.

"Well, Dr. Haddock, since your surgical ties are proving so problematic, we must be grateful for the golden rule." Mr. Bewes

10

raised an eyebrow. "The golden rule, Dr. Haddock?"

"Er, yes. Where there's pus, let it out."

"Exactly. I cannot repeat it enough, never, EVER, sew up an infected wound. Especially true in hot climates. The rest is in here." He thumped an enormous volume onto the table. "This is twenty years African experience - everything you need to know from lancing boils to amputating legs." We stared in horror at the book. "Written by my friend and colleague Maurice King," continued Mr. Bewes in the background.

I shuddered. Surely no one would seriously expect me to amputate a leg.

Further insights into the alarming contents of the book were prevented by the timely ringing of the phone. He snatched up the receiver. "Bewes."

"Mr. Bewes, this really is too much!" shrieked an irate female voice. "A man has just delivered a plastic bag to casualty reception. From your butcher."

"Indeed?" Mr. Bewes held the handset at arm's length.

"It's dribbling something unspeakable all over my desk! I insist..."

"We'll be right there," he said, cutting short any further objections. "So," he grinned. "Time for our practical."

Mr. Bewes marched briskly down the corridor, his moccasins making no noise on the shiny white tiles. Fiona, slim and crisply ironed, glided alongside whilst I trudged behind, wondering if Voluntary Service Overseas actually believed that Mr. Bewes could turn us into surgeons in a week.

"I believe you have something for me?" Mr. Bewes beamed at the middle-aged casualty receptionist. She thrust a Marks and Spencer's carrier bag over the counter.

"Much obliged," he purred and turned back to us. "Let's practice our bowel anastomoses!"

Fiona and I exchanged horrified glances. Mr. Bewes was talking about major abdominal surgery. He could not be serious.

"This way class." He held open the swing door opposite. "The plaster room appears to be free."

Once inside Mr. Bewes eagerly untied the handles of the plastic bag letting a tangle of sheep's bowels slither onto a metal tray.

"My butcher is always most co-operative." We gaped at him. "Come, come, no time to lose. Trouble with your gloves, Dr. Haddock?"

Mr. Bewes handed me ten feet of cold intestines just as I was trying to free my middle finger from the index finger-hole. His slimy offering slipped between my glove-tied fingers, sloshing faecal fluid across my newly laundered white coat.

"Hold the ends up you daft girl. Are you trying to give your patient peritonitis?"

Gulping back our nausea, Fiona and I set to work on the sheep's innards, while Mr. Bewes paced behind us. "Let's pretend that the middle foot is dead bowel that you have just released from a strangulated hernia. Smooth away the bowel contents back to healthy tissue. Good. Double clamp either end with...."

There was a knock. A young nurse peered around the door. "Excuse me, Sir, we need the room for a Colles fracture."

"Please nurse, don't mind us."

Sharing the room with a couple of novices and bits of dead sheep was not quite what the nurse had in mind. She cleared her throat. "Mr. Bewes, I really think..."

Mr. Bewes pulled a cotton screen across the room. " We promise to keep very quiet in this half, nurse."

She shuffled her feet, opened her mouth, clamped it shut

again and turned to fetch her patient with an angry flap of swing doors.

"Where was I?" Mr. Bewes rubbed his hands. "Ah yes, once you've finished the first layer, reverse your stitch and close the second layer."

From behind the screen a wheelchair squeaked in. The young nurse was detailing local anaesthetic injections and manipulation of deformed wrist-bones, while an elderly voice trembled. "Oh dear, oh dear."

"Poor old lady," I whispered to Fiona.

"Dr. Haddock, are you concentrating?"

"What? Yes, of course Mr. Bewes." I closed my ears to the apprehensive patient and went back to my embroidery.

Ten minutes later, I knotted off my final stitch. Fiona's intestines were already neatly arranged on the tray.

"So. The moment of truth is upon us." Mr. Bewes declared with relish. "Have you saved your patent's life? Will your anastomosis allow the bowel contents to pass freely without leakage? Undo your clamps!"

We gingerly released the clamps that had held back the intestinal juices from our newly stitched anastomoses.

"Hold up your intestines to test the join. Excellent Dr. MacDougall, absolutely watertight....Oh dear, Dr. Haddock."

Faecal fluid oozed between my stitches and dripped onto the table.

I couldn't do it.

Well honestly, even with Fiona holding my hand, how was I ever going survive in a hospital in the back of beyond for two years? I was obviously no surgeon. Unfortunately my faint-heartedness left Fiona in the lurch as Zambia needed two doctors. VSO finally salved my conscience by fixing Fiona up with an idyllic new job in Papua New Guinea.

In the meantime I returned to verrucas, colds, bad backs and enough marital misery to convince me that being single was probably a blessing.

In fact I turned out to be quite a good GP, but couldn't stop dreaming of the world beyond my cozy backstreet surgery in York. Until one day, after hearing about Mrs. Jones' twenty year headache for the third time that week, followed by a drug addict calling me a fucking cow for not replacing his methadone script that had allegedly been eaten by his dog, I had had enough. I picked up the phone to the VSO Postings Officer. Surprisingly, prior cowardice seemed not to be a barrier to future employment.

"Glad you've rung, we need a doc in Sierra Leone."

Great. South America, how exotic!

My atlas index sent me to page 36 – Africa? And sure enough, there it was - Sierra Leone, a country the size of Ireland on Africa's western bulge, sandwiched between Liberia and Guinea. I had heard of Liberia, thanks to an unpleasant sounding civil war a couple of months back. Hmmm, civil war a hundred miles from my new home didn't sound very good. Still, there'd been no recent media attention and no news was hopefully good news.

The details of Serabu Catholic Mission Hospital fell through my letterbox the next morning along with a four-page resumé of Sierra Leone.

The name came from an intrepid Portuguese seafarer, Pedra da Cinta, who had spotted the mountainous Freetown peninsula jutting out into the Atlantic Ocean in 1460 and called it Serra Lyoa – lion mountain. Over the next few hundred years various Europeans passed through, largely to pick up ivory or slaves. Now, this was all well and good from a European point of view, until the banning of slavery in 1807, when the British government, rather than allowing ex-slaves to mix with polite white society, decided to ship them 'home'. Of course virtually none of them had originally come from Sierra Leone, and most were at least a generation from standing on African soil. Consequently most of the early shipments died, and those that disease spared were killed off by the indigenous Africans.

The British Government refused to give up and tried to mould the survivors with no common language or culture into a homogenous Christian community, known as the Krios. However, the British were only interested in their colony of Krios in Freetown itself, labelling the rest of the country a mere 'protectorate'. I think that meant that the gold, diamonds, rutile (used for white paint and the coverings of space ships), aluminium bauxite, palm oil (used in making the original Palmolive soap) and piassava (used for the bristles in sweeping brushes) were protected for the exploitation of the British, but history is rarely the strong point of we scientific types. Admittedly they did build a few railways, power stations, hospitals and telephone lines, in exchange for removing the aforesaid goods (or in order to remove them more efficiently). And even set up black Africa's first institute of higher learning, Fourah Bay College, to turn the Krios into teachers and missionaries.

By 1961, the British were well on their way to washing their hands of the colonies and handed Sierra Leone over to Sir Milton Margai, a former doctor (should have been a good bloke then). Unfortunately the reins of power were soon seized by one Siakka Stevens.

Siakka Stevens and his Swiss bank account did very nicely. So nicely that there was not a single railway line, power station or upcountry telephone remaining when he retired thirty years later. Nor was there any opposition (opposition having been conveniently outlawed in 1978) to his handpicked successor, Major General Momoh, commander of the armed forces.

Momoh made his own fortune from the British, the Lebanese and various others with rich pale skins, by coming to an agreement whereby they could help themselves to the gold, and the diamonds and the rutile and the bauxite, without having to worry about little inconveniences like tax. Meanwhile the sixteen tribes that made up the four million strong population of Sierra Leone continued to scrape an existence off the land.

Sierra Leone's only claim to fame seemed to be that Graham Greene had once stayed in Freetown and written 'The Heart of the Matter' about the British colonial days. I noted the title in my diary.

In Graham Greene's day, Sierra Leone was known as 'White Man's Grave' – largely due to the particularly lethal falciparum malaria. White Man's Grave rather missed the point, if you looked at the statistics for the indigenous population. With a life expectancy of 42 and an under-five-mortality of 20% (the world's second worst), the black men, women and particularly children were filling graves much faster than their expatriate counterparts but, then, who cared about them?

That was where I came in. I would care. I would make a difference. I would change those statistics…..

D Day, September 16th: Gatwick Airport

I sat on the toilet at Gatwick Airport and opened a bag of Maltesers. The last couple of months had passed in a whirl of work, VSO courses, farewell parties (eating and drinking to prepare for two years of famine ahead) and packing. Packing to fit two years worth of life into two rucksacks not exceeding twenty-five kilograms. Needless to say, I didn't attempt any more surgery, and the bathroom scales clipped twelve stones. So much for losing weight and, frankly, hiding in the Ladies to avoid check-in didn't say much for the state of my soul. Hmmph! For some reason I thought of Fiona. She'd been very sweet about my pulling out of Zambia, but she never had written from Papua New Guinea.

I popped two Maltesers in my mouth and leaned against the cistern to stare at the Pregnancy Advisory Service number on the cubicle door. Not that I was ever likely to need their services. 'Finding a man' was also looking like a non-starter, what with only two blokes in our group of nine volunteers – a little Cockney mechanic and a married man pushing fifty with a wooden leg.

I rummaged around in the bottom of the bag of Maltesers to find only a crumb of honeycomb left. Pathetic. I crumpled the bag and was about to sling it on the floor when my middle class upbringing got the better of me. I was not a mere smoker who indulged her habit in the toilets and threw her butts in the pan, I was a chocolate eater and we were surely a better breed of addict. I put the wrapper in the sanitary disposal unit and sighed.

My robust exterior and endless jollity belied my lack of self-confidence, but then of course all extroverts claim to be shy. People my size, with the voice to match, are not allowed to be vulnerable. My voice. Ughh, now there was a thing. Too loud and too English. How I longed for a soft Scottish burr like Fiona's. I had spent six years at Dunblane High School and six years at Edinburgh University, proclaiming my Scottishness. After all it was hardly my fault that I had spent my pre-school years as an Air Force daughter (until my father crashed his plane into a water buffalo which inconsiderately ambled across the runway). Nonetheless, Scottish accent or not, I had picked up plenty of good friends along the way. Friends who would not reject me if I never set foot in Africa.

"OK, Gail. You don't have to go." I was right, I didn't. I hadn't checked in, and could easily sneak off before my VSO compatriots even knew I'd arrived. There were other ways of achieving my goals. I could go on a diet, for instance. Hells bells, I could even start going to church!

I flipped open the lock and my rucksacks, crammed to bursting point with bumper boxes of Tampax, rubber gloves and of course Maurice King's book toppled out of the cubicle. The choice between the rubber gloves and a pile of rubbishy bestsellers had been a difficult one, but AIDS mania filled the tabloid and medical press at that time, and Africa's figures were alarming. Catching HIV from a patient during surgery seemed cruel reward for attempting to save the world. Another good reason for staying at home.

"Hi, Gail, you're here!" I jumped. Lindsey, a librarian heading for Fourah Bay College, dropped her bags next to mine and threw her arms round me. "The others are all checking in. They thought you'd wimped out!"

"No way!" I laughed. "Not me!"

"That's what I said," Lindsey giggled in a lovely Scottish lilt that I would have killed for. She was an attractive girl, most unlibrarian-like, also in her late twenties. "Wait for me, would you? This is the fourth time I've been. I'm so excited!"

I watched Lindsey's svelte figure slip into my cubicle then cursed at the mirror. "You've done it now, Gail." My reflection stared back: warm brown eyes, neat nose, cupid's bow mouth and dark glossy hair. Perhaps the straight bob with Cleopatra fringe didn't flatter my square face and perhaps if I ever tried a little makeup….Still, I looked quite young for twenty seven and was a sturdy example of a female Homo Sapien, built to stand the rigors of Africa. Nice teeth too, I was told. I smiled to reveal my best feature. All the better for eating with.

Positive thinking. That was the trick. Visualise yourself as you want to be and it will be so. I closed my eyes to imagine my metamorphosis, two years hence.

There I was, slim and glamorous, an accomplished surgeon, stepping off the plane on the arm of a handsome diplomat, my friends gaping at the swan before them….

"Dream on, Gail." I stuck my tongue out at my reflection and squeezed a spot on my chin. "Just try to survive two years without killing too many patients or sticking yourself with an AIDS infected needle."

At least I still had time to buy another bag of Maltesers.

I exited the Ladies, arms linked with Lindsey, and spotted my fellow VSO's standing in line at the Freetown check in desk, each accompanied by familiar looking bulging rucksacks.

"Kushe everyone!" I waved with unnatural enthusiasm.

"Hey, it's the Doc! Told you she'd show up eventually." Klaus waved back. Good Lord! What had happened to his hair? People called Klaus really shouldn't have a skin head.

Klaus was the Cockney mechanic, despite the name bequeathed by a German father. He was a thirty-year-old ex-rigger, who had worked in Saudi and the North Sea, before adding Sierra Leone to his rather dubious list of workplaces. Half the size of my idea of a rigger, he seemed even shorter with no hair.

"Klaus! Love the hairdo!" I rubbed his shorn head. Buddhist monk or Neo-Nazi, it would undoubtedly prove cooler than my bob.

"No more haircuts needed for two years," he smiled.

"So! Mad Doc Haddock!" Mike with the wooden leg appeared and put his arm around me. "You didn't abandon us in our hour of need?"

"Now would I do that?"

"Course not, glad you're here to tend to all our ailments,"

winked Mike. "Glad you're here too, mate." Mike thumped Klaus on the back. "Rescue me from all these women, eh?" Mike's much younger wife, smiled indulgently beside him.

"No problem, pity we're posted miles away from the delectable Lindsey." Klaus nudged Lindsey's shoulder. Lindsey shook her curly brown hair, held from her forehead with a twist of multi-coloured material and with an easy smile she stuck up two fingers.

"Good odds though, Klaus. Seven to two!"

"Six to one," corrected his wife.

"Of course darling."

"Six to one, and take a look at the one!" I thought, eyeing Klaus unkindly before adding out loud. "So tell me, Mike, what's with all this extra luggage?" I looked down at his two large rucksacks, plus a three-foot oblong box.

"My spare leg."

"Sorry, how could I forget?"

"VSO gave me an extra twenty kilos. In case this one gets eaten by termites."

"A hazard of wooden legs, I suppose."

"Not with my high tensile graphite number. Look." Mike hoisted his trouser leg and unstrapped his leg. "No termites are likely to get this boy. Feel how light it is."

"Twenty kilos?" I raised an eyebrow as the queue shuffled forwards around us.

"Three," Mike admitted. "But good old VSO is too PC to quibble with poor disabled me! So we've got lots of extra books and sweeties packed."

"You are defrauding VSO of valuable funds," a high-pitched Home Counties voice interrupted our banter. Susan was a medical secretary in her early thirties who would be teaching typing to Salonean college girls. Unlike the rest of us who all wore light cotton trousers and a T-shirt, she was dressed in a brown corduroy skirt, brown jersey and high necked lacy blouse, set off by delicate pearl earrings nestling in short blonde curls. "Funds that could be better spent on the Africans we are trying to help."

"Oh Susan," Lindsey sighed. Mike just laughed and strapped his leg back on.

"So Gail." Lindsey said changing the subject. "How did you fit two year's Tampax supply into your bags?"

"Left everything else at home."

"Won't it be the rainy season when we arrive?" asked Susan.

"Ye-es?" Lindsey furrowed her brow at Susan.

"What will happen to all the Tampax if our rucksacks get wet?" Susan put her question in all seriousness as the rest of us collapsed laughing at the thought of the hundreds of expanding tampons bursting out of our bags.

Keen to thwart any potential VSO uprising, the customs men pulled Susan aside at security and started rummaging through her hand-luggage. She obviously looked too innocent to be true. Whilst Susan blushed, the Neo-Nazi mechanic popped his bag onto the conveyor, where it slid unobserved past the TV monitor displaying spanners, monkey-wrenches and all manner of other lethal weapons.

"What have you got in there?" I asked as Klaus swung his bag off the conveyor belt as easily as if it contained a mere change of underwear.

"Tools of the trade. Haven't you brought a set of surgical instruments or something?"

"Only rubber gloves. I can't equip an entire hospital in twenty-five kilos."

"What happens if I need my appendix out, then?"

"I'll use your monkey wrench."

"Ouch," Klaus winced. "So, Doc, here we are on the verge of two years non-stop action and adventure. How do you feel?"

"Probably like you if I really did need to remove your appendix."

"That bad, huh?" he laughed. "Been reading Graham Greene too?"

"Yeah, cheery stuff. What was VSO thinking, putting that on the reading list?"

"We'll just have to get plastered on the plane."

I smiled. Perhaps Klaus was all right, small but perfectly formed, and after all, hair grows.

I had done it now. I was actually on my way to Sierra Leone. I needed a chocolate fix, so pulled the family bag of Maltesers from the sick-bag holder and tugged it open. The bag split and Maltesers danced under the seats.

"Oh no," I sobbed, watching the chocolate marbles roll down the gangway of the climbing aircraft.

"Never mind, Doc," said Klaus. "You can have one of my Minstrels once we've finished our ascent."

"That long!"

"Ingrate!"

"I suppose I'll manage ten more minutes." I gripped the armrests instead.

"A big strong girl like you scared of flying?"

"No. Scared of two years alone in the wilderness."

"You'll be fine. A big..."

"Strong girl like me?" I glared at him.

"Yeah. At least we've got a gentle introduction."

VSO had organized a fortnight of orientation and Krio lessons together in Freetown, before they dispatched us to fend for ourselves up-country.

"Look!" Klaus nudged me. "Drinks already. Fancy a beer?"

"No thanks! I don't like beer. I'll have Drambuie."

"Yugh!"

"It'll go well with those Minstrels..."

"Okay, okay." Klaus pulled his rucksack from under the seat in front.

"Thanks." I reached over to pluck a Minstrel from his bag and spilled my Drambuie over his leg.

"Sorry, sorry!" I frantically rubbed Klaus' sticky thigh with my sleeve, but only succeeded in knocking his beer into his lap. He adjusted himself a little in his seat. "Oh, no. I'm sorry. I'll..."

"Leave it," he sighed. "I hear beer is a good mosquito repellent."

"But mosquitoes probably love Drambuie. Sorry."

"I won't smell so sweet for a long time. Stop saying sorry."

"Sorry."

"For heavens sake, have another Minstrel."

"You've only got one left." I looked pleadingly at him.

"Eat it. It looks like your need is greater than mine. Besides, I've got another packet. In fact, why don't you take that too?"

"Really?" Klaus shot up in my estimation.

"Really, but only if you promise to save them until you get to Serabu."

And he gave me his very last bit of chocolate for two years. I instantly forgave him his haircut and all comments about big strong girls.

2. Two Weeks Grace, One Night's Reality

September 17th: Freetown

The VSO office sat huddled in concrete, two floors above the Red Cross, just off Siakka Steven's Street in the throbbing heart of Freetown. Not a place to linger.

The British High Commissioner certainly didn't hang around, keeping his pep talk focused on the perils of having relationships with or, God forbid, marrying the locals. He wasted no time in asking about our jobs, destinations or worries as obviously British High Commissioners have much better things to do. After a curt goodbye, he tippety tapped down the staircase, past the Red Cross Office and pushed his way through a crowd of Liberian refugees to head straight for his shiny, air-conditioned car. There were no windows in the VSO office, but we watched him through the latticed brickwork that allowed a little air to circulate.

Mike found it all very amusing, but then he was a seasoned aid worker who had already spent a number of years overseas. Wooden leg or not, he was unlikely to have problems. Mike told us the two main reasons for volunteers being pulled out were for motorcycle accidents (not a problem for me, I wasn't going on any motorbike) or psychiatric problems. Well nervous breakdowns weren't my style either. After all I was a stable sort of character, wasn't I?

Of course anybody could be stable when they'd had an easy life like mine: never abused or raped, no major bereavements, no ghastly relationship breakdowns, and even my parents were still married to each other. A spoilt, only child with a cushy, middle class upbringing, that was me. And now it was payback time. Help!

"He's totally ignoring all those refugees!" exclaimed Susan as the British High Commissioner's chauffeur shut him into his cool oasis, closing the passenger door on the smelly, noisy humidity of downtown Freetown.

"What can he do, Susan?" asked Mike.

"He's the High Commissioner, he should help them."

"How, Susan?" pressed Klaus, ever the realist. "He's not responsible for Liberia, and besides he's only in Salone for decoration. The Foreign Office is hardly likely to send its leading lights here."

"Apparently he's just been relocated from Outer Mongolia," whispered Lindsey.

"I rest my case," said Klaus. "At least he's invited all we lowly VSO subjects to his Christmas Party."

Only three months till Christmas. I tried to forget about the bit in-between.

"Did everyone see that bit in 'The Guardian' about Doe?" Said Klaus.

"Who's Doe?" I asked.

"Liberia's president. Don't you docs pay *any* attention to current affairs?" groaned Lindsey.

"No, we leave that to smartarse librarians."

"Well he's an ex-president now," laughed Mike. "Got himself knocked off by the rebels last week."

"And good riddance by the sound of him," added Lindsey.

"Oh dear," said Susan. "Will that bring peace to Liberia?"

"I must say, that civil war did sound worrying."

"How did it worry you then doc, when you obviously don't know a thing about it?" teased Mike.

"Who needs nasty details to be worried about wars?" I retorted.

"Well the Saloneans sound a pretty laid back lot. Sixteen tribes and no wars," mused Klaus. "Sound safe enough for you, doc?"

"That's the only reason I agreed to come."

It is hard to feel chipper when you are emotionally and physically exhausted, and when we finally arrived at the VSO office in Freetown I was exactly that. The two hour introductory tour of the Capital, on top of a six hour flight, four hours at Lungi airport, five hours waiting for the Freetown ferry, an hour on the ferry, and only four hours in bed (or rather on the Field Officer's settee), had been the final assault on our senses, leaving "Oh my God, what have we done?" hanging unspoken in a big black cloud above us all. With the exception of Mike of course, who had done it all before.

Once the British High Commissioner had beaten his retreat, our Field Director, a glum forty-year old with bushy eyebrows shading weary eyes, started to repeat, verbatim, VSO's potted history of Sierra Leone. An overhead fan limped in time to his monotone, and my attention wandered to the one beacon on the horizon of my two year sentence – Nick. Nick was our Dutch Indonesian Field Officer, all multi-cultural designer cool and immaculate grooming. Despite this, he treated us as comrades, rather than naughty school children as already seemed to be the Field Director's wont. They shared us out between them: Klaus, Lindsey, Susan and me at Nick's house (whoopee!) and the rest at the Field Director's (hard luck). Admittedly the Field Director did manage a smile or two for me, which I put down to my dazzling personality, but Klaus said he had no choice - it would not do to alienate even the most dubious of doctors when you lived in White Man's Grave.

The Field Director paused to point out the large map of Sierra Leone, sellotaped onto a cork noticeboard which hung on the yellowing walls of the VSO office. Fifty red pins protruded, scattered around the country, each representing a volunteer. Most were in clusters, like the eight pins in Freetown itself, and four in Moyamba, where Klaus was headed, but there were a few singles, including me in the Southeast.

"The lonely onlies. Look at this poor person." I pointed to a pin, way out East. "Miles from anyone."

"Not any more," said the Field Director. "Panguma Hospital had a new arrival last month. She didn't come with one of our usual batches, so I forgot to put her up. Another doctor, Gail."

"Great. So I won't have to deal with all VSO ailments myself?"

"No. Fiona will help you."

"Fiona....?"

"Yes, here she is." The Field Director pushed another pin in his map. "Dr. Fiona MacDougall, Medical Officer at Panguma Hospital."

"Fiona?" I couldn't believe it. "Fiona's here! What happened to Papua New Guinea?"

"Fell through at the last minute," said Nick. "Panguma was delighted. We suggested she come with you lot, but she was desperate to get to work."

"Typical Fiona!" I laughed.

"She left you a letter." The Field Director waved toward the alphabetical pigeonholes at the front of the office. "I must say," he added, "you're not what I expected of a friend of Fiona...."

Predictably the letter was full of enthusiasm for her job and her colleagues and said I was going to love working in Salone. Somehow I wasn't comforted. It sounded like bloody hard work, and I was singularly unimpressed so far.

September 24th: Week 2

"I'm in heaven," said Klaus, lying between Lindsey and me on soft yellow sand. "A beach that stretches forever, sun on my skin and two beautiful, semi-naked women by my side."

Beautiful? Me? I shivered with pleasure. "Better than Club Med." I sighed. The moment we had seen Freetown's idyllic beaches, we had forgotten all about poverty and suffering. After all, how could it co-exist in a world that had beauty such as this?

"You've never resorted to Club Med, Gail!" said Klaus. There he went again, implying that I was a desirable woman surrounded by suitors. I bristled with satisfaction. He was right, I had avoided Club Med holidays, but not through tasteful superiority. It was those brochures featuring page after page of skinny blonde women draped over rugby-muscled men that scared me off. I wouldn't stand a chance.

"This is awful," said Lindsey, turning over on her towel. "Did you know they filmed the Bounty Bar advert here? How can I write home to tell them about the lush palm trees and the blue sea lapping at my feet without losing all credibility with my friends?"

"Yep, it's a big problem," agreed Klaus. "Not nearly enough suffering to report."

"Kushe, kushe." We opened our eyes to see Mike's hefty body looming over our little ménage à trois. His wife stood by his side with a tray of beers and a single G and T. "How di body?"

"Kushe, Mike. We're just fine," I replied emphatically.

"How di body is the singular form of how are you. We're plural," Klaus chastised.

"Swot!" I grumbled, still smarting from Klaus coming top in the first week's Krio test. Imagine being beaten by a mechanic!

"Smartarse!" agreed Mike. "I'd hoped for a bit of support from my fellow man in the face of all these university-educated women." Klaus just smiled.

"So what is the plural of how di body, Herr Top-of-The-Class?" I asked.

"I have absolutely no idea." Klaus cat-stretched to his full five foot five, then pounced forward to sit cross-legged on the sand. "Do I see beers?"

"Here you are mate, and a double-price gin and tonic for the doc." Mike handed us drinks from his wife's tray.

"Sorry, " I said, "but I really don't like beer. "

"Time you learnt." Klaus offered me his bottle. "There'll be no pink gins and Drambuie up-country."

"I doubt there'll be any beer either. Okay here goes." I was surprised to find how eager I was to override my tastebuds when Klaus' eyes were on me.

"Hmm? At least its cold."

The Venue was the first place we'd found with the luxury of a fridge. It was an enormous raffia basket that housed a beach bar run by members of the enterprising Lebanese contingent. Despite the flimsy walls that had to be rebuilt at the end of each rainy season it did a roaring trade. There were always plenty of thirsty volunteers, eager for a beach break from their upcountry postings: fifty VSOs, a hundred American Peace Corps, numerous priests, nuns and other assorted missionaries, plus various outfits with names like CARE and CONCERN. Whatever the organization, the Venue was the place to be.

"Here's to our first week na Salone." Klaus clinked his bottle with my glass.

"Na Salone," agreed Lindsey, and we all clinked together.

"Isn't Susan joining us?" Klaus nodded towards the small figure huddled over a book in a back corner of the Venue.

"Doesn't drink," said Mike.

"What's she reading?" asked Lindsey.

"Jane Austen," I said. "She was reading it in class. Poor girl can't bear Krio's bastardisation of the Queen's English!"

"Well, I love it," enthused Klaus. "So descriptive."

"A German Cockney's bound to love Krio," teased Lindsey. "You can't quibble with Susan's taste though."

"What?" I asked.

"Jane Austen. She's great fun."

"Great fun?" I mouthed in amazement. Now Susan was

bound to love such books, but real people like Lindsey? Well just wait. Even I fully intended to spend my spare time in the wilderness expanding my reading repertoire. The one book I had not sacrificed for more rubber gloves was an exceedingly small print edition of *Tess of the d'Urbervilles*. I was proud that it had triumphed over other options like Judith Krantz. Hopefully at the end of my two years I too could announce in front of my literary friends that I adored Jane Austen and Thomas Hardy. All part of saving my soul.

"Anyway," Lindsey continued. "Reading tastes aside, I don't think Susan approves of me."

"Or any of us," I agreed.

"Oh, no. She thinks you're fantastic Gail," Lindsey announced. "You're a doctor, you're here to save lives!"

"Hmmph."

"In fact, you've got quite a fan club already," Lindsey continued. "Did I tell you about my granny?"

"Your granny?"

"She saw your picture in the Stirling Observer: *Dunblane Doctor Goes To Africa*. She kept telling me how marvellous it was that the young lady doctor should go to Africa. I pointed out that I was going to Africa too, but that didn't seem to count. After all, *I'm* only a librarian."

"Sorry," I mumbled. I would have to perform well now, so as not to disappoint Susan *and* Lindsey's granny.

"Never mind, Lindsey," laughed Klaus. "Gail's hardly heroic doctor material."

"Hoi, what do you mean?" Heroic doctor definitely fitted into my goals and, although I couldn't quite see it myself, I rather wanted everybody else to think I was wonderful. Especially Klaus, although I couldn't imagine why I should care what *he* thought.

"You're not pompous enough, that's all." He touched my shoulder.

"Hmmph," I grunted. Now, as if the expectations of Susan and Lindsey's granny weren't enough, I'd have to prove myself to Klaus too.

"Come on doc, don't look so glum." Klaus jumped up. "Race you to the sea."

And we ran laughing across the expansive sands, two white bodies, little and large, hurdling over the waves to plunge into the turquoise Atlantic.

The second week passed even more quickly than the first. We were let loose on the vibrant markets of Freetown to practice our newly acquired Krio. Market women, draped from head to toe in tie-died primary colours, tried to sell us piles of dried fish, rice and chillies from their stalls or tempt us with weird vegetables from the baskets balanced on their heads. I managed to buy a huge bagful of dried fish, thinking *bonga* too pretty a name to be given to five-year-old reject sardines that never made it to a cosy oiled can. Klaus of course only went for the mouth-watering options like mangoes and pineapples. Smartarse, I thought, as we walked companionably back for our afternoon Krio lesson at the college.

Two days before the end of our orientation fortnight, Serabu Hospital radioed to say that I was needed ASAP and that they'd collect me that evening. Susan nodded approvingly - no time to waste when there are lives to be saved. My brief surge of self-importance was rapidly replaced by panic - I didn't want to be dragged away from the security of our little group. It would be three months before we would be reunited at the VSO Christmas Conference. Three months of work and God knows what else, and three months before I would see Klaus again.

Whoa! Why was that suddenly a problem?

"Hard luck, doc," said Mike.

"You'll do fine," said Klaus.

"See you at the Christmas Conference," smiled Lindsey. "Don't work too hard."

"I'll write." Klaus gave me a hug. "And you can tell me all about your first op."

"Okay," I whispered. He said he would write!

As I climbed into the front seat of the Serabu Hospital Landrover the driver – Moses – nodded a silent hello and the Field Director handed me a plastic bag stuffed full of money.

"What's all this?"

"Your monthly allowance."

"Good Lord. It looks like I've robbed a bank!"

"Eighty pounds," said the Field Director. "That's Salonean inflation."

"Don't spend it all on gin and chocolate," teased Klaus. His words were lost in a roll of thunder, followed by a curtain of rain swooshing onto the roof of the Landrover. I tried not to think of it as an omen and smiled weakly at Klaus. He gave a little wave, then dashed for cover with the others.

The big strong girl was on her own now.

9pm, October 1ˢᵗ: Serabu Hospital

The rain that had hammered down on the Landrover for the entire journey stopped as quickly as it had started, leaving an eerie silence. After seven hours imprisoned in the suspensionless vehicle being rattled over the most dreadful potholed roads, I was suddenly reluctant to get out.

Eight hours ago I had been surrounded by friends, my hair damp from the sea and my face flushed and salty. Now Moses, the hospital driver, had bypassed the Promised Land and delivered me straight to the gates of hell. My posting.

Well I couldn't stay in the damned Landrover forever, so I

opened the passenger door and jumped straight into a muddy puddle.

"I am Sister Ignatius," said the austere figure in front of me. "Welcome to Serabu Catholic Mission Hospital." She was dressed in a white polyester veil and habit. The kerosene lamp that she held, à la Florence Nightingale, illuminated thin, blue-veined skin stretched over an angular face. Shadowy buildings loomed behind her, shrouded in hot damp mist.

I straightened to my full five foot six - physically half a foot taller and some four stones heavier than Sister Ignatius, so why did I feel so small?

"Er, thank you." I held out my hand. "Gail Haddock."

"You are late, Dr. Haddock." She made no movement towards me. I retracted my hand. "We were expecting you in daylight."

"Sorry," I muttered, unsure as to why I was apologizing for my long uncomfortable journey. Perhaps the pull of my subconscious had slowed the vehicle down, so strong was my desire to remain in Freetown with Klaus and my friends on the beach. Unlike Fiona I certainly hadn't been in any hurry to come to this black concentration camp run by the Ghost of Christmas Future. My future for the next two years.

"Come with me, Dr. Haddock," instructed Ignatius. "You will need food."

For the first time in my life, I just didn't feel hungry.

Sister Ignatius sat across the convent dining room table and watched me eat dry bread and sardines. Finally she spoke.

"Are you a surgeon, Dr. Haddock?"

"Sorry. I'm afraid not."

"I see."

"I'm willing to learn," I offered. Willing, yes - but able? Sister Ignatius fell silent again, so I took another bite of my bread and endeavoured to chew without saliva. The stewed tea didn't help.

"You are here to replace Dr. Pat," she said, as I sipped my tea. "Patients travelled from all over Salone to benefit from Pat's surgical skills." Ignatius paused and looked me up and down. I tried not to slurp. "Why did VSO send me such an inexperienced girl?"

Why indeed? I swallowed my bread and felt the hard lump scrape its way down my oesophagus. "I'm sorry," was all I could say. I *was* sorry. I was sorry for Serabu Hospital, I was sorry for Ignatius, and I was very sorry for myself. Why hadn't I trusted my instincts in the Ladies at Gatwick, or even earlier, when I pulled out of Zambia? I wasn't a selfless hard worker like Fiona, or a surgeon like this Dr. Pat, or an idealist like Susan, or even a confident cynic like Mike - I was a spoilt only child who liked gin and chocolate and running round a squash court. What was I doing here?

"Well then, if you are the best that is available, you had better be a fast learner." Sister Ignatius stood up. "I have a hospital to run."

"I'll...er.. I promise to do my best," I stuttered. For heaven's sake, this wasn't a Girl Guide badge; it was two years' responsibility for hundreds of lives.

"Very well. Mass is at six thirty every morning, if you wish to attend."

I cast my eyes down, unable to find the courage to tell her that to compound my inadequacies, I wasn't a Catholic. Brought up rigidly agnostic, I hadn't even been baptized. Forget my soul, would somebody please save me?

God must have decided to give this poor sinner a chance, and sent a pot-bellied, bearded redhead bursting into the room. My angel of mercy was dressed in a traditional Salonean suit of pink and blue tie-dyed material with a fancy embroidered yoke, which did nothing for his shiny, sunburnt, bald pate, but somehow I couldn't imagine him dressed in anything else. He was a thirty-something Santa on holiday, beaming welcome across his freckled face.

"Ah, now, would I be seeing our brand new doctor?" Irish! Look, Ignatius, this is how the Irish are supposed to be. Gulping back tears of relief, I wanted to throw my arms round him, but found myself already enveloped in an enormous bear hug. "Welcome to Serabu, Dr. Gail!"

"Good evening Alan." Ignatius interrupted. "You will take Dr. Haddock to her house."

"Good evening, Sister." He gave her a curt nod then turned to me. "Alan O'Connor, Assistant Hospital Administrator of Serabu Hospital."

"I'm Gail. Hi." I squeezed his soft pale hand tightly in mine.

"It's grand to have you here."

"She didn't think so." I nodded towards the door.

"Don't be worrying about Ignatius," Alan reassured me. "The staff are all a-buzz over the new lady doctor."

"Oh no," I whispered, my fears flooding back. I could talk to Alan "I...I don't think I can do this job. Sister Ignatius has just been telling me about Dr. Pat. I think..."

"Bejasus! Such talk!" He thumped me on the shoulder. "You'll be grand. Come for a beer."

"I don't really like beer." I knew I sounded churlish, but I was exhausted, I still hadn't seen my house, and I really *didn't* like beer.

"Rubbish. The night is young," Alan continued unperturbed. "After meeting MT, you'll be needing a few beers."

"MT?"

"Sister Ignatius. Maggie Thatcher. The staff call her MT."

I laughed despite myself. "How do they know about the Iron Lady?"

"The World Service. Everybody knows Maggie."

"And I came to escape her!"

Five bottles of Star Beer later, Alan took me on a midnight tour of the hospital. All I wanted to do was crawl into bed, but I was too tired and too drunk to argue.

The hospital looked grim, each ward more unwelcoming than the last, all housed in concrete with kerosene lamps illuminating rows of windows along the sides.

"You'd better know up front that Serabu Hospital, like the whole country, is in dire financial straits," Alan said offering me a cigarette.

"No thanks." I shook my head vigorously. How could he smoke in this heat? "Yes, I've heard about the inflation. You should see the bag of money the VSO Field Director gave me. It's enough to warm the hearts of Bonnie and Clyde." I giggled. Oh dear. That beer was strong.

"I'm afraid it's not funny." Alan was serious for the first time. "The people have no money, so they don't come to us until it's too late. It's disastrous - for our patients and for our hospital. If attendances fall then so does our income."

"But surely you don't charge!"

"Of course we do," Alan replied. "The Catholic Mission isn't made of money. Things are so bad now that unless our finances improve, they'll withdraw their funding in July and that'll be the end of Serabu Hospital."

VSO had made no mention of the fact that my hospital might close before my first year was up. "That's awful," I exclaimed loudly, attempting to cover the shameful thought that I might not be committed to two years after all. So much for saving the world.

"It's fearful, but everybody's mighty excited that you've

37

come. Enthusiastic new doctors are always good for business."

"Oh God!" Never mind the world, was he trying to tell me I was expected to save Serabu Hospital as well? Alan took one look at my face and laughed.

"Are you sure you're not wanting that cigarette?"

"I almost wish I did!"

"Well you didn't drink beer three hours ago," he teased. "Enough gloom. On with the tour. This is Medical Ward and up here is the Administration block that backs onto Outpatients' Department. There's also a small lab for simple tests...."

But I had stopped listening. I was staring at The Body.....

"I don't want you to be thinking that Almamy is typical," Alan stressed after my meeting with the sleeping nightwatchman. "To be fair, I wouldn't stay awake for £10 a month either."

"£10! And I was complaining about £80!"

"He does get three sacks of rice a year too."

"Wow."

"Our staff are all mighty good, you'll see."

"Well I hope I can do them justice." I slurped behind my new friend along the muddy path that led to my house. "So far I've met Almamy, who'll be telling everyone I can't even fix a simple hernia, and Ignatius. Well, I bet you never realised those two had anything in common."

"Enough! We'll be turning you into a surgeon within the week."

"I doubt it," I grunted and sidestepped a small pond.

The path was cut through long wet grass that brushed against my legs, soaking my dress and plastering it to my thighs. Muddy water splashed my shins and trickled back down to my leather sandals, which were now so soft that my feet slid off the soles and chafed against the straps.

There was a damp sweet perfume in the thick air that reminded me of Klaus soaked in Drambuie. I smiled. I was actually going to miss the little mechanic.

"Don't you have a torch?" I asked Alan.

"No batteries. I hoped you'd bring supplies from the land of electricity."

"I've two spare sets and a torch at the bottom of my rucksack, wherever that is."

"Don't worry, Moses' taken everything to your house," Alan reassured me. "But always hang onto your torch. You don't want to be standing on any snakes or driver ants." He certainly knew how to cheer a girl up. "Now then, here we are. Chez Dr. Gail."

We stood outside a big dark bungalow, the last building on the compound some five hundred metres from the wards. The moon picked out silhouettes of three tall palm trees standing behind my house, casting their shadows protectively over the corrugated iron roof. My personal guards.

"Is that all for me?" I had been expecting some sort of mud hut. This was bigger than my own York semi - currently overrun by lodgers. Oh dear. I had a sudden vision of my living room redecorated with black flowery wallpaper, but put it quickly out of my mind. There was enough to worry about right here.

"The volunteer doctors often have families."

"I'm young free and single, I'm afraid."

"Lucky you. The biggest and best house on the compound, all for our new doctor." Alan slapped me on my back.

"Only me and my two rucksacks to fill it."

"Your keys, doctor."

I fumbled with the lock, opened my door and vainly flipped the light switch.

"Forgotten that electricity bill again!" Alan smacked his wrist.

I peered inside and could just make out two easy chairs, a sofa and a table lurking in the shadows.

"Your bedroom's second door after the toilet." He pointed into the darkness. "Sleep tight. Don't let the mosquitoes bite. Pa George, our cook, will be up to see you in the morning."

"We have a cook?"

"Of course."

"I haven't come to expand the British Empire. I'm sure I can cook for myself."

"You'll be too busy saving lives."

"I don't want a servant," I persisted.

"So you're good at cooking rice and mashed cassava over a three-stone-fire?"

"I can learn."

"Concentrate on learning your surgery," Alan retorted. "Besides, Pa George will be delighted to work for a doctor again. Pat's departure left him stuck with me, a mere administrator."

"Hmmph."

"Goodnight." Alan kissed me, scraping my cheek with his beard. "God bless." And he ambled back down my path singing *Danny Boy* in a surprisingly angelic voice. I stood alone in a strange black house. My new home.

3. What For Chop Today?

A machine gun knocking catapulted me into morning from the haven of my bed. Pa George stood barefoot in the doorway, arms folded. He looked me up and down. With my British reserve, I tried to observe him a little more surreptitiously.

"What for chop today?"

Neither of us were aesthetic examples of our race. He had a ploughed field for a face, his head driven forward on a stringy neck, led by a big nose and protruding bottom lip. A gargoyle carved in charcoal, I thought unkindly. However, judging by his expression, Pa George was thinking equally unflattering thoughts about me. What did he make of my podgy body, still clad in the mud-splattered sundress I had fallen asleep in some five hours earlier? And what about my bloodshot eyes and breath, still heavy with the fumes of Alan's hospitality? All I wanted to do was collapse back into bed, but Pa George's sinewy frame looked ready for anything.

"What for chop today?" he barked again. I assumed he was asking me what I wanted for lunch.

"Er...er," I stammered. Pa George pursed his lips and his black eyes challenged mine from deep weather-beaten sockets. Sweat popped out in globules over my forehead. Come on, Gail, remember your Krio, think of a dish. There's no Klaus to help you now.

"Um.....plassas?" I hoped plassas was good.

"Bonga forty leones." He said thrusting out his hand. "Rice ten leones, cassava leaf eight leones, pepper four leones, onion twenty leones, palm oil thirty leones." It took me a minute to realize that this was the shopping list.

"Uh..., okay. I'll just go and find my money." I'd put it all in one of my bags. Now there was a point. Where were they?

According to Alan, my rucksacks would be here. However, like most doctors, I did not trust administrators - especially not

41

Irish ones with a wicked sense of humour who dressed in pink and blue tie-dyed pyjamas.

Feeling Pa George's eyes on my back, I turned to search my new abode for my elusive possessions. The sparse furnishings left little hiding place. Flimsy cotton curtains tried to soften the window bars and rusting mosquito mesh but they were no match for the stream of sunlight that was further fading an unsavoury mustard velour sofa. At the other end of the living room, a large table was covered with tie-dyed material that looked remarkably similar to Alan's suit.

Before I could ponder further on Alan's taste in clothing, I spotted my two muddy rucksacks through the open door to the kitchen. Moses had propped them against a chest-high, black and red oil drum that sat by the door. A thick black crack cut the concrete floor in half. Oh dear, I hoped the rest of the house was structurally sound. I was about to step over the crack when it moved. I recoiled. Good Lord! Ants!

My pulse gradually slowed down allowing my mother's biology teacher gene to kick in. Such big ants and *so* many! I bent down for closer inspection. Each one made of large and small glossy black beads, all in perfect formation, their mission, to stop me getting to my money. Well *I* wasn't going to be beaten by a couple of formicidae.

Taking a deep breath, I reached over and carefully lifted up the smaller backpack. I pulled out the plastic bag stuffed with money and something fell to the floor. It was the last of Klaus' Minstrels. The ants were delighted. They congregated around the Minstrel, and started to rock it from side to side. Once enough of them had taken up position, they hoisted their massive prize aloft and bore it away. I watched, helplessly mourning the passage of my only remaining bit of chocolate.

Pa George had finally moved from the doorway and was

42

now standing, hands on hips, in the living-room. Neither the ants nor my Minstrel were of any concern to him.

"Here we are," I said, hoping to sound efficient, "your money for the shopping." He plucked the proffered one hundred and twenty leones from my hand and started to count.

"Onion twenty leones." Pa George' huge callused hands thumped one twenty-leone note on the table.

"Bonga forty leone." He counted one twenty on top of another. Bonga? Surely he wasn't planning on feeding me that awful dried fish I'd seen in the market?

"Rice ten leone...." He paused and straightened up.

"What's wrong?"

Pa George shoved the money back across the table and refolded his arms firmly over the corrugations of his chest. Bewildered, I picked up the grubby notes and turned each one over before grasping Pa George's problem. These were all twenties and rice was *ten* leones. Fishing in my plastic 'purse', I found a ten leone note, handed it over and counted out the rest of the money into separate piles to the exact value of each remaining item. Pa George seemed satisfied, he took the money, grunted and slammed the door behind him. What was that Alan had said about Pa George being delighted to work for me? We hadn't even said hello.

I stepped outside and my pupils constricted painfully in the morning sun. The cloudless blue sky bore no hint of the rain that had pummeled the Landrover last night. I stood and watched Pa George march bandy-legged off to market through steaming knee-high grass. The rubber plants and palm trees, lush and abundant at the end of the rainy season, obscured my view of the wards, but I could hear a distant bustle of activity. It wasn't comforting to think I was going to become part of that action.

Before I could do anything, I had to empty my bladder - Pa George' arrival had left no time for such things. I wandered into the bathroom, disturbing a couple of cockroaches that scuttled behind the toilet, and sat gingerly on the plastic seat.

Once relieved, I pulled the chain but nothing happened. I pulled again. Nothing but a dry clatter. I tried the tap but again nothing. I looked around. There was no bath, only a large bucket of water, a jug and a plughole set into the floor. Fair enough, I'd have a bucket bath and change my filthy dress. The toilet would just have to wait.

Washed and wearing a crumpled but clean dress, my body now craved rehydration. I went into the kitchen in search of drinking water. The tap in the kitchen was no more use than the one in the bathroom, so I lifted the wooden lid from the oil drum. Flecks of rust and dead flies floated unappetisingly on the surface of the water. Great. Turning round, I spotted a two-foot water filter in the corner. I opened its little tap and filled a glass tumbler. Thankfully it looked quite clear, so I drank long and deep. Next to the water filter was a plastic bag containing two bread rolls, a banana and two processed cheese triangles. Good old Alan. I knocked back another two glasses of water, then returned to the living room, taking big bites out of my breakfast.

"You must take care of the ants." A six foot beanpole arose from my sofa.

"What?" I jumped.

"Je m'excuse, but the ants, they will like this too much." The beanpole pointed to the trail of breadcrumbs I'd left on the floor.

"Yes. You're right. I've already met the ants." I thought of my precious Minstrel. "But who are you?"

"Dr. Jean at your service." He bowed.

"You're Jean?" I exclaimed, trying belatedly to hide my

surprise. So this was the Medical Superintendent of Serabu Hospital? He looked no older than me, with a boyish face split by a beaming smile and topped by a mop of straw. His shirt lay open at a rather scrawny, unshaven neck and its tails hung out of baggy shorts that sagged to his knees. Beneath, two hairy stilts ended in prehensile toes poked into yellow flip-flops.

"Bonjour, bonjour." He stretched out a long arm to shake my hand.

"Hi. Bonjour. I'm Gail."

"Welcome, Dr. Gail. Sister Ignatius told me that you have arrived."

"What else did she say?" I asked anxiously.

"Rien du tout. I make not big conversations wiz the sister." Jean grinned and I giggled with relief. He continued, "And you have met already Pa George?"

"I think that's who it was."

"Ah yes, Pa George also makes no big conversations. So you have taken your breakfast, yes?"

"Mmm," I confirmed, swallowing my last mouthful of banana.

"And the 'angover, it is a little better?"

"Yes, yes, I'm fine," I nodded, rather alarmed that my new boss thought that I looked as bad as I felt.

"So we make our ward rounds?"

"Yes of course, but um, what do I do about flushing the toilet?" I asked, embarrassed.

"I am sorry but the 'ospital water pumps do not work for one month now. You must pour the dirty water from your bucket bath into it this evening."

"Oh. Okay."

"On y va?"

"Yes. Let's go," I said, trying to sound keen.

The sun blazed down on Serabu Hospital, which was a big improvement, but even prisoner-of-war camps must look better in daylight. Six whitewashed concrete blocks were dotted over two acres of roughly grassed ground, each roofed with corrugated iron and windowed with a series of metal bars and mosquito mesh.

"Where's Sister Ignatius?" I had half expected her to be shouting out orders in the middle of the compound.

"Generalement, MT comes not to the wards," said Jean. "She stays up there, in Admin. " He pointed to a larger block, with an open-fronted waiting area, set slightly up a hill.

"The 'ospital has been here since thirty years," Jean explained as we walked between the buildings. "First it was a clinic only. Then one year Sister Hillary built a ward and the next year anozzer then anozzer. Now there are one hundred ten beds, the outpatients and the nursing school."

"Sister Hillary?"

"You have not heard of Hillary? The Irish Sister Doctor?" Jean was amazed.

"Sister Ignatius told me about the wonderful Dr.Pat," I ventured.

"Ah yes, Pat was very good, but for six months only, and there were many doctors before Pat. No, Sister Hillary was Administrator, Surgeon, Doctor and Politician at Serabu for thirty years. She is a big legend."

"Did she go back to Ireland?"

"No, she lives in Bo and runs Primary Health Services for Southern Region."

"Oh." I rubbed my eyes. All these wonderful people. I couldn't cope.

Jean told me more about the hospital and its history, but I gave him only half my attention. I was captivated by what was going on around me. Nurses dressed in crisp white uniforms bustled past, patients meandered to and fro. Strings of bedsheets, patched to rival Joseph's Technicolor coat, hung drying outside one of the wards. A family of five were making use of the shade cast by the sheets to have their breakfast. They sat cross-legged on the rough cut grass and dipped their hands into a communal food bowl as three goats grazed nearby.

"They are so poor now that the women, they buy the onions one quarter at a time," Jean was saying, his eyes joining mine on the family eating their meal. "Salone has diamonds, gold, rutile and bauxite mines, but the people, they have nossing."

"So where does all the money go?"

"To the Lebanese dealers, to the mining companies and corrupt government ministers. Did Alan tell you that Scrabu has not enough money?"

"Yes, he said that people can't afford the fees and Serabu may well close."

"C'est vrai. The hospital has had the big struggle since Sister Hillary left. Admissions went up when Pat came, but she returned to America." He shrugged. "Serabu is too far from any place. Even the locals call it Serabush."

"Serabush!" I laughed. "So why didn't they build it closer to Bo?"

"Serabu is the Archbishop's home village."

"I see."

"When there were roads and railways it mattered not, but now, ha!" Jean shrugged. "Now the Archbishop never visits and, probably, the 'ospital will shut after the review next July. C'est pas juste!"

"Oh," I said and we crossed the compound in silence. We stopped outside a shelter made out of sheets of corrugated iron held up by wooden poles. Underneath, seven women tended big black pots that bubbled on top of open fires, whilst children scampered perilously between the flames.

"Voila the kitchen!" It didn't look much like a kitchen to me. "Regarde the fires. Here the women make meals for sick relatives."

"Kushe kushe, Dr. Jon," called the cooks.

"Una kushe," he replied with a wave. "Dis na Dr. Gail."

"Kushe, Dr. Gay," the women chorused.

"Kushe," I replied with a smile. A pot-bellied child with swollen limbs ran up to Jean from behind the twists of wood-smoke.

"Bua, Dr. Jon." The little boy held his arms out to Jean.

"Bua Sule." Jean bent down and swung Sule up to sit on his hip. "Sule's twin died of measles last week."

"Oh no," I sighed. "Kushe, Sule." The child caught my eye and buried his head into Jean's stubble.

"But Sule is better now." Jean smiled. "Bi gahujena, Sule?"

"Kayingoma," answered the little voice, muffled by his protector's bony shoulder.

"Is that Krio?" I asked, puzzled.

"No, Serabush is Mendeland. Mende is a language very difficile for the poomuis."

"Poomuis?"

"White people."

"Oh. Well this poomui can't even get to grips with Krio, never mind Mende," I said. "And Krio is just English with no grammar."

"Ah non." Jean wagged his finger. "Krio is a tongue wiz her own history…" Three goats sauntered across the compound to explore the bins outside the latrines. "Allez-vous en!" he bellowed. The goats scampered off and Sule, still clinging to Jean's neck, burst into tears.

"Pardon, Sule. Osh osh." Jean bounced the boy up and down and soon brought the smile back to his face. "Eh bien. To Surgical Ward?"

I stood on the chipped brown tiles that partially covered the floor and looked at the yellowing paint peeling from the walls of Surgical Ward. Twenty rusty metal-framed beds were lined up on either side of me, their occupants lying directly on patched and taped brown rubber mattresses. Where were the sheets?

A thin cotton screen failed to conceal a nurse giving an enema to a curled up victim. She scooped up a jugful of soapy water from a bucket, poured it into a large plastic funnel connected to her patient's rear by three foot of half-inch plastic tubing, then held the funnel aloft like the Olympic torch. As the water ran in, I clenched my buttocks in sympathy.

On the neighbouring bed an old woman fed her sick husband from a tin cup and spoon whilst a child slept on the floor beneath the bedsprings, curled up alongside a blackened cooking pot. Another nurse dished out pills from rows of identical little bottles sitting on a rickety trolley. She made her entries on the paper charts that hung on the bedposts, oblivious of the patients who lay moaning on their sheetless beds.

At least the ward was clean. An old man, holding a bundle of twigs that served as a brush, was bent double, sweeping under the large wooden cross that hung over a crack in the wall at the end of the room.

"Eh bien, here comes Dauda, charge nurse on Surgical," Jean announced, waving his long arm at a rather chubby nurse who appeared pushing a trolley piled with foul smelling bandages.

"Dauda, this is Dr. Gail," Jean introduced me.

"Kushe, Dr. Jon. Kushe, Dr. Gay. Welcome."

"Thank you," I replied, hesitating to shake Dauda's extended hand, which was covered with the unsavoury evidence of his toils.

"Oh, sorry-oh," Dauda chuckled, revealing a broken front tooth, the only harsh angle in his plump round face. He removed his rubber glove. I smiled and shook.

"Can you do small small surgery, Dr. Gay?"

"No," I sighed. "But I can learn."

"Ah." On hearing my unsatisfactory reply, Dauda turned his attention straight back to Jean. Crushed, I studied the broken tile by my sandal. I felt almost as demeaned as that poor patient having the enema. And as if that wasn't enough, I was as hot as an Old English sheepdog locked in a car on a summer's day. Wiping the sweat that clung to my eyebrows and upper lip, I squinted through the condensation collecting under the face of my watch. Nine-thirty. Was that all? I had scarcely survived an hour. "We are quiet today, Dr. Jon, no big big problems," Dauda continued. "You can make your round this afternoon."

"Fine, Dauda. On y va, Gail?" Jean touched my shoulder. "I will show you theatre next."

I was pleasantly surprised by the operating theatre, which was old-fashioned of course, but in good repair. There were clean white tiles, a proper overhead operating light, and best of all, an air conditioner. I positioned myself to get the maximum benefit and luxuriated in the stream of cool air blowing up my skirt.

"Tiange is our scrub nurse. Tiange, here is our new doctor, Dr. Gail." Jean introduced me to a small woman in a thin blue cotton theatre dress. Her uniform was topped with a little green theatre hat, tied on with frayed tape, which failed to cover a cluster of braided hair that poked out of the back. Nature had not blemished her smooth black skin, but man had scoured symmetrical sets of three one inch scars at the corner of each eye, like parallel crow's feet. Tiange was unlikely to acquire crows feet the normal way, the woman looked like she had never smiled in her life.

"Kushe, Dr. Gay. Can you do surgery?" she asked in a husky voice. Oh no, not again.

"No, but I can learn," I repeated. This was not the answer Tiange wanted to hear. She went back to cutting up gauze, not even

50

troubling herself to look up as we left.

"Pat said Tiange was the best theatre nurse she had ever worked with," Jean told me.

"Well Tiange didn't think much of me. Nobody does." I said miserably. "They all want a surgeon, someone who will boost attendances and save the hospital." Someone like Sister Hillary or Dr. Pat or Fiona, I thought bitterly.

"Ah yes," Jean agreed. "They believe the scalpel can cut out devils."

"Well I'm not going to be any use, am I?" I snapped.

"Doucement, Gail. I also could not do surgery when I came. You will learn."

"But I can't!" I blurted. "Oh what am I doing here? Maybe I should go home now and stop wasting everybody's time."

"No, no. Please stay," begged Jean, alarmed at my outburst. "I need your help. It is six months since Pat left."

"What?" I exclaimed, shocked by the sudden desperation in his voice. "You've been the only doctor here for six months?" No wonder he looked so thin.

"Listen well." Jean clasped my shoulders. "Two per cent only need surgery. You can help ninety-eight per cent, even if you never go inside the operating theatre. Do you know why Sister Hillary left?" I shook my head. "Enfin, she believed the Community Health Team do more good than clever doctors, by vaccinating the children and teaching the mothers to boil their water," Jean paused from his speech to take breath. "You are a woman. The pregnant ladies will come to ante-natal clinic to see a woman."

"Good." I was glad I might be good for something.

"Yes," Jean mused. "Perhaps now we will see the difficult cases before they have laboured for three days and have already a dead baby."

Jean's cynical words horrified me at first, but I was soon to realize that he was only stating harsh facts. A student nurse, with hair braided in elaborate fingerprint swirls and whorls against her scalp, ran up to us. "Dr. Jon, Dr. Jon, you get for come to Maternity. We get one woman with afterbirth that no want come out."

"A retained placenta?" I asked. This was quite a common problem, even in Britain. If the afterbirth wasn't removed, the mother wouldn't stop bleeding.

"Yes," agreed the student. "We de go?"

Jean followed her to the cramped labour room. I squeezed in behind.

A midwife stood tying the mother's legs up to wooden poles so that Jean could do his examination. A fly landed on the mother's knee as she lay naked on the bare rubber mattress with her legs suspended in the air. No one flicked it away. She stared silently at the wall as blood poured between her legs. Her baby lay dead in a metal tray on the floor.

I let out a little cry and backed into the corner of the room. I wasn't prepared for a stillbirth - the student had obviously not thought it a relevant detail. My whole gaze focused on the little purple hand that hung over the edge of the tray. I could see its fingernails. Perfectly formed miniature fingernails.

The student was chatting away to the midwife in a blur around my head. I could hear Jean shout, "She is bleeding too much," and the snap of rubber gloves being hastily pulled on. I just couldn't take my eyes off those tiny fingernails.

"We have to get this afterbirth out quick quick." Jean's voice again. The midwife kicked the tray with the baby under the bed to make space for Jean.

"Oh, no. Don't," I sobbed, but nobody was listening to me. The midwife forced the mother's knees apart and Jean thrust his hand inside the young woman's womb to grab the placenta. Thinking that I would be sick, I covered my mouth and looked around for the door, but the midwife had yanked a trolley out of Jean's way and it was blocking my escape. I shot a guilty glance at the patient, but her head was still turned to the wall. There was no escape for her either.

"What about the anaesthetic?" I gasped, appalled.

"We're running out....... have to save it......can.......usually.....do these...... without.......Voila!"

Jean pulled out the ragged afterbirth, a pound of liver grasped between yellow rubber fingers. The midwife rubbed the mother's lower abdomen releasing a final gush of blood that trickled onto the floor.

"Bon. Now she will be okay." Jean dropped the placenta into a bucket then gently lowered the mother's legs. He picked up a bloodstained length of material from the floor. This was the lappa that she had worn around her waist to walk to the hospital, which Jean now used as a sheet. He squeezed his patient's hand and smiled reassurance, but the young woman's gaze never left the wall

"We go to C Ward, yes?" he asked me.

All I wanted to do was go home, but could find no words to argue. I nodded my assent with my hand still over my mouth. Then, turning my back on the mother and her dead baby, I stumbled out of Maternity Ward behind Jean.

Children's Ward was full of toddlers with malnutrition. Malnutrition with or without various other diseases. Jean let children who had tummies so swollen that they looked pregnant clamber all over him. Watching him, so at home with his young patients, helped me to compose myself. After twenty minutes I was able to start up conversation again.

"You're very good with the children, Jean."

"Myself, I have two pickins," he said, tickling a little girl's tummy as he examined her. "When we are finished, you will meet Francoise and les enfants."

"Thank you. I'd like that." I smiled, thankful that there might be a haven of normality somewhere in this dreadful place.

"Would you like to make examination of this little girl with malaria?" Jean asked.

"Of course. Kushe." I smiled at the frightened yellow eyes in front of me, then bent over to examine her abdomen. She let out a shriek, rolled off the bed and scuttled underneath.

"Oh dear." I was stricken.

"Oh, Dr. Gay," laughed the nurse. "The pickin is scared of poomuis."

"Isn't Jean a poomui too?" I asked.

"Dr. Jon a black man now." The nurse gave Jean a hug. He blushed.

"Don't worry Gail." Jean dropped to his knees and started to play peek-a-boo with the toddler under the bed. She started to giggle. "Probably MT is the only other white woman these pickins have seen."

"I see." I was not consoled by the comparison. "But doesn't your wife ever come to the wards? Didn't you say she was a nurse?"

"Francoise helps the Community Health Team in the villages. She is mozzer to two babies. She likes not to come to C Ward." Before I could comment, he looked at his watch. "Ah. We must go to theatre before they close the generator."

"So when do we have electricity?" I asked, trying hard to keep up with the whirlwind of information. At least the electricity supply was a non-emotive topic.

"If we have diesel then there is electricity from eight o'clock until midday, then from six until ten in the evening."

"What about emergencies?"

"Then we must turn the generator back on. MT likes it not.

Diesel is too expensive. But we look forward to the emergency operations."

"Why?" I was struggling to think of how emergency surgery could be a treat for anyone.

"Cold water."

"Cold water?" I was puzzled.

"Eight hours of electricity will not keep our fridges cold, but extra generator time gives beautiful cold drinking water." Jean licked his lips as though dreaming of a five-course slap-up meal.

Lansana was waiting for surgery. He had limped ten miles to the hospital with a huge festering wound in his buttock. I couldn't see how he had managed to walk across the room, never mind make his way unassisted from his village. He told Jean he had shot himself a week ago.

"How can you shoot yourself in the backside?" I asked as we scrubbed up.

"Lansana was shooting monkeys and fell on his gun."

"Some sport." My sympathy ebbed.

"It is no sport. They shoot monkeys for food. But yes, c'est vraimant difficile to get such a wound by yourself. Dauda thinks he was, how you say, shooting where he was not allowed?"

"Poaching?"

"Yes. Dauda says that probablement he was shot and had too much fear to come to the 'ospital in case they found him."

"Who?"

"The chief's men."

"How can they punish him any further? Surely he can't survive this?"

Tiange and Jean rasped their scalpel and curettes against bone, dolloping rotten tissue and chinking bits of shotgun pellet into a metal dish. My stomach churned as the operating theatre filled with the stench of rotting meat. I didn't strain too hard to watch.

An hour later Jean picked out the last splinter of bone, leaving a cavity big enough to hide three oranges. "We can give Lansana antibiotics, but Mozzer Nature, she will be the one to heal this hole."

Mother Nature would have to come up with some sort of miracle to close that crater, but since I had no better suggestions, I made no comment.

"Now I go for lunch," Jean announced. Squeamishness obviously wasn't the cause of Jean's skinny frame. "Pa George, he is cooking for you?"

"I think so." I assumed that making lunch had been Pa George' intention.

"Good. Then we meet on TB ward at three?" Jean held the theatre door open for me to step outside. The oppressive midday heat was only small relief from the odours within. It was autumn back home, my favourite season. Oh! to fill my lungs with clean frosty air and jump into a pile of crunchy golden leaves, watching my laughter condense into little puffs.

"The TB patients will be very happy to have a new lady doctor" added Jean. Well, that made two things I was good for.

4. Oh Lord, Give This Patient Well Body

".... and we hope that Dr. Gay able give this patient well body. Tenki ya. Amen." Peter, the nurse anaesthetist, cast his eyes in my direction as he finished his supplication to the Almighty. Sheepishly I laid my scalpel down - a naughty child reaching too eagerly for her knife and fork before grace.

Lunch had been interrupted by my first ever, surgical patient. She had a twisted ovarian cyst, which Jean said would be a nice easy one for me to start with. I wasn't so sure. My patient was only numbed from waist to toes with a spinal anaesthetic, leaving her conscious and able to hear every word of the prayer. Still she looked trustingly up at me. A droplet of sweat trickled down the inside of my spectacles. I was scrubbed so couldn't wipe it away.

"This is a Catholic hospital." Jean's eyes smiled reassurance above his faded surgical mask. "Peter prayed before Sister Hillary's cases too."

I nodded and smoothed the rubber gloves over my trembling, stumpy fingers, but no magical pair of rubber gloves was going to transform them into a surgeon's lithe hands.

Tiange slapped a scalpel into my palm. I swallowed, nodded, and made my first incision. The blade barely broke the skin. I tried again, but snaked off to the left, tried to pull the knife back on course and nicked a blood vessel that started to spurt over my glove.

Tiange clamped the bleeder with one hand and prised the scalpel from my fingers with the other. Sent off in the first minute, I could only watch from the sidelines as Jean sliced cleanly through the abdominal wall so that he and Tiange could remove the off-purple melon that had once been our patient's ovary. Tiange reluctantly allowed me back on in the closing minutes to sew together the last layer of skin with a needle and thread that my grandmother would have refused to darn socks with. I still managed to snap it.

"This is last needle." Tiange sighed. I reached to take it from her but she pulled it away fractionally. "I will finish the work." She announced and sutured the ten inch wound together in under a minute. My eyes were transfixed on the premier division embroiderer's nimble fingers, partly with admiration, but mostly to avoid catching the eye of Jean, or the patient.

My only achievement was to hold back the sobs long enough to escape from the operating room.

Alan lay draped across my sofa, Star Beer in hand. Today he was wearing a green and yellow tie-dyed suit that clashed horribly with the mustard velour.

"I need a gin," I wailed.

"Star Beer?"

"I don't like beer." I whined, blowing my nose.

"Bejasus. Last night you were after drinking five bottles." Alan pulled himself up to a seated position.

"I thought it rude to refuse. Oh God….." I dropped my head in my hands.

"The first day is always the hardest. Go on have a beer."

I took the warm bottle, flipped off the gold star lid, then moved the blue and gold paper label aside to check for creatures within. "Peter actually prayed in front of a fully conscious patient!" I complained, wiping a smear of glue from my hand. "Talk about inspiring confidence."

"We all need prayers," came a voice from the corner.

"Oh, hello," I said, self-pity momentarily forgotten when I noticed the gaunt, yellow-eyed stranger in my sitting room.

"Hi. I'm Tom." He held out a clammy hand, which I shook ever so carefully. "Malaria, I'm afraid."

"Tom teaches at our nursing school."

"Are you alright, Tom?"

"Much better, thank you, Dr. Gail," he said, although the evidence pointed to the contrary. "Are you enjoying Serabu?"

"No! I wanted to save lives and be a better person and I'm just useless," I howled. "I'm no Sister Hillary"

Tom looked alarmed at my response but Alan just furrowed his sweaty brow. "Forget all that and drink your beer."

"People are starving? How can I drink beer?"

"And stop wallowing in Catholic guilt. Guilt is self-indulgent and destructive."

And yesterday I had thought of Alan as my angel of mercy? "I take it you're not one of these religious types yourself?" I glowered.

"Me? I'm going to be a priest."

Alan looked rather satisfied at my horrified expression and took a deep swig of his beer. Tom excused himself and staggered back to bed.

"Vegetarian," sniffed Alan. "He'd rather get malaria than swot a mosquito. And he forgoes the healing properties of Star Beer too. Drink up."

There was nothing else for it. I finished the bottle, just as Pa George thundered in from outside and dumped two soot-blackened pots on the table. He piled our plates with mounds of soggy rice followed by green gunge.

"What's that?" I exclaimed, my eyes fixed on the bright orange oil that was seeping under the rice and heading for the edge of the chipped plate.

"Plassas," said Pa George. "I de go." And he went. I looked in dismay at the steaming cowpat before me. Alan burst out laughing.

How was I ever going to survive two years of this? At least I might lose some weight!

"Dr. Gay, you get body," said the first patient on TB ward.

"Yes, Dr. Gay really get body," agreed a skeletal man in the bed opposite. Twenty male heads nodded their approval.

"What are they saying, Jean?"

"They say that you have the woman's curves. Notto so, Mr. Kpukoma?" Jean turned to the Charge Nurse, a kind eyed man with scattered curls of grey hair who scarcely reached Jean's shoulder.

"Yes, yes, Dr. Jon. Dr. Gay is fat," Patrick Kpukoma agreed enthusiastically. My jaw dropped, accentuating my double chin.

"This is a very big compliment in Africa," Jean said reassuringly.

"Hmmph!" I straightened up, lengthened my neck and sucked in my tummy.

"Dr. Gay get fine body," Mr. Kpukoma grinned.

"A big 'ealthy woman is a big prize for a Salonean man. Especially for these patients wiz dry cof."

"Dry cough?" I asked.

"Krio for tuberculosis," explained Jean.

"Yes, but *dry* cough?" Back home a dry cough was an annoying tickle without any gratifying phlegm. But here? The first patient coughed up his soul to half fill a tin cup with guacamole green sputum, then proudly displayed his efforts. I balked. "Jean, how can you call that *dry* cough?"

"Ah. Dry means thin."

"Dr. Jon dry." Mr. Kpukuma held up Jean's scrawny arm. "And Dr. Gay get body!" He squeezed the soft flesh above my elbow.

"Fat," I snapped. Twenty men with concentration camp physiques, looked at me accusingly. "Skinny cough," I mused. "What a good name for TB."

Perhaps it was time for the big strong girl to revel in her plentiful coverings.

I spent the rest of my second day making myself as inconspicuous as possible in the hope that Jean wouldn't suggest I actually lay hands on a patient. Thankfully, he let me observe quietly, content with throwing me little titbits of advice and information. Jean's caring manner really impressed me, as he did what had to be done within the confines of Serabu's meagre resources. But clinical abilities did nothing to boost my confidence. I had been a good GP, although that was easy, with a hospital full of consultants only ten minutes down the road. Why hadn't I stuck with my strengths?

The next patient arrived, ushered in by his four wives. I smiled at the old Pa. He had a lump the size of an orange where his right testicle should have been.

"Tumour," said Jean, palpating the normal testicle dwarfed by its malignant neighbour. "But I think it spreads not, we need only remove the bad one."

"Can *you* do that?"

"Bien sur. It is not too difficult." Jean turned to his patient. "I very sorry Pa, but we get for pull you ball."

It cannot be easy for a man to hear he will have to lose a testicle. I waited for the anguished howl.

"No problem, Dr. Jon." Came the cheery reply. "Pull all two. I get nineteen pickin."

"Nineteen children!" I spluttered once our patient had left to arrange his admission. "Don't you have *any* family planning?"

"This is a Catholic hospital!" Jean sounded affronted. "Besides that's only five children per wife."

"Of course." I bit my tongue. Had those VSO courses taught me no tolerance? "Sorry."

Jean's eyebrow raised a fraction. "Fais-voir, Dr. Gail." He unlocked his top drawer.

"Condoms!" There were enough to service the whole population of Serabu twice over.

61

"We smuggle them from Freetown. MT sees not the women weak from ten, fifteen, twenty pregnancies with no food for the children they have. Twenty percent of the pickins die before they reach five." Jean shook his head as he continued. "The women get desperate and go to the, how you call, 'quacks,' for abortion. Then they come, bleeding and infected." Jean sucked in his breath. "You should go home and unpack. Then come to meet Francoise at six."

"Okay," I replied, although I didn't want to unpack. That would imply that I was staying.

Glad as I was to leave the wards, my house gave no comfort. It was not, and would surely never be, home. This oppressive heat was sapping my energies and it was too hot to lie down without a fan. More air could circulate if you stood upright. I fiddled with the dial on my compact short wave radio and found the World Service, that faithful companion of displaced souls like myself, but all it had to offer was a programme on tapestry. What I really wanted was a 27inch screen showing *EastEnders*, or even *Neighbours*, and a large box of Thornton's chocolates on my knee.

What was I going to do? *Tess of the d'Urbervilles* was about as inspiring as tapestry and the nearest phone was in Freetown, one hundred and seventy miles away. I would have to make do with writing letters. Of course, I would write to Klaus.

I had soon filled three sheets of paper with doctor's scrawl. Pausing to flex my cramped fingers, I skimmed through my efforts. Oh dear. The long list of complaints wouldn't enhance that heroic doctor image that I wanted to put across. I couldn't have Klaus knowing how pathetic I was being, so scrunched the sheets into a ball and threw it into the bin. Fiona? No - her letter from Panguma had been so enthusiastic. I was interrupted by Alan making faces behind the mosquito mesh.

"Lunchtime, Dr. Gail!"

"Already? There's no rumble from my tummy?" Nevertheless, Pa George clattered in and slammed a pot on the table.

"What's for chop today then?"

"Potato leaf plassas," snapped Pa George and stomped out of the room.

"Look at that oil," I whispered, eyeing the soggy green mash with the bright orange palm oil floating a centimetre thick on top. No wonder my hunger signals had gone on strike.

"We're poomuis," Alan explained. "Extra oil for the rich white man."

"I'll ask him to cut down?"

"What? And insult him?"

"Hmmph." Alan was right. After our inauspicious start, I couldn't afford to get on the wrong side of Pa George. "Anyway, this looks just like yesterday's."

"Yesterday cassava leaf. Today potato leaf." Pa George returned with the plates, his grasp of English was clearly better than I'd assumed. "What for chop tomorra?" He thrust his chin forwards.

"Er..." I backed away. "What do you suggest, Pa George?"

"Crin-crin."

"Okay. Crin-crin."

"Crin-crin eight leone, onion twenty leone, pepper four leone...."

Alan was sniggering again.

"Okay, so what's crin-crin?" I asked as soon as Pa George had gone.

"Oh, it's like cassava leaf, only slightly greener."

Francoise, cradling eight-month old baby Geraldine at her breast, handed me a glass of freshly squeezed orange juice. She wore only a sleeveless white blouse, tie-dyed shorts and flip-flops but still managed to look coolly elegant, despite unevenly cropped blonde hair (presumably Jean's work), and unshaven legs covered with mosquito bites.

"Jean says you are doing well," she smiled.

"Huh?" I spluttered on my orange juice. I had taken Jean for an honest man.

"It eez very hard at first. Jean also could not do the surgery when we came. Please. Have some more orange."

"Thank you." I waved the flies from the mouth of the jug and refilled my glass. We sat outside their house as the sun set behind a palm tree and Jean played football with two year old Matthieu, and four Salonean children.

Matthieu, ghostly white next to the shiny black skins of his team-mates, was splodged with gentian violet dabbed across an assortment of spots and scabs. He bent over to pick up the ball, revealing a two-centimetre boil on his bottom.

"Viens, Matthieu. Qu'est que c'est, mon petit?" Francoise gave the boil a gentle squeeze with her free hand. "Tiens, c'est la Tumbu."

"Tumbu fly?" I looked more closely at poor Matthieu's bottom.

"Let me show you how to treat Tumbu. Un moment."

Francoise returned with Geraldine on her hip, holding a pot of Vaseline.

"Vaseline?"

"Fais voir." Francoise smeared it over Matthieu's gobstopper boil.

"Ne bouge pas, mon petit. Vaseline cuts off the maggot's oxygen, then we wait."

64

"Huh?"

"The Tumbu must come for air. Regarde."

The boil erupted and a juicy prawn wriggled out.

"Yugh!"

"Voila, Matthieu." Francoise flicked the larva on the floor and squashed it under her flip-flop. Matthieu ran off to continue his game.

"Madame Tumbu likes very much to lay her eggs in the seams of underpants." Francoise explained "Pa George must iron your underwear to kill the eggs."

"Pa George isn't ironing my knickers!"

"Eh, bien. If you know how to use a charcoal iron...."

"So, Francoise, how long have you been here?"

"Two years. We arrived when Matthieu was a baby."

"What about Geraldine, you surely didn't have her in Serabu?" I gasped, but Francoise's attention had been diverted by delighted squeals. Her husband was trotting round the grass like a tame giraffe, giving the children rides on his shoulders.

"He is 'appy that you have come, Gail," she continued. "Look. He laughs again!" I was about to thank her for her kind words, but something in her change of manner made me hesitate. "Dr. Pat left six months ago, and from then, Jean has had no day off...."

"Six months is an awfully long time," I agreed. Two days had been a long time.

"He is very tired, yes?" Francoise leaned toward me and I gulped, realising where this conversation was going. "Jean very much needs a break". I nodded dumb agreement. "We have been waiting for you so we can go on 'oliday for one week." Francoise hesitated. "Gail, I want to ask you ......I ....We...."

"Francoise, not yet." Jean appeared at his wife's side, with Matthieu still perched on his shoulders.

"Mais oui, Jean." Francoise placed a hand on his arm. "You

65

are getting ill. You need to sleep, you must rest."

"But it is too soon."

My head turned from Francoise to Jean and back again.

"And we must think of Matthieu...We would like to go next week," she blurted.

"Next week," I repeated dully.

"I know it will be difficult, but Matthieu...." she looked at her little boy scratching the angry prickly heat on his tummy. "The sea breezes will make his skin better."

"Yes, of course." I attempted a nonchalent smile.

"No, Gail. It is too much," Jean protested feebly.

"It's okay. I'll manage," I announced without thinking. Never one to say no, how could I refuse? Jean was exhausted – six months alone, and that poor little boy. But how could I agree? Good God. A whole week alone. Next week?

5. Is That Why They Sent You Here?

"What for chop today?"

Roast beef, pink in the middle, horseradish sauce, crispy roast potatoes, lashings of gravy, mange tout peas and perhaps a smooth dark chocolate mousse for afters.

"Plassas," I sighed. A full week and I was still here! The trouble was I couldn't bring myself to abandon Jean before his break. And then there was Klaus, and Lindsey's granny. What would they think if I wimped out within a week?

"Cassava leaf, eight leones, rice, ten leones, onion ten leones." I cringed at the thought of more mashed green leaves spiked with bonga, smothered in bright orange oil. If God would deliver me some chocolate, then my soul was his forever. "Palm oil ten leones, bonga twenty leones. What's your name?"

"Er, Gail. Gail Haddock," I replied, trying to keep a straight-face. "And yours?"

"George Williams."

George Williams? "Pleased to meet you, Mr. Williams." We shook hands solemnly.

"Do you have family?" This was progress. Conversation!

"I get one wife an one girl-pickin."

"How old is your little girl?"

"Two rainy seasons."

"And what's her name?"

"Dr-Pat."

"Doctor Pat?"

"Dr. Pat fine doctor," he stated.

"Yes. Yes. Of course."

"Do you get pickins?" he asked.

"Er no. I have no children."

"Do you get man?"

"No. I have no husband."

"Is that why they sent you here?"

Great, just great. Incompetent, undesirable and barren. Well Dr-Marvellous-Pat might well have boosted their attendances and saved their hospital from closure, but not me. I was evidently not the knight with a shining stethoscope they had hoped for.

My paranoia was symptomatic of a more general misery. Prickly heat and mosquito bites battled for possession of every inch of my body, fungus grew in the moist hiding place along the bra line beneath my breasts and the armpits of my clothes were turning yellow as palm oil literally seeped from my pores. Tom had told me that palm oil contains more cholesterol than virtually anything, so to add to the insult of having to eat the stuff (in double, poomui doctor quantities) my arteries were hardening by the minute without a single piece of chocolate passing my lips. It just wasn't fair! AND Jean was going on holiday tomorrow. Bloody Hell!

Perhaps I could give my prickly heat its medical title, milia rubrae (Latin for little red spots), and pretend it was a serious tropical disease that required an immediate medi-vac. Who could argue with the only doctor?

MT, that's who. After twenty years in Sierra Leone, even an administrator could no doubt spot prickly heat from 200yards, regardless of fancy names. With Jean away, MT was never going to allow her hospital's only remaining doctor to leave, no matter how useless she proved to be.

I wasn't exactly homesick. Returning home so soon without a very good excuse seemed rather pathetic and besides, as Pa George had so rightly pointed out what was there for me at home? No husband and no children. And apart from a slight loosening of my waistband, my big goals were further away than ever.

It was ten o'clock on Saturday morning and Jean had given me the day off to calm myself before the storm. Relaxing was out of the question, so I rubbed the mould off my leather sandals, strapped them on and headed down to Alan's. He answered the door in a gara dressing gown, fag in hand.

"Not dressed yet," I exclaimed. "It's gone ten!"

"Jaysus, that early? What do you want at this unearthly hour?"

"I thought you might fancy a walk."

"Is the girl mad?"

"Come on, I'm getting cabin fever."

"Cabin fever? You've only been here a week!"

"I know, I know. Please, Alan, I need you to cheer me up."

"I'll put on my shorts."

I followed Alan's frighteningly pale legs down the path that formed the outer boundary of the hospital compound on one side and a series of mud houses with corrugated iron roofs, set between the ubiquitous rubber plants and palm trees, on the other. The path led onto Serabu's main street, a red latterite road dotted with puddles. A goat stopped to take a drink, then sauntered off between the houses made of the same job lot of concrete, rusting roofs and rotting wooden shutters as the hospital. The children called "poomui, poomui", then ran to hide behind trees or toothless grannies. White man, white man. I smiled and waved.

"Spot the newcomer," teased Alan and, right enough, by the time we reached the market square my jaw was aching with smiling so much and I was beginning to understand why the queen looked so grim.

Serabush's market was nothing like the jostling hub of Freetown - seven ramshackle stalls displaying only stingy piles of rice, bonga, cassava leaf and quartered onions - certainly nothing I was tempted to buy. We just smiled and said kushe to the disappointed vendors.

Beyond the market the road ran alongside a stream where naked children splashed happily in the shade of the lush greenery.

"Oh, lets jump in!"

"No! What would they think of Serabu's new doctor cavorting with the Assistant Administrator in her birthday suit?"

"Who cares?"

"And you don't care about schistosomiasis, giardiasis, amoebic dysentery or larvae migrans either?"

"Smartarse," I sniffed. "Why don't you do Jean's job this week?"

"I faint at the sight of blood."

A little further upstream, three women were washing their clothes against the stones with bars of soap.

"Have you met Sesay?" enquired Alan.

"Oh yes, the maintenance man."

"Well, they are his wives."

"What?" I spluttered. "All of them?"

"All three!"

"Humph." I snorted. "Well they seem to get on very well." I added, watching the women laugh together as they spread their lappas out to dry on the bank.

"Like having extra sisters."

Humm, and to think that I'd always wanted a sister.

"How does anything dry in this humidity?" I added out loud.

"The same way things get washed in the dry season when there's no stream left."

"But our nurses are so crisp and white. Is there a hospital laundry?"

"You're joking, with our fancy electric water pumps broken for six weeks? The nurses are responsible for their own uniforms, and the patients bring their own sheets. Fortunately you and I have Pa George."

"Okay, okay, so you were right about him too."

Three miles uphill we reached the Junction, where the road met the main road to Bo. There were several people milling around with trays of bananas, oranges, groundnuts and little plastic bags of home-made ginger beer on their heads. We chose to give our custom to a painfully thin lady whose eight month pregnancy was grotesquely exaggerated against her six stone frame. She introduced herself as Musu. She was desperate to make a few extra leones after the recent death of her husband and before the imminent arrival of her first baby. We immediately bought another four oranges, which she peeled for us to squeeze straight into our mouths.

"Why all these vendors?" I asked Alan as Musu sliced the top off a tenth orange. "I can only see two houses."

"They're waiting for the poda-poda to Bo."

"Poda-poda?"

"The local bus. It means slowly-slowly," Alan explained. "You'll see."

And slowly slowly, right on cue, a poda-poda creaked down the road. It was a rusty truck, sardine packed with people peering out from the metal grills that ran along the sides, and a roof that was piled high with more people, firewood, sacks of sweet potatoes, the occasional goat and bits of old furniture. Needless to say it all looked very precarious.

The poda-poda lurched round the side of a pothole, then wobbled to a halt. A couple of people jumped down from the roof and helped an old lady out of the back. Four other people squeezed themselves into her place. Musu passed her oranges to the other passengers through the grill, and they passed out their money. It was a race against both time and the other sellers to get rid of as many oranges as she could before the poda-poda pulled away. We watched the truck creak around the corner, and set off back to the village.

Alan took me through the back courtyards of the village where the concrete buildings that fronted onto the main street gave way to houses of mud and stone. Children scampered barefoot in torn knickers whilst a woman cooked. She was a classical Mende beauty, with high cheekbones, slimline nose and a dimple-faced baby strapped to her back. I gaped with horrified admiration as she lifted a rice pot directly from the fire with her bare hands. Turning she gave us a beautiful smile with her full friendly mouth. She looked awfully familiar.

"Kushe Dr. Gay, kushe Alan."

I blushed. Serabu's matron was dressed only in a black stripy bra and lappa, whilst we stood, uninvited in her kitchen.

"Kushe, Betty," breezed Alan, without a hint of embarrassment. "How were you ever managing to lift that off the fire without gloves?" He pointed to the pot filled with bubbling plassas.

"Training. If I cried when I touched the hot pot, my mother hit my hands with a stick."

"That's awful," I cried.

The child torturer in question turned out to be an elderly woman who was pounding a five-foot pestle into a giant mortar.

"Kushe," I nodded curtly at Betty's mother, who nodded back.

"What's she doing?"

"She must pound the cassava leaves for one hour to get the cyanide out."

"Cyanide!"

"But you don't need a cook, do you Dr. Gail?

"Shut up, Alan."

"Hillary got funding to send Betty to the Liverpool School of Tropical Medicine" Alan led me back through to the main street. "She knows, unlike most Saloneans, what a cold and lonely sort of paradise the affluent West can be."

"So she understands what I'm going through."

"Not that she'd be saying anything bad about your homeland, but we're mighty glad she hated it and came home."

"She's super with the staff and patients. Even MT's civil to her."

"MT knows that Serabu slumped as much because of Betty's year out as Pat's departure, so she can forgive a bit of pre-marital baby-making. In fact our MT's quite gaga over Hindolu."

"You're joking."

I left my friend to stagger back to his own house muttering that he'd be up for lunch when he'd recovered, and continued home. A young lad intercepted me.

"Kushe Dr. Gay. You want bananas?" The boy, no more than ten years old, pointed to the bunch of bananas on the tray perched on his head.

"No. Look at all these bananas!" I had already bought four bunches in an effort to spread my custom up at the junction. How many did these people think I could eat?

"You want groundnuts?" he persisted, determined to make a sale.

"Oh, okay. How much?" He took his tray down to show me his wares. The peanuts were fresh and almost juicy looking. "Twenty leones." He took the tray from his head and used a rusty tomato puree tin to measure out my nuts.

"What's your name?" I asked, watching him make a little paper funnel to pour them into.

"Nurse," he said.

"Nurse?" I raised an eyebrow.

"Nurse Sankoh." He handed me my parcelled groundnuts. "Twenty leones."

"Well thank you, Nurse."

He put the tray back onto his head, and put my twenty leones into his sandshoe. He was the first child I'd seen with shoes - selling groundnuts must be good business. I put the nuts into my pocket and returned to my house.

I went straight to my water filter and downed three glasses. Taking a fourth, I flopped on my sofa and listened to Pa George clattering around outside. I knew I should be grateful for Pa George, but the smell of plassas was making me nauseous.

Aw fo do. There might not be any cheese or chocolate, but at least I've got groundnuts, I thought, unpackaging the nuts. Just a minute. This looks a bit familiar. I stared at the wrapping.

The paper was covered in my own scrawl - it was my discarded letter to Klaus.

"And what is our Dr. Gail studying so intently. A letter?"

I jumped. "Alan! I didn't hear you."

"A love letter!"

"Hoi!" I clutched the letter to my chest.

"Let me see, let me see."

"It's not a love letter," I protested. "It's just an unfinished letter I threw out. That boy, Nurse, has wrapped my groundnuts in one of my own letters!"

"So why did you throw it out? Scared it might be too slushy?" Alan fluttered his hand against his heart. "Go on. Send it!"

"No, I didn't want him to think me a whinger."

"Who?"

"None of your business."

"Well it's half of Serabu's business now!" laughed Alan.

"Oh no, I've complained about everyone." I groaned. My popularity ratings were low enough already. "I just can't believe they rake through our rubbish."

"Of course they do, we poomuis are terribly wasteful," Alan said casually. "Never mind, literacy is less than 17% and your writing is illegible."

"I hate you."

"Of course you do. Now then, I think we've earned our beer today." Alan produced two bottles from behind his back. "I'll make the toast. Hillary and Pat, eat your hearts out, there's a new doc in town. Slainte!"

"I still hate you. I have nightmares about those two. Did you know that Pa George even called his daughter after Dr. Pat? Literally Dr-Pat?"

"Oh don't you worry doc, Pa George'll be singing your praises soon enough."

"I doubt it," I snorted. "But don't you think he looks old to have a two year old?"

The door burst open and Pa George stormed in carrying the rice pot.

"I'm not old. I'm just ugly!"

6. Locked Out

Jean drove off to the beach with his family, leaving me with a
chicken. Lansana, the man with the gunshot wound, had presented
him with it as a thank you for the miraculous healing of his buttocks.
Well, if he had survived, perhaps there was hope for us all. I stood
watching as their truck bounced out of the compound, with the
chicken clawing my legs and the hand of doom gripping my gullet.
It gave an extra little squeeze when Tiange thrust the Theatre keys
under my nose.

"You no get for lose those keys, Dr. Gay, others are not there."

"Can't you cut more?"

"If we take those keys to make other set, we get for leave
theatre open. MT say the thiefmen go thief everything."

"Who would steal theatre equipment?"

"The quacks able look like real doctors, the drapes make
fine sheets and you able melt scalpels and forceps for cooking pots."

"You're joking!"

But Tiange didn't joke. "We go see back."

Pa George's cold plassas was waiting for me when I got home. I
christened the chicken 'Tikka' in eager anticipation of a change of
menu, threw her some rice to fatten her up, and flopped onto my
sofa and opened Tess. The big words in tiny print blurred in front
of me. Oh why hadn't I brought a glossy bestseller and why oh
WHY had I agreed to be the sole doctor in the Chiefdom for a
whole week? To punctuate my mood the heavens opened. Rain
battered on my corrugated iron roof, pounding in unison with my
head. I paced round the living room, sat down, picked up my pen to
begin a letter home, chewed the end, doodled a couple of smiley
faces on the envelope, stood up, walked to the window, was sprayed

by rain flying through the mesh and sat down again. I gave my faces bodies, then put a monkey wrench in the hand of one and embellished the second with a fringe, ponytail and stethoscope. I drew a big heart round both. Klaus and the doc.

"Gail, what are you thinking?" I scribbled out the unlikely lovebirds, reopened Tess, attempted a few more paragraphs but, irritated with beautiful heroines, threw it down again. I tried unsuccessfully to appease my chocolate craving with a banana then fiddled with my radio for the World Service. The classical concert might have been enjoyable if my radio had been any bigger than a cigarette packet. Now what? My toenails needed cutting - my how fast they grew. Toenails cut, I looked at my watch yet again. Twenty-to-ten. At last, a reasonable time to go to bed.

Now this wasn't as easy as it sounded. My narrow single bed was smothered with a king-sized mosquito net hanging from wires that strung across my bedroom with as much excess as possible tucked tightly under the mattress. None of those little bloodsuckers would find a way into *my* bed. Unfortunately with all those spare folds, neither could I.

The World Service theme tune –Lillibolero tinkled out for the ten o'clock news. Instant darkness. Why did Sesay have to be so blooming punctual with the generator curfew?

Blindly, I tried to fight my way through a false opening in the net curtains from hell, eventually pulling their suspension wires from the wall, leaving me drowning in a cloud of foaming mesh. I'd left my torch in the sitting room, so I fumbled around for a candle on my bedside table. Of course there were no matches to hand, which was probably fortunate, as I was hot and sticky enough without everything going up in flames. Praying that braving the mosquitoes for one night would not mean White Woman's Grave, I curled up naked and sweaty on the mattress, clutching my sheet like a security blanket.

The rain had stopped, but the toads still grommeted ectastically outside my house, punctuated by the drip-drip from my overfilled gutters. In the distance I could hear the rumble of rhythmic drumming from a secret society gathering somewhere in Serabu village. As a poomui, I would never be privy to any information about the secret societies, but since membership seemed to involve genital mutilation for both males and females, ignorance was probably bliss. The drums blended with the occasional groan of thunder that after an hour or two became almost soothing.

Light suddenly flickered through my cotton curtains. I bolted upright and went to the window, expecting to see Almamy standing on my doorstep with his kerosene lamp, come to fetch me for some dire emergency. But there was no Almamy, just some distant flashes of lightning. Finally I dozed off.

When Almamy really did start banging on my door, I was deep in dreamland, skiing after Klaus down a snowy Scottish hillside. Totally disoriented, I jumped out of bed and tripped over the voluminous mosquito net that covered the floor. Bang bang bang.

"Okay, I'm coming." I felt around for my dress.

"Dr. Gay, come quick quick." Bang bang bang. It was too dark to find any clothes so I wrapped my nude body in my sheet and stumbled through to the living room.

Almamy was still knocking on the door when I opened it. He stopped to thrust a note into my hand and held his lamp so I could read the childlike writing on the crumpled paper:

Jeneba is eight months pregnant. She get convulsions.

"Shit!" I grabbed the theatre keys, rammed on my flip-flops, and flew to Maternity, my makeshift toga flapping at my ankles.

I arrived on Maternity, my sheet splattered with mud and

was faced with a heavily pregnant teenager having violent seizures.

"Kushe Dr. Gay," said Laygby. "Dis Jeneba. She get eclampsia."

"Eclampsia." I took some deep breaths. I'd never seen it but eclampsia was one of those conditions hammered into medical students as pregnancy's greatest danger. The textbooks describe how the blood pressure soars and the fluid leaks into all the bodily tissues causing widespread swelling. It had turned Jeneba's normally slim body into a grotesquely overinflated rubber doll, swamped with excess fluid. Fluid also leaks into the brain, and this, combined with the rapidly escalating blood pressure leads to convulsions then death. In the West mothers-to-be wonder why their doctors and midwives make such a fuss over blood pressure. Here, convulsing in front of me, was the reason.

My sheet was slipping, so I tied it more firmly over my breasts to steady myself for action. With no Jean to call upon, two lives now depended on me. Help!

"Laygby we need intra-venous diazepam," I announced in my calmest voice.

"Diazepam don finish, Dr. Gay."

"What do you mean, finished?" I hissed.

"Don don. Aw fo do."

"What? No!" I nearly screamed. "Don't give me aw fo do. What about hydrallazine?"

"Don don, Dr. Gay," repeated Laygby.

"Damn. Find some from another ward. Break into pharmacy. Anything. Just do it quickly."

Laygby ran out with her lamp leaving me with two assistants: a fellow pregnant patient and Jeneba's mother. First I needed to secure venous access for the drugs, so Jeneba's mother clamped herself round her daughter's convulsing legs while my second assistant tried to restrain her arm for me to slip the cannula into her vein. My assistants whispered urgently to each other in Mende. Even if we had a communal language, there was nothing I could say to reassure them. Jeneba and her baby would surely die.

Things had seemed bad enough, but then Jeneba jerked uncontrollably and knocked over our remaining kerosene lamp. In the blackness, I felt for my torch, burning my hand on the overturned lamp. My curses conveyed their meaning without literal translation, and the room fell silent.

Moments later, Laygby burst into the dark room, clutching the necessary drugs and her lamp. We looked over to our saviour, standing in a dim pool of light, with a unified desperation.

"Well done Laygby," I said, trying to force brisk confidence into my voice. "Draw up two vials of diazepam and put that lamp here so I can find my torch."

"No problem, Dr. Gay."

Two hours later we finally calmed Jeneba's fits and eased her blood pressure down, but the only cure for eclampsia is immediate delivery of the baby. Without all the swelling, Jeneba would normally be a tiny girl and she had a very big baby. I knew what I had to do.

"Laygby, we need to prepare for a Caesarean Section."

"No problem, Dr. Gay."

You might not think it's a problem Laygby, but then you haven't seen me with a scalpel. "Can you get the theatre staff?" I added out loud.

"No problem. I go look for Almamy."

Almamy was asleep outside Surgical. Laygby tugged off his woolly bonnet and sent him to rouse the theatre staff from their homes in the village. No telephones in Serabush.

Tiange and Peter, who lived in the first two houses by the hospital, arrived within ten minutes. "Where theatre keys?" Tiange yawned.

"The keys? The keys," I muttered, looking hopefully first at Laygby then the grandmother. I patted my belly and hips, as if expecting to find pockets in my bedsheet-dress. "Where are they? Where are the keys?" I pleaded. Laygby shook her head and Tiange rolled her eyes to the ceiling. Peter scanned the table and floor with his torch and shrugged. The grandmother turned from me, clutched Jeneba's hand and started to moan rhythmically. Now she knew this poomui would never to save her daughter.

I dropped to the floor and crawled under the bed with the torch. They all stood and gaped.

"Well, help me look for them, dammit."

We scoured the path to my house for the keys, but our lamps and torches were no match for the puddles, mud and grass. We'd have to break down theatre's doors, which with big metal framed doors, would certainly cause considerable damage. Oh God, MT would never forgive me.

The last person on Almamy's emergency call out list was Sesay for the generator. Fortunately Almamy, for all his faults, always knew which wife Sesay would be with and, even more fortunately, Sesay had a separate set of keys for the generator room.

Laygby and Peter were lifting Jeneba onto the theatre trolley just as the comforting rumble of the generator flooded us with light. And lo! There were the elusive theatre keys, pressed deeply into Jeneba's left buttock.

Once in theatre, Jeneba's swollen flesh obscured the space between the vertebrae for Peter to pass his spinal needle. He was distraught. "I no able feel the bones-self. Five years don pass since I miss a spinal, Dr. Gay."

Good Lord, imagine giving a spinal to a patient with eclampsia – totally contraindicated, but our alternative was ketamine and that was even worse.

"Let me try," I offered. I had spent a year as an anaesthetist in York, so spinals were one thing I was actually good at. Usually.

Jeneba's skin was like playdough, with Peter's fingerprints and the deeper imprint of the theatre keys, the only landmarks. This was going to be a stab in the dark but finally God smiled on me. The needle popped through the coverings of the spinal cord and slipped into place and I injected the local anaesthetic with ease. For the first time since arriving at Serabu Hospital, I felt a glimmer of confidence.

After a quick check in Maurice King's book, Tiange and I scrubbed with a bar of soap and bowls of water taken from the theatre drum, put on our patched green gowns and rubber gloves and prayed.

"We pray that Jeneba and her baby can be saved this night, tenki ya. Amen."

"Amen," I whispered into my mask. Tiange placed the scalpel firmly into my hand and I made my incision.

Mr. Bewes said a beginner should give themselves plenty of room, so I cut deep and straight and long. I worked down through the layers of waterlogged skin, muscle and fibrous coverings of the abdominal wall until I reached the womb. Blood oozed from every level, but Tiange pressed arterial clamps into my hands and I found myself calmly tying off the bleeders.

We were quickly upon the womb wall, and my hands trembled as I made a tiny incision through the paper-thin tissue to reveal a curl of damp hair at the nape of the baby's neck, immediately below my blade. Tiange took the scalpel and I pulled the womb wall open with my fingers and plunged my hands deep into Jeneba's pelvis to grip the baby's head and ease it out. I could feel the womb tearing around my wrists as I pulled the body of a floppy blue baby boy from Jeneba's abdomen. My heart sank as I felt desperately over his chest wall for a heartbeat. There was none.

The room was silent apart from the snip of Tiange's scissors as she cut through the umbilical cord. I handed the lifeless bundle to Laygby who dashed over to the resuscitation table. Should I help her or should I stay and try to repair the gaping mess that lay before me? The baby was surely dead already, but maybe I could still save Jeneba.

"Help me, Dr. Gay. He no breathe," called Laygby.

"Tiange?" My eyes pleaded with the scrub nurse for guidance.

"I can pull the placenta Dr. Gay. You go look the pickin."

I left Tiange to remove the afterbirth and went to join Laygby, who was now doing mouth to mouth on the tiny mite. Peter had laid out a miniature rubber endotracheal tube and a rusty laryngoscope. The laryngoscope may have illuminated the vocal cords of the very first baby delivered by Sister Hillary thirty years ago, but its light was not coming on today. "Come ON!" I slammed the piece of equipment against the table. The bulb flickered and I took my brief opportunity to slip a tube into Jeneba's baby's windpipe before it went out again. Laygby connected an ambu-bag to the end of the tube and I squeezed the bag gently but rapidly to pump air into our patient's little lungs. Laygby massaged his heart with her fingertips, tapping out compressions over his breastbone like a Morse code operator.

"Can you connect up the oxygen, Laygby?"

"No oxygen, Dr. Gay."

"WHAT ....? Of course not. Sorry. I knew that."

I kept pumping the bag until my fingers cramped. I swapped hands and kept going. Laygby did the same with her heart massage. Tiange had removed the placenta and put some clamps on the edges of the womb, then covered the open wound with a warm damp cloth until I could continue. The minutes passed.

Just as I was about to give up and return to Jeneba, I felt a little resistance as I pumped the bag.

"Wait." I stopped and watched. The bag sucked in a fraction

of its own accord, then a little more.

"The baby's coughing!" I squealed with delight.

"And I able feel his pulse," added Laygby.

"Let me feel, Laygby." I pushed Laygby's hand away in my eagerness to confirm her report. The little heartbeat tapped my fingers from under his left nipple, slowly at first, then fifty, sixty, ninety and finally one hundred and forty beats a minute.

"Laygby, you're right!" I shrieked. "He's made it.The young survivor started to take his own regular breaths through the endotracheal tube. I pulled out the tube and he coughed, then let out a furious cry. It was music to my ears.

Peter helped me into a new pair of gloves. Spurred on by the baby's cry and Tiange's instructions, I took my time and sewed Jeneba's womb up, Tiange telling me where they usually put the knots.

An hour later, I bounced out of theatre into the dawn of a new morning, my head nearly too big to get out of the door. I'd saved a life! Two! Wait till I told Fiona! And Klaus! And Lindsey's granny!

It would not be a discrete little wound that could hide under a bikini but fortunately, in a society keen on tribal markings, a large and ugly scar seemed to be something to be proud of.

7. Break A Leg

The next evening Jeneba's baby screamed for his dinner while his mother lay unconscious. This wasn't good.

"This pickin is hungry." Fatmata, the student nurse, took the baby and put him to his mother's breast as she lay in a coma. But no matter what angle she tried, he wasn't going to latch on.

"Any formula milk?"

"No. No milk, no bottle," Fatmata answered. I should have been pleased that Western marketing of bottle milk hadn't reached rural Sierra Leone, but on the other hand this baby needed feeding.

"Well, he'll have stores for a few days," I said, uncertainly. And then what? If his mother died, which was looking very likely, what would become of him? Deflated, I went to continue my evening round on Surgical.

Two men were just arriving with a young woman in a native ambulance - a rope hammock, slung beneath a wooden pole balanced on their heads. As they gently lowered the patient onto the bed, I recognised her - Musu, the pregnant orange-seller from The Junction. Life hadn't treated her kindly, not only had she lost her husband, leaving her near-starved, but now she had a broken leg. Her tibia and fibula jutted out at a sickening angle through mud and blood and the trauma had started an early labour. I turned to the first 'ambulanceman', and was surprised at the Good Samaritan. "Almamy! Did *you* just carry Musu all the way from the Junction?"

"Yes."

"Three miles! On your head!" Quite a feat for anyone, never mind for the terminally lazy Almamy. I was so impressed, that I didn't ask what he was doing at the Junction when he should have been on duty an hour ago. Probably doing a bit of his own business to the poda-poda passengers. "So what happened to Musu?"

"That man in the poda-poda no pay Musu," he said. "An the poda-poda don begin go. Musu don chase am."

"Musu was chasing the poda-poda for her money?" I could visualise the heavily pregnant young woman desperately trying to get her few leones.

"Yes Dr. Gay, and dat poda-poda don turn over."

"Trapping Musu underneath?" I shuddered. It had to happen.

"Yes Dr. Gay."

Cringing, I made my plan.. I'd have to get a spinal in, clean out all the muck and dead tissue, pull the bones straight and support it in plaster. Not that I had ever put a cast on. Mr. Bewes should have let us help that old lady with the fractured wrist instead of making us play with sheep's intestines. But this was no time for wishful thinking, Musu's contractions were coming hard and fast. I needed to do whatever I was going to do quickly. Giving birth with a dangling broken leg would be agony.

"Kushe, Musu, I want fix that leg...." But Musu wasn't interested in my explanation. She just clicked her fingers at the peak of each contraction.

"Can we get theatre ready, Dauda?"

"Yes Dr. Gay. Almamy, go call theatre staff."

"No problem."

Almamy trotted off, and reappeared within minutes accompanied by Tiange and Co. We manoeuvred Musu onto the theatre trolley and headed towards the operating room. An old woman stood in front of the doors blocking our way.

"Kushe Ma, er, can I help?" She didn't utter a word. Nor did she move out of the way.

"Who's this?" I mouthed to Dauda. Short of mowing the old woman down with the trolley, I was a bit stuck.

"This is Musu's mother."

"Ah." I nodded to the unfriendly face. "What's the problem?"

"She wants the Native Healer," explained Dauda. After all, everybody knows that broken legs go to the Native Healer.

Well, I tried logical explanation, pleading and cajoling, and when that failed, shouting and stamping my foot, but Musu's mother was not going to let me put on even a temporary backslab. Spoils the magic apparently. Tiange leaned against Surgical's doorway, peeling an orange and the patients grinned delightedly at the entertainment.

Five hours later Musu's baby arrived, bottom first as predicted. I had only ever watched a breech delivery as a medical student, and it hadn't looked too easy. Okay, okay. The obstetrician had used the lithotomy position, so Fatmata helped me hoist Musu's legs up onto poles, which left her foot hanging by its tendons. I grimaced in sympathy, but had to concentrate on my part of the job. Then the obstetrician had eased the hips downwards....there. A limp body slid out, leaving the head stuck with the arms pinned up against the ears in surrender. God, this wasn't looking too good. Four minutes, I had four minutes tops if I wanted to deliver a live child. Arms, he hooked down the arms, didn't he? Musu's mother holding the two halves of her daughter's broken limb steady, glared at me. Taking a deep breath, I reached inside Musu to pull down first one then the other of her baby's arms. Now it was dangling by the neck. Musu clicked her fingers a little louder as I twisted the head round....and up... and plop, out popped out a little girl! The baby cried, I laughed with relief and Musu beamed. But still her mother did not smile.

The next morning, Musu was asleep on the bed, her baby asleep by her side and her mother asleep under the bed. Laygby had propped two sandbags on either side of Musu's leg for some support. The baby stirred so I picked her up.

"She's beautiful, what's she called?"

"Laygby."

"After you? How lovely." I smiled at the little bundle.

"Musu did not name her pickin after me," the midwife said.

"No? Well anyway, it's a pretty name. Perhaps if I ever have a little girl, I'll call her Laygby."

"Oh no, Dr. Gay, you must not!"

"Why not?" I asked, surprised at Laygby's uncharacteristic adamance.

"Laygby means 'I was born after my father has died.'"

"Oh." I bit my lip. "Sorry. Do we know why he died?"

"He don dry," said Laygby. "He no get money for come na hospital."

"Well Musu's losing weight too. We need to start her on charity feeding and get Latif to check for HIV and TB. Can you arrange all that Laygby?"

"No problem."

"Meanwhile, what about this broken leg?"

Just then Betty appeared in Maternity's doorway with a tiny, stooped old man wearing a gara suit much like Alan's. He was carrying a raffia basket over his arm. "Dr. Gay, this is Pa Kamara."

"*This* is the Native Healer?" I blurted. Where was the six-foot witch doctor covered in warpaint, dressed in feathers, black cloak and a headpiece with perhaps a monkey's skull set into the front? I was rather disappointed and vaguely insulted that my medical skills had been spurned in favour of this unprepossessing character. Betty led the elderly gentleman to Musu's bed.

Musu's mother jumped up, prodded her daughter awake, guiltily hid the sandbags under the bed and stood to attention. Pa Kamara nodded, put down his basket and motioned for Laygby to bring him a bucket of water. I sidled towards the door, not wanting my poomui presence to interfere with the magic. Betty caught my hand and mouthed, "You can stay."

Amidst much chanting, Pa Kamara rubbed what looked suspiciously like plassas into the broken leg then dragged his hands, sodden with the green gunge from the thigh to the foot, pulling her leg in line, but as soon as he let go it flopped back to its unnatural right angle. After a dozen pulls and humming a higher note he ran his hands up the skin from her foot to her thigh, gradually straightening her leg. Musu lay still and silent, although the procedure must have been agony. Her mother offered her no comfort, standing several feet from the bed, ramrod straight and expressionless while Pa Kamara climaxed with an enormous groan and shoved the ends of the broken bones together. I was the only one to wince. Then he tied a series of little twigs round the fracture site with twine. Even I had to admit he that he did a very neat job.

Just when I thought he had finished, he reached into his basket and pulled out a chicken. The bird, which had been quite silent until now, had a flurry of justified panic. Pa Kamara held its body under his arm and snapped its right leg in two. He resumed his chanting while splinting the chicken's broken leg with a tiny piece of cloth and twine.

"When dat fowl walka, Musu go walka," he announced, setting the squawking chicken on the floor to hop to refuge under the bed. Poor thing. Suddenly I saw Tikka, tied to a rope outside my house, innocently pecking at her rice, and went off all ideas of chicken for lunch. Pa Kamara picked up his basket and left.

There was still work to do, so I bent over Jeneba in the neighbouring bed. This was day three and the swelling that had so distorted her body had receded, revealing the fine features beneath. Sleeping Beauty lay without an eyelid flickering, nor finger twitching. I cuddled her baby.

"Poor little thing. He's not going to have a mother, Laygby."

"Jeneba will recover."

"Says who?"

"Sister Hillary say we must never give up."

Unfortunately, we don't all have Hillary's midas touch. I sighed. "This little one won't even have a name."

"But yes, Dr. Gay. He is called Problem," said Laygby.

"Problem? You can't call a baby Problem!"

"He is called Problem."

"Well then Problem, why are you so happy today? Have you found some milk?"

"Musu don feed him fine," said Laygby.

"What?" I turned back to the emaciated young woman, who could scarce have stores to sustain herself and her own baby, never mind that of a stranger. And what if her husband had died of AIDS and she was also positive? But Problem needed food, and was there a choice?

Problem didn't think so. He burped and Musu smiled.

8. Let Them Eat Cassava

Laygby went to MT, holder of the purse strings, to plead for Musu to have charity feeding. But MT said there was no money. I was in the middle of Outpatients when Laygby returned with the news, so scrawled "MUST HAVE CHARITY FEEDING" in big black pen across her chart and sent it back. Laygby returned to say Musu could have free treatment, but she would have to find her own food.

"But Pa Kamara's treating her leg, not us. And she's feeding Jeneba's baby." I stormed up to Admin.

"Sister Ignatius. I insist we feed Musu."

"I would be grateful if you would knock before entering, Dr. Gail." MT fixed my eyes with hers, shrivelling my confidence.

"But she probably has TB, she's lost her husband and has a baby to nurse. Two babies in fact." My voice was getting shriller. I had never been good at being assertive. "She cannot live on water. We must feed her."

"There are too many charity cases. We have already delivered her baby for free."

"But she and her baby will die of starvation." I was pleading now. I needed to steady myself and reclaim the advantage with some logical argument that might appeal on a financial level. "If they die, we've wasted time and money." Yes, that sounded better. "Two lives saved will look better on the Annual Report than two added to the mortality figures," I added with sudden inspiration.

"Very well, Dr. Gail," she said, briskly signing the chart. "But if you have any more such cases you can feed them yourself." She stood up. "Now if you will excuse me."

I was dismissed.

Back in Outpatients I turned my attention to Ma Kpukoma's infertility..

"Kushe, Dr. Gay! Kushe Ma Kpukuma!" AJ, a first year student nurse, swaggered into the Outpatients office.

"AJ. Can't you knock!"

"I get for translate for you."

"Sit down AJ."

"We go see back Ma Kpukoma." He waved at my retreating patient. "She no able born pickin, notto so?" continued AJ once the dejected lady had gone. Serabu Hospital had never heard of confidentiality. "But she lucky-oh."

"Hardly lucky, AJ."

"But Pa Kpukoma has not left her."

"I should think not!"

"Oh but he no get boy pickin. He get for take other wife."

"AJ!"

The cocky young student shrugged. I bit my tongue, after all polygamy was the norm, and I couldn't do without a translator. "Just try to be kind AJ."

As the hours passed I became increasingly suspicious of AJ's ever-lenghtening monologues that sprang from my simple sentences.

"AJ! What are you saying?" I hissed when a man with inoperable liver cancer left the room with a cheerful thank you.

"I translate fine for you!"

"AJ, I have no doubts about your linguistic ability, but why was he so happy?"

"He was glad to meet you Dr. Gay!"

"AJ......" I glared at him.

"I don tell him the iron tablets go make him better," he announced proudly.

"AJ, no they will not! He's terminal."

"But if he does not have fine blood, he will not get better."

"True, but….." I thumped the table in exasperation. "Look, you're a first year student whose job is to translate, not transform what I say into something you think sounds better. DO YOU UNDERSTAND?"

"No problem, Dr. Gay," he beamed back. Before I could strangle him, Laygby appeared for Antenatal clinic.

"Women's business," said AJ. "We go see back."

"Phew! Okay, Laygby, who's our first patient?"

"Na me.".

"You are? Well congratulations," I said, looking at the outpatient card. Three months pregnant. Hang on a minute, one stillbirth, five Caesarean Sections.

"FIVE Caesarean sections?" I exclaimed. Three Caesareans was pretty much the limit in my book, partly as the increasing scar tissue makes it technically very difficult, but mostly because the womb wall can weaken to the point of rupture (and uterine rupture is a catastrophe that will kill mother and baby). Laygby would never survive a normal labour, and Jean would be gone in six months, so it would be up to me to perform her sixth Caesarean. Hopefully I'd be better at it by then.

"My first baby died after many days of labour. Sister Hillary saved my life."

"I promise to look after you Laygby, but this baby has got to be the last one."

"But you are not allowed to do sterilisation, Dr. Gay."

"Says who? Your man?"

"No, MT. This is Catholic hospital."

"MT isn't having her sixth Caesarean section. Nor will she be in theatre. What do you want, Laygby?"

"I wanted to be sterilised last time."

"Right. We will call it tubal ligation and hope MT doesn't notice. Are you staying for the rest of the clinic?"

Alan was in his usual position, when I went back for lunch, reclined on my sofa with a beer, listening to the World Service.

"Don't administrators ever do any work?" I moaned.

"Shhh. Listen."

"What?"

"Maggie Thatcher has been thrown out!"

"What? No. Really?" I turned up the volume.

"..and Margaret Thatcher leaves number ten Downing Street with tears in her eyes...."

"Well, well, well," I said. "Good riddance."

"Have a heart, Gail," Alan teased. "Don't you feel sorry for the poor old dear? Her life's work in ruins."

"She's left plenty of lives in ruins."

"Forgiveness, Gail."

"Alan O'Connor, just because you are going to be a priest and ooze virtue, please don't expect it of me."

"I thought you were trying to save your soul?"

"I've got enough problems just now. So who's Prime Minister then?"

"Some chap called John Major."

"John....?"

Before I could ponder further on the identity of the mystery man who was now running my homeland, Pa George dumped a large black pot of plassas on the table with his usual verbal constipation.

"Oh please let's eat Chicken Tikka," begged Alan.

"No. We're keeping her for eggs."

Mustapha took health education and childhood vaccinations to the remote corners of Bumpe chiefdom. He was one of the first nurses to be trained by Sister Hillary but, despite his thirty years loyal service, Mustapha was particularly unpopular with MT. Perhaps it was because he was a Muslim, or even worse, because he was always fetching non-paying patients from his Community Outreach Team.

"Sorry-oh, Dr. Gay. I bring you one patient from the villages."

Pa Bangura stood, barefoot, leaning against the Landrover, his black skin ashen and the palms of his hands milky pale.

"Kushe, Pa. Can I look?" I asked. Battling with every gasp of breath, the old man just nodded. I pulled down his lower eyelid to look at his sheet white conjunctiva and felt the racing pulse at his wrist. He was so anaemic that he'd gone into heart failure.

"We need Latif."

"Latif don check his blood count already, Dr. Gay. Three grams."

"Three grams! Mustapha, are you sure?" I was not really questioning Latif, who was an excellent laboratory technician, but in the UK, a blood count of six grams would normally be a ticket to the intensive care unit. Pa Bangura shouldn't really be alive.

"Three grams," Mustapha repeated.

"Who can give blood?"

Jean had told me to avoid transfusions where possible, because of the risk of infection. AIDS was not the only infection we were worried about (although it was an increasing problem and we didn't entirely trust our HIV test kits) but also hepatitis, malaria and bacterial contamination during the transfusion process. With our pathetic refrigeration, a blood bank was impossible, so Pa Bangura's only hope was for us to find a donor.

"He only has one wife. Look at her," Mustapha nodded to the back seat of the Landrover. A pale old lady sat patiently.

"Latif had better check her blood too," I sighed. "What about children?"

"All the pickins don die. There is no other relative to donate."

"Oh dear. What happens now, Mustapha?"

"Latif will go to the village. He get a list of donors."

97

"Good, well let's get Pa Bangura into a bed on Medical and organise a transfusion."

"But Dr. Gay, Latif get for pay the donor."

"How much?"

"Each pint, one thousand leones."

"He'll need at least three. I don't suppose Pa...." I looked at the old man's torn shorts, and bare, skeletal chest.

"No. You must get the money from the charity fund," said Mustapha. "Sorry-oh."

Alan was on admin duty in the afternoons, so hopefully that wouldn't be too much of a problem.

"Kushe," I greeted Moses in the front office, having swapped his driver's hat for that of records officer.

"Kushe, Dr. Gay. How di body?" he said in his soft voice.

"Fine. Is Alan in? I need three thousand leones for blood."

"Alan don go to Mokanje this morning," Moses sympathised. "MT is on duty. Sorry-oh."

"Damn," I muttered under my breath. "What's he doing at the Mines anyway?" The Swiss-owned bauxite mining company was just over an hour's journey away in Mokanje. Alan and I argued over the Mines' ethics, but there was no doubt we had a symbiotic relationship. Serabu Hospital looked after the Mines' employees and their families, including twenty expatriate families, and the Mines regularly helped us out with things like barrels of diesel or spare sheets of corrugated iron.

"The Mines' people don radio today. They say they get parts for the water pumps."

With the water pumps down, I knew what a priority it was to fix them before the dry season, but I wanted Alan right here, right now.

My best bet was to bring Pa Bangura with me to Admin, so MT could see his condition for herself.

"Sister Ignatius, his blood count is dangerously low, he must have a transfusion," I explained, with the breathless old man propping himself up on the corner of the table in the back office.

"Let him pay for a donor," MT said, not looking up from her accounts.

"I beg ....Sister....I get........ no pickin...........my wife..........no well...." Pa Bangura gasped.

"No." MT did not have heartstrings that could be tugged. "You had a charity patient only yesterday. Aw fo do."

"Sister Ignatius, this is not a lost cause, but a life we can save," I begged. "Pa Bangura will do very well with a transfusion and iron treatment."

"Then let him eat more cassava leaf." This was her final word as she left the office with a swish of her habit.

"Marie bloody Antoinette!" Nuns are supposed to shelter heroes from Nazis, not turn sick old men away from hospitals! I kicked open the back door. "Find him some blood Moses, I'll pay for it."

I stomped out.

We may have rid ourselves of the real Maggie Thatcher, but who was going to oust Serabu's own?

9. A Woman's Life

MT had opened a vein of bad-temper that I never knew I possessed. Self- improvement? Huh! Well God could just forget my soul and start work on hers. Jean was due back in a matter of hours and once he arrived, I was going home. Home home. In the meantime I still had to finish off my rounds.

Maternity Ward did nothing to improve my mood. It looked like my surgical meddling had only made things worse. Jeneba remained comatose, and no matter what Sister Hillary might have said, I wished she'd just pass away quickly and peacefully, rather than put her family through any more suffering. Musu was feeding Laygby and Problem beautifully, but what if she did have AIDS? She gave me a lovely smile, but her mother sat stoney-faced on the edge of the bed.

"Doesn't that woman ever smile, Laygby?" I blurted out. "I've agreed to the Native Healer, I've made an enemy out of MT for getting *her* daughter on charity feeding, and I've brought her grand-daughter into the world after quite a tricky breech delivery." What was I looking for? Gratitude? YES!

"She did not want a girl pickin for Musu."

"What?"

Traitor! Speechless, I walked out.

Patrick Kpukoma came running over from Medical, waving a chart.

"Now what?"

"Dr. Gay. You get for sign for the blood."

"Blood?"

"For Pa Bangura-self."

"We've got blood?

"Yes, Mustapha don give one pint and Moses go give his blood this evening."

101

"Oh well done! Well done." I couldn't believe it. They were marvellous. "You don't need me."

"Oh, Dr. Gay!" Patrick Kpukoma blushed through his dark skin.

Well maybe they didn't, but I was so touched by the staff's kindness to an old man that I decided that I just might stay after all.

Jean returned that evening with a healthy covering for his ribs and his little boy with skin back to baby's bottom quality. He also brought me three letters from the VSO office. My granny's petunias hadn't survived the recent frost and our squash team seemed to be doing depressingly well without me, but what was this third envelope with only my name on it?

I ripped it open to find a double page torn from a jotter, and scanned through the four sides covered in tiny script to find the signature. Klaus!!

Opening a bottle of Star, I settled into my sofa to read a list of complaints longer than my own: no water, no electricity, no funds, no tools, no spares, a workshop full of broken vehicles, cockroaches, driver ants, prickly heat and so much plassas that he was worried he might have jaundice because his palms and soles were turning yellow. I laughed out loud. At least I was not alone.

Next morning we were on the scrounge for another pint of blood for Pa Bangura.

"Tom offered, but he's too anaemic."

"Quelle surprise. This man has always the malaria. Pah! He eats not even the fish."

"So, where to find another candidate…." I had just spotted Alan wandering towards Admin, which conveniently backed onto the lab. "Quick!" I dragged Jean into the lab.

"Kushe, Dr. Gay. Kushe Dr. Jon." Latif looked up from his

microscope. "Wetin do?"

"Kushe, Latif. We need your services."

"No problem."

"What blood group is Alan?" I nodded through the window towards the bleary eyed red-head, still suffering no doubt from the excesses he had been forced to endure during his trip to the luxury Mines Compound in Mokanje.

"Yes, Dr. Gay. I have the staff list." Latif lifted a chart off the wall. "O positive, Dr. Gay. Like Pa Bangura-self."

"Great. Get him boys."

Latif and Jean hustled Alan into the lab and were draining blood from Alan's arm before he had time to object. He promptly fainted. Betty appeared with a cup of tea and Jean produced a piece of chocolate he'd brought from Freetown (and had been keeping very quiet about) which brought Alan round as swiftly as he had fainted. Latif resumed his business of blood letting and Alan swooned again, but this time with one eye half open.

"Perhaps another piece of chocolate might rouse him, Jean?" I suggested.

"Moses don put his admission notes in the three-stone fire," whispered Betty as we watched Pa Bangura sitting cross-legged on his bed the next day, sharing a bowl of Pa George's leftover plassas with his wife. Twenty-four hours, three pints of blood and six little tablets for the hookworm later the old man was transformed. We'd treated his wife too.

"All they need now Dr. Gay are a couple of months of iron tablets and some flip-flops to stop the hookworm burrowing in through the feet."

"A big success," smiled Betty. "You deserve some time off. Come to the celebration this evening, Dr. Gay."

"I'd love to. What sort of celebration?"

"The girls are coming out," Betty explained. "I come for you eight o'clock?"

"That will be nice. Eight o'clock," I agreed, but she was gone before I could ask what she meant by coming out.

"So what is it? This Coming Out?" I asked Alan over our plassas. "The girls spend two weeks in the bush undergoing their initiation. When they come out of the bush, they are accepted into society as women available for marriage and everybody celebrates."

"Like debutantes?"

"Yes, except I don't think debutantes get circumcised."

"What?" I exclaimed.

"All the women get circumcised here. Jaysus, you're a doctor. You must have seen the evidence."

"Well, yes." I had seen the scars. Irregular lines of raised, lumpy scar tissue where once there was a sensitive clitoris, running down the upper vagina to the urethra.

"So why the big surprise?"

"Why's Betty inviting us to celebrate such an awful thing?" I felt a bit sick.

"It's a big event. We should feel honoured that Betty trusts us enough to invite."

"I'm not going."

"You'll insult Betty."

"It's collusion."

"It's education. Come on Gail. You've got to work with Betty and the others for the next two years. It's a big party."

"You mean they party round these poor girls whilst they lie screaming and bleeding as some man hacks away their genitalia with razor blades!"

"No, no. They've done all that already in the bush. At the Coming Out all the girls get to wear their new clothes and are presented to society. Besides it's the women that do the circumcisions."

"Women do it to each other?"

"They do it to remove all trace of man. It's a sacred passage to womanhood."

"God."

"Will you come?" Alan leaned towards me earnestly. "Please. Betty wants you to come, I know. Don't you see. She needs you to understand."

"I won't understand."

"Try."

"Okay," I sighed. "Okay."

Betty arrived exactly at eight o'clock. She looked great, with her hair tied up in a colourful head-dress that matched her gown and lappa. The gown was a loose-fitting, knee-length poncho made in a heavily sheened deep green cotton targeted with several golden tie-dyed circles and richly embroidered in white thread across the yoke. The lappa was made out of the same rich green, but was quite plain. She wore fake gold sandals and large gold leafed earrings. I felt very dowdy in my short-sleeved blue denim dress.

"Oh Betty, I need some new clothes."

"Ma Kpukoma will make gara for you, then we visit the tailor," said Betty. "You would look very fine in the gown and lappa. You get body."

Okay, okay. I am fat. I should be proud to get body. And Betty was right, I probably would look good in a gown and lappa. At last, a fashionable outfit that would cover my bulges.

"That would be great," I replied with a determined smile.

"We de go?" Betty asked.

"Yes, let's go. We bumped into Alan was marching up the path wearing a new gara suit. This one was navy blue with purple tie-dye.

"Love the new suit, Alan."

"And you ladies both look marvellous. Shall we go." Alan offered us an arm each and we made our way to the village.

It was a beautiful night, stars littered the sky around a slither of a moon, with no clouds or street lights to detract from their glory. We could hear drumming and singing long before we reached the market-square. The main street was packed with people dancing, all dressed in multicoloured gara. They danced to a beat, played out by groups of drummers on goat skin drums and children with sticks on coconuts or rusty tins. There were six or seven 'devils' working their way through the crowds, although I thought they looked more like dancing haystacks strewn with multicoloured pom-poms. They twisted and cavorted like erotic dancers in front of both men and women. One gyrated under my nose, then rubbed his belly against mine.

"Oh!" I gasped and stepped back. He did it again. I giggled anxiously.

"He wants you to give him money," Betty told me.

"Oh he does, does he?" I replied. "Where am I supposed to put it? Down his grass skirt?"

"He won't mind where," said Alan, slipping my devil twenty leones. The devil twirled round in appreciation then brushed his body over mine again.

"Good Lord." Afraid of spending my two years in Serabu under a curse, I hastily handed over twenty leones. My devil took the money in his teeth, tossed his straw head-dress in appreciation, then picked another victim.

AJ appeared from behind a devil, clutching a two-gallon

plastic container and three chipped cups.

"You want poyo?"

"Tenki-ya," Betty smiled, and took two of the cups. Alan took the third. AJ poured cloudy liquid into each.

"What's that?" I asked, taking a sniff of the cup Betty handed to me. "Urgh." I recoiled. It smelled like diluted vomit.

"Poyo. Palm wine." Betty smiled and drank her cupful down in one. AJ filled it up again.

"Palm wine?"

"It's the fermented sap from palm trees. It's good. Drink it." Alan drank and AJ refilled.

"Hmm," I said dubiously, sniffing again. It didn't smell any better. AJ smiled encouragement, poised with his container. There was no escape. I would have to drink. I threw the poyo over my taste buds and swallowed, concentrating hard for a few moments to make sure it stayed down.

"Well done." Alan slapped me on the back, making me gag. Alan gave AJ fifty leones to top me up and I gave the student a sick smile. AJ grinned and moved on through the crowd in search of more customers.

By then we had reached the market-square. The stalls had all been dismantled and in their place were fifteen makeshift armchairs, covered with gara. On each of these thrones sat a girl dressed in white, holding an umbrella. Their heads were bowed and their eyes covered by cheap plastic sunglasses in fluorescent pinks and greens, obscuring expressionless young faces.

"Sunglasses!" I hissed to Betty. "Why those awful sunglasses?" I was stunned. I could imagine some gum chewing pre-pubescent American wearing them, but not here. This was a celebration of an ancient tradition that I could only begin to comprehend or forgive in the context of its deep cultural roots. But the sunglasses made a mockery of the whole thing.

Your mother tells you it is the most important occasion of your life. You get new clothes. You will become a woman. You able ask for anything."

"Sunglasses?"

"The girls want sunglasses," Betty explained.

"Have you... did they do it... to you, Betty?" I was horrified. Betty was so well educated. She seemed just like me. How could her parents do such a thing? I knew her family were stout Catholics.

"Of course."

"But isn't it just the Muslims."

"No. We must all be initiated."

"Why? Why didn't your parents stop it?" I demanded.

"The mothers are too much frightened. If a girl is not initiated, she is not clean. If she is unclean, she cannot marry and will never belong to her society."

"But look at you Betty. You are the matron of Serabu Hospital. Everybody looks up to you. How would anybody know if you had been initiated or not?"

"They would know," Betty said simply. "I would not be in such a position if I had not been initiated."

"It's awful." I shuddered. I wanted to ask her what it was like, but I couldn't. Betty met my questioning gaze.

"The girls look forward to initiation," she explained.

"But do they know? Do they know what will happen?"

"No," said Betty, sadly. "Nobody tells you what go happen."

"Good God." I looked at the girls in their longed for sunglasses and wanted to cry. Some were fully-fledged women, yet a few could be no more than seven or eight. "But some are just children!"

"It is 'spensive to initiate a daughter. If you able pay when she is young, the men know you get money and she will marry better."

108

"Poor kids. Can't you refuse?"

"It is hard. No mother wants her daughter to be an outcast. I was very happy when Hindolu was a boy."

"Oh Betty."

I thought of Musu's mother's disappointment at having a grand-daughter. And Betty, getting hit over the wrists as a girl for crying when she picked up the boiling pot. And Laygby bearing another child at great risk to her own survival. And Jeneba. God, Jeneba. All I had to worry about was being manless and a bit chubby. I shuddered.

If I was a Salonean woman, I wouldn't want my baby to be a girl either.

"What for chop today?" Pa George was thumping on my bedroom door. "You are too much late."

"Okay, I'm coming." Urgh, that poyo! I tentatively pulled my dress over my thumping head and went to open the door. Pa George thrust a dead snake under my nose.

"Look," he said. I recoiled. This was no way to treat a girl with a hangover.

"Yes, Pa George, I can see." It was over four-foot long and had shiny leaf green skin.

"I kill this today outside you door," he announced proudly.

"Thank you, Pa George. Is it poisonous?"

"Very poisonous."

"Oh. What do you call this kind of snake?" I asked, thinking I should know for future reference.

"This is green snake."

"Of course."

"What for chop today?"

"I'll leave it to you Pa George," I answered, giving Tikka a saucer of water and some rice. I wondered when she'd start laying eggs. Abruptly, I looked up and shouted "But not the snake." Pa George shrugged and arranged his trophy on the doorstep instead.

Jean was striding up my path. "Bonjour, bonjour. Come quick."

"Sorry I'm late. Is there a problem?"

"Viens." I trotted behind my Medical Superintendent to Maternity. He held the door open for me. I froze in the doorway.

Sitting in the bed opposite was a beautiful young mother, tucking into a plateful of plassas whilst a baby slept at her breast.

Jeneba? Jeneba!!

I was speechless.

"Jeneba, this is Dr. Gay," said Laygby.

"Kushe, Dr. Gay," grinned Jeneba. "I gladdi to meet you."

I burst into tears.

10. A Christmas Carol

Two months in Serabu and only on page ninety of *Tess Of the d'Urbervilles*. Tsk tsk. At least I had managed to save a few lives.

Jeneba and Problem, the first two notches on my stethoscope, had long since been discharged, although I would have happily kept them on Maternity for ever, just for the ego boost. The other good news was that Problem's wet-nurse was HIV negative, although she did have tuberculosis. But dry cough was treatable and Musu was now two stones heavier. The broken-legged chicken was hiding under her bed on TB ward while she nursed baby Laygby. Pa Kamara appeared from time to time to rub in a few more herbs, but there was still no smile from the grandmother from hell.

I turned to page ninety one.

"Open the door for the children,
Open the door for the ch-il-dren,
Open the door for the children
Christ is born today."

Glad of the distraction, I opened my front door. Eight schoolgirls clapped their hands and banged their home-made drums, wiggling their hips in patched dresses that either brushed ankles or scarcely covered bottoms. After the opening number, they abandoned their rehearsed classroom English and lost themselves in the rhythms of their own Mende carols. The first of December obviously qualified as carol singing season.

Patricia Kpukoma was the ringleader, and thus bearer of the group's one kerosene lamp, which swung dangerously as she danced. The song finished and they reorganised themselves into a neat line. Sixteen hopeful eyes twinkled at me from glowing faces. Full of Christmas cheer, I gave them twenty leones each and they skipped off delighted.

"You gave them how much?" exclaimed Alan.

"Twenty leones."

"Each?"

"Of course, each. Come on, Alan, it's Christmas!"

"Hah! Just you wait. Christmas is three weeks off yet."

The dry season had well and truly begun. The deep green palm trees and vegetation that lined the laterite roads were turning autumnal in colour, but it was with red dust blown by the wind rather than any natural process. Tikka was also beginning to look a bit barren - she still hadn't laid any eggs.

God gradually turned up his thermostat and my prickly heat reared its red spotted head again. Only fourteen days before I would be able to expose my skin to the cooling sea breezes of Freetown's beaches. My bucket bath gave temporary relief, but I felt guilty about using a whole bucket of water while the pumps were still broken. Thank God for Pa George. I didn't care if a smile never crossed his weathered brow as long as he found me some water. I even spotted him carrying buckets to his own house. A man carrying water for his wife was virtually unheard of in Serabu! I resolved to give Pa George, Salone's first new man, a large Christmas bonus.

But I was not to be the only one giving that Christmas, my first present arrived that evening.

"Dr. Gay, you want beef?"

Pa Bangura stood on my doorstep with a large sack slung over his shoulder, almost unrecognisably healthy after our first meeting.

"Kushe! How de body Pa?"

"I tell God tenki, Dr. Gay. I get fine blood now." He pulled down the lower lids of his eyes and I peered approvingly at healthy pink conjunctivae.

"Very good Pa."

"I bring you beef."

Beef? Since my arrival in Salone, I hadn't seen a single cow, but before I could ask, Pa Bangura tipped an Alsatian-sized rat onto my kitchen floor. It lay like in typical dead rat pose, feet in the air with a blind goofy-toothed stare. I stared back at it, edging my foot out from under the metre-long tail that had flopped over my sandal.

"Fine beef, Dr. Gay. I catch him today," announced Pa Bangura proudly.

"Beef?" I finally found my voice.

"Na so." He was obviously very pleased with his present. "For you."

"Tenki Pa, but you should eat this yourself. Plenty iron for you and your wife." This impressive specimen was certainly nutritious, and might well have been very tasty, but *I* wasn't eating it. Pa Bangura looked crestfallen.

"I don't know how to cook it." I said trying another tack. "Pa George has gone for the weekend." This should work better – we poomuis were known to be incapable of doing anything practical for ourselves. Pa Bangura cast his eyes down. Oh hell. "Pa, this beef better for you, it get plenty protein and plenty iron." I tried a final time to convince him that his need was greater than mine.

"Tenki ya, Dr. Gay. We go see back." He stuffed the rat back into the sack and slouched back down the path.

I sighed and sat down to Pa George' plassas. It looked surprisingly appealing.

Alan was furious. "It's the greatest insult to refuse a gift!"

"Sorry, but rat!"

"Or monkey, or snake. Besides it was a cutting-grass, more of an overgrown guinea pig than a rat and they're actually rather good."

"Rat, guinea pig…" I shook my head.

"You can't afford to be rude, and you certainly can't afford to be fussy. Just cos you've got plenty of stores…"

"Alan…" I warned.

"And I'm SO SICK of plassas! Won't you get Pa George to cook Tikka? She's never going to lay."

"No!"

We sat in silence on my doorstep until Nurse Sankoh, junior entrepreneur, sauntered into view.

"Dr. Gay, you want egg?"

"Eggs! Great!" Nurse's timing couldn't have been better. "How much?"

"Forty leones." He produced two from his pocket and I handed over the money. Nurse put it in his shoe and ran off.

"You shouldn't just buy eggs from Nurse without checking them." Alan sniggered.

"What for?"

"Chickens."

"Huh?"

"You've got to check for chickens." Alan took the eggs and plonked them into a cup of water. "Yup. They're floating." He cracked them open to a tangle of feather. "Chickens."

"Aww." I cringed.

"Aw fo do." He threw them out of the door. "Never mind the eggs, we've got a more serious problem. Our beer's don don."

"Well it's only two weeks before the High Commissioner's Party," I said Chicken foetuses instantly forgotten, I hugged my knees with excitement. "Perhaps I can buy some in Freetown? No silly idea, I'd never get it back on a poda-poda."

"Off jaunting to Freetown already?"

"Excuse me." I jabbed my finger into his chest. "All VSOs are expected to attend the annual conference."

"Oh my."

"And look at you. Always off to Mokanje."

"Urgent hospital business," Alan sniffed.

"Yes, I'm sure there's lots of business to be done at the Mines' swimming pool."

"Ah well, it's amazing what donations and price reductions you can get with the personal touch." Alan tapped his nose smugly.

"So why aren't our water pumps fixed then, if you're so good?"

"Jaysus, I've already got MT on my back. You try finding spares," he sulked. "That's it!"

"What?"

"Your excuse to get the hospital Landrover to go to Freetown. You can find spares for the pumps and bring back as many crates of Star as we can find money for."

"We ought to be saving our money to feed a TB patient or two, then I'd never have to cross swords with MT."

"Jaysus, you sound like Tom. Don't start feeling guilty, Gail. You'll always have more than anybody here. Most people back home could buy fifty pints of blood a week, feed the whole TB ward and still have enough for a drink. The way I look at it, the longer you keep your sanity, the longer you'll stay and the more good you can do."

"You'll be a very popular priest, Alan."

We went back to my doorstep, cradling our cups of water, just as Pa Ali was walking past.

"Dr. Gay, bua."

"Bua, bise, Pa Ali," I replied to the tiny old man who came at dawn and dusk to tap poyo from the palm tree behind my house. He wore only a ragged pair of shorts, revealing his leathery skin stretched over stringy muscles.

"Bise, bi gahun yena?" he asked, beaming at me.

115

"Kayingoma. A bia be?"

"Kayingoma. Malo-hua."

"Malo-hua."

Our greeting routine was now as much a part of my daily rhythm as Pa George' plassas. 'Hello. Thank you, hello. Thank you, how are you? Thanks be to God, what about you? Good-bye'.

"He's far too old to be climbing that tree." I watched as the wiry little man hung off the prickly side of the palm tree, suspended by a loop of woven cane. He dug a sharp hollow metal pipe into the tree and released the sap into a large plastic container.

"It's his living. From God to Man."

"What are you on about now, Alan?"

"Poyo comes straight from the tree, from God to Man. Which means the 'tee-total' Muslims drink it quite happily! And even guilt crippled volunteers can justify it."

"You'd have to be desperate to drink that stuff," I cringed, remembering AJ's offering at the Coming Out.

"Listen, we *are* desperate. Pa Ali, how much for that poyo?"

"Protein. You all need plenty protein." I started my regular Friday afternoon nutrition nag on TB ward.

"You give me mericine, Dr. Gay. Protein too much spensif," complained Ibrahim, six weeks into his treatment, and still only nudging five stone.

"Those tablets and injections just won't work unless you chop plenty protein. Beef, fish..."

"Too spensif, Dr. Gay, too spensif." Ibrahim chewed his kola nut, Africa's answer to speed. Kola might assuage his hunger, but it would still leave him starving.

"Well spend your money on beans and groundnuts rather than kola then," I persisted. "You must eat protein. Look at how

116

well Princess is doing." I nodded towards the pregnant Liberian refugee that we had managed to get on charity feeding a week or so earlier. But as soon as the words were out of my mouth I realised that I had chosen the wrong example.

"But Princess get charity feeding!" Ibrahim exploded into a coughing fit.

"We no get charity feeding, Dr. Gay!" The others rallied to his cause.

"Give we all charity feeding, Dr. Gay, then we all get fine body."

"Sorry-oh, we can't feed you all," I shouted above the outcry. "Aw fo do."

Oh why oh why had I mentioned Princess? Patrick Kpukoma glowered at me. I mouthed sorry and beat a hasty retreat.

I ran straight into Nurse, lurking outside TB ward.

"Psst. You want egg, Dr. Gay?" he whispered. The appeal of an omelette was too strong to question the origin of his eggs too deeply, but if I was to be the recipient of stolen goods, I wanted to check them first. I marched Nurse up to my house and this time his eggs sank.

"Okay Nurse, I think these are good."

"Forty leones, Dr. Gay."

"No. Those others were not good. Twenty."

"Forty leones," Nurse insisted.

"Twenty."

"Okay, Dr. Gay. Thirty."

"Very well. Thirty. But no more eggs with chickens in them," I said assertively, ever so proud of my little bargaining triumph.

Alan was right about the carol singers. Alan was right about everything. They flocked to my door by twos, by tens and by

117

twenties. Nurse, who now supplied me with a daily egg, kept reappearing, singing loudly in the front row of half the groups. No wonder he could afford shoes.

Adults and children sang 'Open the door for the children' and I foolishly did as instructed. VSO had not allowed for carol singers in their calculation of monthly living expenses, so I had to gradually reduce my donation, but obviously insufficiently to dissuade the next group. And the next. And the next.

I was almost relieved to find Almamy knocking at my door late one evening.

"You get for come to Maternity," he announced, chart in hand.

"But this is a C Ward chart."

"They call the pickin Maternity."

"Sorry." I looked more closely. Maternity Sankoh, aged five. She was very sick with pneumonia.

"Aisha, can you draw up the antibiotics whilst I put in an IV line?"

"No problem, Dr. Gay." The young nurse dashed off to find the drugs trolley, leaving me by Maternity's bedside.

The little girl sat all alone on the bed. Perhaps her mother had gone to get water and would return soon. Propping herself forwards on her thin arms her chest wall heaved up and down. She desperately needed oxygen, but we had none, so all I could do was hope.

"Osh, osh," I said and tried to take Maternity's hand, but she would not uncurl her fingers from the determined fists that made her props, so intent was she on sucking in each breath. And where was her mother? It was very unusual to find a child alone. Feeling very inadequate, I went to bed. Only six days to Freetown.

Klaus was serenading me in my dreams. I sang along, banging a drum. The tune slowly turned into 'Open the door for the children'. Bang bang bang. I beat my drum and sang 'Open the door for the children'. It was louder now, Bang bang bang.

"Open the door for the children." Knock, knock, knock. My eyes snapped open.

"Open the door for the ch-il-dren."

"Oh no." I moaned and squinted at my watch. Half past one!

"Open the door for the children." Bang bang bang. I pretended not to hear.

"Jesus Christ is born."

"It's the middle of the night. Go away," I yelled from under my pillow. The singing stopped for a second, then continued.

"Open the door for the children."

"Go away!"

"Open the door for the ch-il-dren."

"FOK-OFF!" I screamed at the top of my lungs. Footsteps shuffled off.

Our Krio teacher had informed us, reliably I hoped, that *fok-off* was acceptable Krio for get lost. Jesus himself shouts it in the Krio Bible to rid the temple of the wheelers and dealers. At least I had made myself understood.

MT would have been proud of me.

11. Nurse

"You don enjoy the show last night, Dr. Gay?"

"What? Those bloody carol singers at one in the morning!" I retorted, embarrassed that word of my bad temper had got round.

"No, no, Dr. Gay, the video."

"The video?" What was Dauda talking about? Surely there were no videos here.

"In the church hall, Dr. Gay," AJ chirped into the conversation. "The Liberians brought a video. Only a hundred leones to get in."

"Oh, I see."

Refugees from Liberia's brutal civil war were fleeing over the border in their thousands, and were sheltered in Salonean homes, sharing the already meagre resources of their host families. They brought with them horrendous stories of the atrocities being committed by the rival rebel factions led by Prince Johnson and Charles Taylor. Both men claimed to have liberated the country from the brutality of the president, but had so far proved at least as brutal if not more so.

The Saloneans gave thanks that they were not and had never been involved in such a terrible war. On the other hand the Saloneons had never been as prosperous as their sophisticated neighbours. And those refugees who had escaped early in the conflict, had brought belongings that Saloneans could never have dreamed of – such as televisions, videos and portable generators. An enterprising refugee could certainly make a nice living from showing videos in village halls.

"So what was the video?" I asked.

"The Killing of President Doe," siad Dauda, enthusiastically.

Typical, I thought, a Rambo movie. Then I stopped, remembering far off news bulletins. "Wait, wasn't he President of Liberia?"

"Yes. Prince Johnson don kill him," said AJ.

"Was it some kind of documentary then?" I asked, hopefully.

"Oh no, Dr. Gay! The rebels don torture him then they don kill him and they don make a video!" AJ enthused.

"Oh," I said, feeling suddenly sweaty and light-headed. Good God, a snuff movie.

"Sorry-oh, Dr. Gay."

"No problem," I gulped, assuming Dauda's concern was over my change in colour.

"We are sorry we did not tell you about the film," Dauda continued. "You could have come with us!"

"That's quite all right, Dauda." I found my voice. "There's enough blood on Surgical."

"There was plenty plenty people there, Dr. Gay," raved AJ.

"Mmm hmm." My hand was still over my mouth.

"Sold out," nodded Dauda.

"Indeed." This was probably the first time any of them had seen a television, I told myself. They would have been just as excited by *The Sound of Music*.

"He was a bad bad man, the President," said Dauda.

"So I understand."

"Yes, he killed hundreds. Thousands. He deserved to die, Dr. Gay."

"I'm sure. And these rebel-saints? How many have they killed?"

"Prince Johnson don cut off his ear," AJ continued, ignoring my last comment.

"And then he ate it!" added Dauda. This was too much for me. I left them to their enthusiastic conversation, went outside and threw up.

We big strong girls are not usually squeamish, but Betty sent me home for a lie down.

A hundred yards from my house, I spied a small figure bent over in the undergrowth outside my back door. It looked like Nurse Sankoh. I squinted against the mid morning sun to try and make out what he was doing - pinching Tikka's eggs!

"Hoi. Nurse!" I hollered. Startled, he sprinted off. I tried to make chase but an eleven stone white woman was no match for a wiry Mende boy at the best of times, never mind with churning innards. My mind filled with all manner of un-Christmassy thoughts which were never likely to get souls saved, but I was forced to let Nurse go.

Eggs were not the bargain I had thought at thirty leones.

After a cup of water and a banana, I was ready to face TB ward. I wasn't ready to find Patrick Kpukoma rollicking Musu's mother.

"Patrick, Patrick! Why are you shouting at that woman?"

"She don thief two cups of water from the water barrel!" His black face was purple with outrage. "For Musu."

"Two cups of water?" I glared at our normally placid Charge Nurse. Musu's mother was not my favourite lady, but really! "Patrick, this woman's daughter has TB, a broken leg and a newborn, and you are shouting at her for fetching a drink of water?"

"She has a bucket. She get for go to the well."

"But it's hot and she's old, have a heart."

"The well is too far and we nurses are too bweezy." There was no doubt that since the rains had stopped and water could no longer be collected by barrels under the guttering, student nurses had been sorely put upon to fetch water from the village well, a good mile away.

"You're as bad as MT. Let this lady have her water, Mr. Kpukoma," I pleaded. "As a Christmas gesture."

"No. She must fetch her own."

"But…" I stopped. Patrick wasn't going to give in. He'd obviously carried one bucket of water too many that week. "Who's first on our round then?"

Ibrahim smiled sweetly at me from the first bed, then resumed his lunch, spooning something out of a sort of cup. My jaw dropped.

Monkey brains alfresco, straight from the skull. The blood rushed from my face and the whole ward burst out laughing.

"Protein, Dr. Gay," Ibrahim announced, mouth full. "You tell us we must chop plenty protein."

Four days, only four days to Freetown.

Maternity, the little girl with pneumonia, was sleeping peacefully on C Ward. The antibiotics had worked their magic and she was breathing normally. I smiled and bent to stroke her head, but stopped with my hand poised above the sleeping child's tight curls. Bloody Nurse Sankoh was sitting on the end of the bed.

"Aisha, what's that little thief doing here? Touting stolen goods to the patients?"

"Nurse is Maternity's brother." Aisha replied quietly.

"What?" I looked more closely at the boy. He had been crying. "Of course," I whispered, ashamed of myself. Nurse and Maternity Sankoh, children of Serabu Hospital.

"He don sit with Maternity all night," Aisha continued. "Until she breathe fine."

I nodded, then managed to clear the lump in my throat to speak a few banal words. "She'll be fine now, Nurse."

"Tenki-ya, Dr. Gay."

"No problem," I said, and paused. I still had not seen the mother. "Um, Nurse, is your mother here? Maternity's mother."

"I am her mother," said Nurse.

"Oh." I furrowed my brow. "What about your father?"

"I am her mother and her father," stated the ten year old boy.

"Nurse looks after Maternity," explained Aisha. "He don tell me he try to make plenti money so he can send her to school."

"Oh." Was all I could say, before stumbling out of the ward in tears, vowing in future to buy as many eggs as I could from Nurse.

12. The Junkie

Ibrahim was poorly. The monkey had got the last laugh, but I bit my tongue and bent to examine his abdomen. The pressure of my fingers was obviously too much and he vomited all over me. I tried to catch the worst of it with his chart.

"Fatmata, I need a bucket of water," I cried, holding the young man on his side with one hand and clutching the vomit-soaked chart with the other.

"Sorry-oh, Dr. Gay. Water don don."

"What! Why is there no water?" I shouted, dripping hands extended.

"Sorry-oh. I don only use one bucket all shift."

"Then wake up Almamy and send him for some more."

"Almamy will not fetch water, Dr. Gay. He say he needs to be available for emergencies."

I pictured him, snoozing peacefully under his woolly bonnet. "This IS an emergency!" Vomit dripped over the side of the bed onto my foot and I began to understand Patrick's stance that afternoon. Only three days to Freetown, Gail.

Fatmata threatened Almamy with MT if he didn't fetch a bucket of water. He returned with the goods in five minutes.

"Well done, Almamy. That was very quick." I gave praise where praise was due and set about washing my hands.

"Very quick. Really very quick," agreed Fatmata as she started to wipe the floor, shaking her head.

"Yes, you're right.....too quick almost," I started, but was cut short by Laygby

"Where is Almamy?" she thundered. We looked up questioningly at the irate young woman.

"Almamy. Where is he?" Laygby fumed. "He don thief my water. Now there is none on Maternity."

Fatmata shrugged and carried on mopping the floor. I made a diplomatic exit to bed.

One day to Freetown, I hummed as I sauntered down to Surgical.

"Urgh!" An overpowering smell of rotting flesh enveloped me as soon as I opened the door.

"Kushe, Dr. Gay, this is Gasimu," said Dauda. "His leg don rot."

"Kushe, Gasimu," I forced myself to say. The man lay directly on the brown mattress, surrounded by sodden, stinking, gauze swabs. I didn't add 'How di body?' The answer was blatantly clear. The infection had eaten down to the bone of Gasimu's foot, and the flesh from his calf was sloughing off in black and green strips. Betty had put a plastic sheet under his leg, which seemed to be turning to liquid before my eyes.

"Gasimu get diabetes," explained Betty. I nodded.

"Tiange is setting up theatre," said Dauda. I nodded again.

"Latif say his blood sugar is forty. Too much high. Dr. Jon gone look for insulin," Dauda added as he slipped in an intravenous cannula. I nodded.

"Will I give the antibiotics?"

I carried on nodding dumbly and concentrated on writing up the medication, gulping back another wave of nausea.

"Ah Gail, tu es arrive. We are ready for you." Jean breezed in and slapped me on the back. "You will have to amputate."

"What do you mean, ready for *me*?" My vocal cords jolted back into action.

"Well you are the expert on amputations now, yes?"

"What? NO!" Last week I had amputated three fingers crushed in a boat propellor.

"Oui. You have amputated three fingers more than myself."

"Hell's bells!" I looked at Jean in horror. He shrugged and handed a bottle of insulin to Betty. "Thirty units. Latif will check his sugar in an hour."

"No problem, Dr. Jon."

"Merci, Betty. We take him to theatre as soon as his sugar is stable," Jean said, briskly writing his instructions on Gasimu's chart. I gazed at him in disbelief. Surely he wasn't serious?

"Eh bien, Gail. Shall we find your big book of surgery?"

"Oh hell, oh hell, oh hell," I repeated as we reread Maurice King's three short paragraphs that claimed to cover everything one needed to know about amputating a leg. "I'm not up to this Jean. We should clean it up so at least it doesn't smell, then leave well alone."

"If we cleaned out all the necrotic tissue, we would leave only bare bones. Amputation is his only hope," said Jean.

"He doesn't stand a chance." I shook my head.

"You have reason, Gail. We have only four bottles of insulin," he confessed. "It is too expensive for us to keep. One patient's supply for a year could fund the whole hospital for two months. We do what we can with tablets."

"Oh."

"Diabetes is rare in Africa," continued Jean. "The diabetics are like the junkies, travelling the country, searching, stealing and begging for their insulin."

"But if we have none, then who does?"

"A little bit in a clinic here, or a pharmacy there," Jean shrugged.

"That's awful. Poor Gasimu. It looks like his searching has come to an end."

"We should not give up without trying." Sister Hillary's legacy still lingered in Jean's words. "You can buy some more insulin in Freetown, peut-etre?"

"Okay," I sighed. "You're right, we can't leave him like this."

"We do not have any saw." Tiange said, standing in the doorway.

"No saw? Nothing?" Jean asked.

"The Gigli saw," she suggested.

"Quoi?"

"The cheese wire," I told Jean, remembering the frightening device she'd handed me last week. "Bloody hell!"

"Then we must do this option," announced Jean, pointing at the third paragraph "'Amputation through the knee'."

"Hmmm."

"It says it is most easy. No bone needs to be cut. Just to cut the ligaments and disjoint the bottom from the top. Pas de probleme."

"No problem," I repeated.

In fact it was surprisingly easy. After only forty minutes we were sewing the skin flaps over the stump whilst Peter wrapped up the leg and took it away. Most 'waste' was dropped down the pit latrines, but a leg was surely too big. Peter could deal with it. I didn't want to know. I just stood admiring our neat finish.

That evening I returned to the freshly aired ward, with all the patients back in their beds.

"Tenki ya, Dr. Gay. Plenti tenki." Gasimu clung to my arm and wept.

Nobody ever went to Freetown without a shopping list. Mine was as follows:

1: Insulin
2: HIV test kits
3: Spares for water pumps
4: Everyone's Christmas mail
5: A few thousand condoms
6: Beer.

128

I mentioned the first four items to MT, hinting at the difficulties of carrying them back to Serabu on a poda-poda. It would, of course, be nearly impossible with items five and six. Amazingly she agreed. She would go to Freetown herself for the water pumps and bring me back home. Gosh, my surgical prowess must have really impressed her. Alan, eavesdropping from the back office, gave me the thumbs up, smacking his lips at the prospect of more beer.

But I still had to make my own way to Freetown.

My journey started at dawn with an hour's walk to the Junction when thankfully it was still cool. By seven thirty, I had joined the poda-poda queue forming under the lone palm tree that offered the only shade. Three women, two babies, a toddler, two teenage lads, an old Pa and a goat greeted me. I smiled back and sat on my rucksack, hoping I wouldn't squash the gown and lappa that Serabu's tailor had made especially for me from Ma Kpukoma's hand-dyed gara. I wanted to look my best for the High Commissioner's Party - you never knew who might be there.

"Kushe, Dr. Gay. You want orange?" I looked up into the hard eyes of Musu's mother. She was looking after her daughter's patch.

"Tenki ya."

She peeled off the outer skin, sliced off the top and handed it over. Never being one to roll a toothpaste tube from the bottom, I grabbed it by the middle, threw my head back, and squeezed the juice straight into my mouth. Delicious. I tossed the skin to the Pa's goat, who munched it down. I handed over the money for another.

At noon a poda-poda finally appeared, by which time frustration and eight oranges had given me indigestion. Musu's mother had done a roaring trade from the queue of thirsty passengers and the goat was also looking pretty pleased with itself. The driver prised in my travelling companions, their luggage and the goat, but refused to let me on board.

"Place not there," he said, shaking his head at the fare I held under his nose.

"What?" My stomach acid production doubled "But you've just let all these people on!"

"You poomui woman no go manage," he added simply.

"Of course I'll manage. Let me on," I demanded. What was this strange form of racism that suggested that poomuis were too soft to tolerate the journey when they had waited over four hours like everybody else and there was unlikely to be another poda-poda coming along that day and they had friends to meet, seas to swim in and a High Commissioner's Party's to attend. Huh?

Remarkably, my saviour turned out to be Musu's mother who ordered two lads to climb onto the roof, leaving a tiny space for me on a bench down the middle. Once squeezed in, I was sardine-canned from all four sides by bodies, from underneath by the goat and three chickens, and from above by the metal roof bowing under the weight of the boys on top.

"Tenki ya," I said, rather uncertainly to Musu's mother. She nodded back.

Thirteen hours later, my body contracted into the foetal position, I wished I had heeded the driver's warnings at Serabu Junction. Poomui or not, I never wanted to get into a poda-poda again. Thank God for MT, my angel of mercy, for promising me my own personal seat in the Landrover for the return journey.

But I had arrived! The big city! I needed to find my VSO comrades, so armed with my torch to avoid the potholes and storm drains of the dark streets of central Freetown, I picked my way to the VSO resthouse.

Gosh, I was looking forward to seeing everyone again. Even Mike. Perhaps he'd show me his stump, so I could compare it with Gasimu's. I quickened my step. Wait till I told them all that I was a surgeon now. I had saved lives! I had amputated a leg!

13. The High Comissioner's Party

Not unreasonably for two am, everybody was fast asleep. It was probably just as well, for I was truly exhausted. I crawled through the mosquito net of the last bunk in the resthouse and within seconds had joined my friends in the land of slumber.

Morning came and I opened my eyes to an escapee from Hammer Horror hovering above my mosquito net - the shaven head was cracked and peeling, with blood oozing from the sores around the corners of the lips.

"It's Mad Doc Haddock! They let her out!" Cried the head.

"God!" I sat up abruptly and pulled the netting aside. There stood Klaus, as cachectic as my TB patients, clothes hanging from his body and his skin covered with the most dreadful eczema.

"What happened to you? You look awful!"

"Great bedside manner, doc. You, however, are the absolute picture of health," he said, trying to smile through the sores.

"You mean I haven't lost an ounce?"

"Yep. Still the same big strong girl."

"Hmmph!" I was going to complain further but he really did look a mess. "What are you doing about that eczema?" I asked, almost kindly. "You should go home."

"Na. Fiona's given me a prescription for some lotions and potions." Klaus put his arm round an unfamiliar looking girl beside him. With her cropped hair and sensible glasses I assumed she was one of VSO's old guard.

"Kushe." I held out my hand. "Gail Haddock."

"Gail!" she spluttered. "It's me!"

"Huh!" I reached for my glasses under the bunk. "Goodness, Fiona! You're nearly as bad as Klaus!"

"Lost my contacts, cut my hair and can't stand plassas. You look great, though!"

"Well yes, I probably do, compared to you two. You three," I corrected, spotting a waif sitting in the corner, peeling an orange. "Kushe, Susan! And there's Lindsey, Hi!"

I squeezed Lindsey and Fiona tightly, and Klaus a little less tightly in case he should snap, and they introduced me to some of the more established VSOs who were down for the conference. There were nurses, teachers and even a tailor known as Squeeze-Box Tim (for reasons that became obvious at the party).

Tim taught tailoring at a vocational college, far out East in Kailahun, whilst his VSO housemate Samantha taught secretarial skills. They'd been in Salone for two years already and it was obvious it had become their home now. Sam even had a Salonian boyfriend and Tim had a crush on Tracey, a black American Peace Corps.

So relationships were possible. I had been having doubts, surrounded as I was by professional celibates. Good for Sam though. That was one in the eye for the High Commissioner and his dire warnings. Meanwhile, I had spotted a three-inch boil under her arm that needed sorting.

"Where there's pus, let it out." Fiona and I quoted in unison.

"After you, Gail."

"Help!" Sam looked anxiously from Fiona to me.

"You'll feel a lot better," I assured her whilst Klaus set a pan of water on the stove and started boiling up one of his razor blades.

It is always satisfying squeezing pus out of nice juicy boils and Sam's was no exception. She grudgingly admitted to feeling better whilst Fiona and I sat down to compare Panguma and Serabu.

"I'm so jealous!" laughed Fiona. "Amputating a leg, I can hardly believe it!" I preened a little but attempted modesty by saying nothing. She had a real surgeon that she could send her major cases to, only ninety minutes away at Segbwema Hospital.

"Listen. Segbwema's going to give me some surgical training

at Easter," she continued. "Why don't you come too?"

"Great!" I enthused, immediately planning ways to get time off. Jean would cover me, no problem, he was leaving in May and owed me a week anyway, but I would need to put a business case to MT – something along the lines of improved surgical skills attracting more custom. "Now, how to get there...?" I mused.

"I'll take you," offered Klaus.

"What? Really?" I said, delighted, then paused, "How?"

"I've done myself up one of CARE's old Honda trail bikes. I'm not spending two years fixing up all their vehicles without doing one for myself now am I?"

"Klaus Von Hondabenda!" exclaimed Lindsey. "Your own transport, you lucky sod."

"A hundred and fifty miles on the back of a motorbike? On these roads?" I wasn't so sure, but hey, anything would be better than a poda-poda, and I'd be with Klaus. I smiled. "It's a date!"

"Easter, then Doc?" We shook hands.

"If you haven't been medi-vacced by then." I eyed his skin.

"Nah. I won't be joining Mike."

"What do you mean?"

"Don't you know?" Lindsey exclaimed gleefully. "Mike and his wife have gone home in a huff."

"Home home?"

"Last week," Klaus added. "His project collapsed after he sacked half his staff in the first month. The rest walked out."

"Really? I said, suppressing a snigger. "Any relation to MT?"

"MT?"

"Maggie Thatcher, my boss."

"Maggie Thatcher?" asked Lindsey, and off we went for a happy few hours comparing stories.

Fiona's prescription for Klaus' eczema wasn't available in any of Freetown's pharmacies, so he had to make do with potassium permanganate soaks in Nick's bath, which turned both him and the bath first purple then splodgy brown.

"You really should go home, " I suggested mildly. "Get out of this dreadful climate."

"Naw. Too many beautiful women here," he smiled. Gosh! Did that include me?

"It's tempting though, decent food, decent beer, a game of squash...."

"You play squash!"

"I love it."

"We'll have to play." Why was I so excited by this sudden revelation of common ground?

"Naw. Wouldn't want you to embarrass yourself." He smiled a knowing smile.

Gosh, he must be good. He was usually such a modest chap.

"A coaching session then."

"You find the court and I'll play."

"You're on!" I agreed enthusiastically, although I couldn't imagine who would build a squash court here. "But a sweaty game of squash is the last thing your skin needs. I'm being negligent, not telling the Field Director to send you home."

"Don't you dare!"

"He'd never let him go," Sam piped in. "He's far too useful." Klaus had apparently already wired up the VSO office to its new generator, fixed the water supply in the rest house and mended the VSO Landrover.

"A bit of air conditioning would help," said Fiona.

"I'll just have to hang around the Lebanese supermarket."

"Or get yourself an invite to the High Commissioner's compound," Lindsay suggested. "They must have spare rooms."

"He'll be lucky," Squeeze-Box Tim snorted. "Scruffy VSOs like us are allowed in for the annual Christmas Party and that's it."

"They'll think I'm trying to infect the High Commissioner with the plague and bounce me at the doorstep. Aw fo do."

"We'll lynch 'em if they do," said Tim. "There's more of us."

"Cheers, mate," Klaus laughed. "Perhaps I'll just go for some sun, sand and salt water treatment. Anyone coming?"

"Yes," chorused twenty voices. The Health, Education and Politics on the Conference agenda could wait.

The High Commissioner's party was a scene taken straight from the last days of the Raj. I only spotted five black faces, Sam's boyfriend Fatoma, who was AJ without the swagger, Tracey, Tim's date, and three waiters. By rights we should have stuck by our VSO principles and boycotted it completely, but principles are there to be broken at the prospect of unlimited free food and booze.

A tall black waiter dressed in a white suit with gold trim handed me my fourth pink gin. I giggled and accidentally sloshed some onto the speckled marble floor. The waiter raised an eyebrow. I flashed him a smile and hastily slipped out onto the white columned veranda to join the others on the lawn.

Everybody was dressed in competitively garish outfits. Everybody, that is, except Susan, who still wore the same high necked lacy blouse and brown corduroy skirt that she had had on in the check-in queue at Gatwick, only now they hung limply from her body. Poor Susan. All that worry over her Tampax was wasted as stress and weight loss would surely have put a firm halt to her menstrual cycle.

The rest of the girls wore dresses made from an assortment of stunningly coloured gara material, or the gown and lappa with head-dress. Tracey's was the best of course, since she had her own pet tailor to make it for her. Tim had made himself an immaculate gara suit in rich blue and green tie-died circles, but even he was upstaged by Nick, an Adonis in a white robe of shiny embellished material, trimmed in gold. Klaus, in comparison, was a pale Belsen refugee in what looked like embroidered brown pyjamas, but at least his skin looked better. He was laughing at Tracey, a natural comedienne, telling us how she spent her first weeks shouting back at the Saloneans "Sister, I'm blacker than you!" when they insisted on calling her a poomui too.

"Tracey's only in Sumbuya, Gail," said Klaus.

"Hey girl, you're my nearest neighbour - come and visit."

"That'd be great. I'm sure Tom would lend me his push-bike for a weekend."

"Woah, it's still twelve miles!"

"No problem! I'd walk it for an excuse to escape Serabu."

"Well then, second weekend in January?"

"Great!"

Everybody was happy, swapping experiences and invitations to visit. Even the Field Director looked relaxed and almost handsome with a pretty brunette on his arm.

"Who's she?" I asked Nick.

"His wife. She teaches at the blind school in Freetown."

"Gosh, imagine being blind here. Life's hard enough."

"Well, Suzanne will know. She's blind too."

"Really. Now that is brave."

"Her husband looks after her, and half the children at the blind school too. Your Field Director's always taking children to Connaught Hospital with TB or broken bones. Pays their medical fees too."

"He does?"

"Yes. He's always worrying about some child or other."

"Leaving him no time to worry about us volunteers," I snorted ungraciously.

"Ah, but you are big and strong, Gail. Nobody need look after you," laughed Nick.

"Yeah."

"Dance?" Nick held out his hand. I perked up.

He whirled me around the impossibly green lawn of the High Commissioner's humble home. The grass was framed with palm trees and beautiful flowering shrubs and stretched down towards the horizon, blending with Freetown's coastline below. Behind us the chatter of guests and the gentle hum of the generator accompanied Tim's accordion.

The waiter called us to dinner, and oh boy did we feast. My VSO comrades joined me in hoovering up turkey, real potatoes, brussels sprouts and Christmas pud. We even raved about the cabbage. Ecstasies over cabbage? The High Commissioner and his wife looked on, smiling with a mixture of indulgent patronage and disgust as their buffet table was reduced to crumbs and their drink's cabinet dwindled.

We wondered just what High Commissioners did all day, but with our heads woozy with alcohol and our bellies full, we were glad to see that ours was fulfilling at least one useful function.

There were several other expatriates at the party, presumably to provide moral support for the High Commissioner. They clinked their ice cubes in long glasses and made polite conversation with the plucky young people from upcountry.

Susan avoided the expatriate contingent completely, refusing to be associated with their Capitalist exploitation and Colonialist attitudes, but as far as I was concerned they were just another audience to whom I could boast about amputating legs. I gave them the full olfactory-visual experience in between mouthfuls of mince pie.

"...all I can say is diabetes is bad enough at the best of times, but I'm damned glad I'm not diabetic in this country," I proclaimed. One of the middle-aged ladies in the group then announced that she had been diabetic since childhood.

"Oh." I choked on my mince pie. Tact had never been my strong point.

"Never mind dear. From your story, I too am glad to have been born in Britain," she said, more kindly than I deserved.

"Where do you get your insulin?" I asked tentatively. Having dug my hole, I might as well jump in to get the information I needed. My last three lunchtimes had been spent unsuccessfully touring the pharmacies in Freetown for insulin. Even the pharmacist at Connaught Hospital, the main government hospital, had laughed in my face at my request.

"I brought my own supplies. I'm only visiting my son for two weeks," she explained. "I don't let diabetes interfere with my social life, although I can't eat quite as many mince pies as you dear."

Touché, I thought, wiping the dusting of icing sugar from my upper lip. "You're very brave."

"Not at all, I've been treated like a queen for these two weeks at the High Commissioner's oasis. I'll be sorry to return tomorrow."

"Tomorrow?" I asked, my brain slipping slowly into gear through the fog of gin. "Forgive me for sounding rude - well, even ruder than I've already been - but would you, er, have any spare insulin?"

"Yes," she smiled. "Six bottles. My GP told me to bring triple supplies."

"Sensible GP."

"Would you like to pick it up tomorrow morning for your patient?"

"Oh, yes please!"

The High Commissioner spoke to each one of us individually - for a least a minute.

"So what do you do?" he asked.

"I'm a doctor at Serabu Hospital."

"Indeed. That must be very interesting."

"Yes, I..." But he had turned to Squeeze-Box Tim. Hmmmph. I had had longer conversations with Pa Ali, and we only shared ten words of common language. Perhaps the High Commissioner had been talking to the diabetic lady's group. They had probably warned him that if he wanted to avoid twenty minute monologues on rotting legs and cheese wires, then on no account should he give the big girl in the blue and purple tie-dyed tent any opening whatsoever. Klaus was the only one to engage him for any length of time.

"So, Mr. High Society," I teased. "What was all that about?"

"I was telling him he should consider solar panelling, He seemed very interested," I had to agree. "But what do you know about solar panelling?"

"I did a module at university."

"You went to university?" I hadn't meant to sound quite so surprised. "Where?"

"Cambridge. Oh, there's Lindsey, she promised me a dance."

Well, well, well. Handy, intelligent, modest....

"You'll have to come to Serabu to discuss solar panelling. Diesel's so expensive....." I started conversation as soon as they left the dance floor. Perhaps the boy just needed an excuse to visit.

"They call him Mr. Electricity at his project," said Lindsey, slipping her arm through his.

"Very good!" I laughed over-heartily, with one eye on Lindsey's fingers resting on Klaus's forearm.

"Yeah, Serabu sounds like fun, I've got my bike, and it's only eighty miles from Moyamba, " he mused. My heart leapt into my throat. "I know, Lindsey can come too, up from Freetown."

139

"Great!" said Lindsey. My heart slumped back to its rightful anatomical position. Why couldn't Lindsey come another time?

"Great," I agreed.

"Good, it's another date then." Klaus smiled and turned to Lindsey. "Are you on for another dance?"

"Absolutely," said Lindsey. I smiled idiotically as he led her back onto the dance floor, then glugged down the remains of my gin and went to find the drinks waiter.

Next morning I woke with salt caked into every pore and the nausea of a woman two months into a twin pregnancy. It was small consolation that morning sickness was not something I was ever likely to suffer, if my record to date was anything to go by. With a determination borne of rejection, I had out danced and out drunk everybody at the party. I had challenged Klaus to a dance and dragged him onto the floor for a Strip the Willow. I did take a certain satisfaction in flinging him from partner to partner as we spun down the set, which, I am sure, is against all rules of attracting men.

Now, feeling wretched, I crept out of my bunk and tiptoed to the bathroom. At least there would be no competition for a bucket bath from the snoring bodies behind the mosquito nets, so I spun the taps wide open. Not a drop. So much for the big city.

I stuffed my sweaty gown and lappa into the bottom of my rucksack and put my slightly less smelly dress on for the journey back to Serabush. MT had given me a noon deadline, which left four hours to pick up the insulin from the diabetic lady and then find my way downtown to the National AIDS office for HIV test kits and condoms. There was no time to say goodbye to anyone, which was just as well since maintaining jollity would be hard this morning.

Leaving my sleeping comrades at the resthouse, I started the two mile walk back up to the High Commissioner's compound. My mind was too busy with the implications of last night to notice my aching feet, battered and blistered from hours of barefoot dancing.

Why shouldn't Klaus fancy Lindsey? She was, let's face it, the most attractive girl in the group. And nice. And funny. And clever. And probably a squash international too. But why should I care anyway? They were probably just flirting, as we had all done from day one. We were just a group of fond siblings, that was all.

"Silly me, " I said to myself, as I gave the security guard on the Compound gate the handwritten letter requesting that I be allowed to pass. He waved me towards one of the back buildings.

"Good morning," I chirped, my jovial façade firmly reapplied.

"Well, it's the dancing doctor. Good morning. I must say I didn't expect you so early." She looked me up and down, but managed to stop herself from actually sniffing. "Come in for a shower."

"Great," I replied, too excited by the prospect of my first shower in three months to take offence.

"The bathroom's this way." I followed her eagerly through the air-conditioned apartment, to the strains of Beethoven coming from the hi-fi system in the corner. The bathroom was a sanctuary for a smelly VSO, with its clean white suite trimmed with gold, shower cubicle, flowers in a vase on the windowsill, soft powder blue bath mat and six matching towels on the rail. Soon I was revelling in the massaging force of water, the hot needles, helped by copious amounts of moisturising shower gel flushed the sweat out of my pores. Humming along to Beethoven's sixth I worked my hair up into a satisfying lather, rinsed it off, then doused my scalp in almond conditioner. Then I rubbed myself down in one of the oh-so-soft towels, losing myself like one of those babies in fabric conditioner advertisements, and wrapped myself in the bathrobe that hung on the door.

"That was heaven," I said, surfacing a clean pink some thirty minutes later.

"Glad you enjoyed it, dear. Lemonade?"

"Please." I accepted the long frosted glass, and flopped onto the cream cotton sofa. I slurped my cold cold drink and listened to the ceiling fan swishing gently round. My hostess brought me her six bottles of insulin, two freshly baked bread rolls with real butter from the Lebanese supermarket and a large piece of fresh pineapple. Life in Sierra Leone was not hard for everyone.

An hour later, I was delivered back to the VSO office by her son's driver. I popped in for a final check for Christmas mail. There was nothing new from home in my pigeonhole, but there were four little notes:

'Had to get an early poda-poda if I'm to make it to Panguma today. See you at Easter. Love Fiona.'

'Where were you this morning? We've gone to the Crown Cafe for breakfast. Love Lindsey.'

'How's the head Doc? See you at the Crown. Love Klaus.'

'How'd you get up so early? Hope to see you at the Crown. Guess what? Lindsey tactfully rejected Von Hondabenda last night, but everybody is still friends. A little birdie tells me you might be relieved. My lips are sealed. Love Tim.'

I tore the notes into shreds and threw them in the bin. Tim was right, I should be relieved, but instead I felt somehow insulted.

And how did Tim know anyway? I didn't even know, something to do with being a fellow sufferer of unrequited love, or had I been that obvious? How embarrassing! The therapeutic effect of my morning shower evaporated. At least I wouldn't have time to face them at the Crown for party post-mortems. I scribbled super-cheery little Christmas messages to leave in their slots, then made my way heavily out of the office, down the stairs, past the cluster of refugees outside the Red Cross Office and along the street to Connaught Hospital for my midday rendezvous with MT.

14. No Socks, No Sex

The National AIDS Office was deep in the bowels of the faeculant Connaught Hospital. A hand-painted banner greeted me:

"WOMEN, NO ONE FOOT SUCKS, NO SEX!"

"Huh?" *Foot* was Krio for leg, and *one foot* was the penis. No penis sucks, no sex. Goodness, what was it suggesting? Oral sex to avoid AIDS?

Our own HIV posters, assiduously vetoed by MT, depicted couples holding hands with no hint of a kiss, never mind fellatio. Smiling at the thought of AJ and the rest of the students trying to design our sweet posters without mention of sex or condoms, I jumped when a little man flung open the door.

"Kushe, kushe. Welcome to The National AIDS Office!"

"Oh, kushe. I'm Dr. Gail from Serabu," I said looking round the cubby-hole. It was filled from floor to ceiling with boxes of condoms. Before I knew it, I was the caretaker of a good number of them and a box of HIV test kits.

"Thank you." I dusted off the box of test kits, searching for the expiry date. "But, er, aren't these out of date?" I was sorry to sound so ungrateful to one so generous.

"Aw fo do," he answered, his grin never wavering. "No more 'til Easter-time."

There was no time to argue, it was already noon and MT wouldn't tolerate lateness. Unable to face another poda-poda journey, I dashed to Connaught's main entrance, balancing boxes of condoms like a waiter clearing up after a Greek wedding. Puffing, I spotted Moses rattling round the corner in the Landrover.

"Kushe, Dr. Gay." Moses jumped down to open the back.

"Kushe, Moses. How di body?"

"I tell God tenki. I get your beer." He said pointing to six crates strapped to the roof.

"Six! I only gave you money for three. Yours?" I asked doubtfully.

"Too spensive for me." Moses smiled.

"For MT? No! Really?" MT reclined across my imagination with a bottle in one hand and a bible in the other.

"Quick, Dr. Gay." Moses suddenly grabbed my arm. "MT de come."

I threw the thirty bumper boxes of condoms into the back seat and hastily covered them with my newly purchased yellow and green gara.

"Dr. Gail, you are here. I could not find the required items for the water pumps." MT was not one for small talk. "I hope you were more successful."

"I have everyone's mail and some insulin, but the HIV kits are out of date."

"No use, Dr. Gail, no use at all," she tutted. "Latif has tested 3% of our potential blood donors as positive. How can we combat the scourge of this terrible disease with inadequate testing?"

"There are other ways," I suggested, settling myself innocently against my condoms. "At least they're less out of date than our current batch."

"And when is the next delivery?"

"Easter."

"Well I'm quite sure we will not be wasting fourteen hours of diesel coming down again." MT lifted her tiny frame into the front seat and arranged the layers of her dark grey, ankle length, polyester habit. Little wonder she was bad tempered. I was sweating in my knee-length cotton dress.

"Back to Serabu, driver," she instructed, straightening her veil for action. Poor Moses had been driving round Freetown at her beck and call all day without a break. He sighed and put the Landrover into gear.

146

Failing to get the spares for the pumps had put MT in an even worse mood than usual. I was only slightly comforted by the thought that even she had to suffer bucket baths and dispose of her bodily wastes without water. My head thumped and my stomach churned, so I half-leaned out of the window for some air while the beer bottles clinked accusingly in their crates. Hour by hour we crept closer to Serabush in miserable silence.

One year, nine months to go. Bloody hell. Look on the bright side Gail, that's one year nine months to convince Klaus of your charms. Or one year nine months for him to convince Lindsey of his charms. Not that she was the only competition - female volunteers far outweighed the men, both in the VSO and American Peace-Corps' ranks.

Aw fo do. Remember Gail, you amputated a leg! You are a surgeon, you can be proud of yourself.

The proud surgeon stood on the bare concrete floor of her bathroom, looking at the trickle of water dampening the bottom of a bucket. Seven and a half, dusty, nauseating hours in a Landrover and there wasn't even enough water for a bath. Welcome home. My shower at the High Commissioner's only that morning seemed as long ago as my last soak in a hot bubble bath in Scotland. It was already dark and I was too tired to think about fetching any water myself, so went to bed coated in grime.

Next day I put on a clean dress to disguise my dirty body and went straight to Gasimu's bed, eager to see how my first amputee was progressing.

"Kushe, Gasimu. How di body?"

"I tell God tenki, Dr. Gay. How di Freetown?" he smiled weakly.

"Fine." I shook his hand.

Dauda appeared with the dressing's trolley. "I get for do Gasimu's dressing."

"Good," I replied, watching Dauda peel back the layers of gauze.

But it was not good. Gasimu's stump was swollen and leaking pus.

"You'd better remove the stitches," I whispered.

Dauda did as I bid and I hid behind him with my hand over my mouth. The whole wound fell open, revealing a writhing mass of maggots. I froze, transported into a horror movie with all my boastful words being shouted back at me from the screen.

"AJ, do ya, bring me water," said Dauda calmly.

"No water," AJ replied.

"Then fetch some from the well," Dauda ordered.

"But the well is ten minutes walk!" AJ, king of the student nurses, did not want to demean himself with women's work.

"Quick quick," Dauda snapped. AJ glared at him, but marched out of the ward to find a bucket. "Don't worry, Dr. Gay. I go clean the place," Dauda added kindly. "You go to Maternity."

"Thank you," I whispered and lurched for the door, unable to look into Gasimu's tortured face.

An hour later, Dauda and Betty had cleaned and dressed Gasimu's leg with fresh white gauze. Perhaps I should have left the maggots in to debride the wound? Too late now. Gasimu, pale and sweaty, still managed a smile for me.

"Insulin don don," Betty whispered.

"I brought more from Freetown," I stated flatly.

"Tenki ya, Dr. Gay." Gasimu grasped my hand, obviously understanding every word that we were saying but I looked away. I couldn't accept his gratitude.

We had been so pleased with our tidy, impressive looking wound. But that neat little line of stitches had been our, and more importantly Gasimu's, undoing.

"Never sew up an infected wound" Mr. Bewes's words hammered against my skull. *"Where there's pus, let it out."* His fist pounded the table.

"The bone-self don begin rot," Dauda told me once we had left the room.

"We should have amputated further up." I grimaced.

"You are trying, Dr. Gay," said Dauda.

To try was a great compliment in Sierra Leone, whatever the outcome, but perhaps sometimes it's better to give up gracefully. Oh why had I ever come back from Freetown? There had been plenty of flights that would have taken me home in time for Christmas.

Home. I leaned against the doorway of Surgical. No one need know I had been a failure in Africa. I would just write "three months in Sierra Leone" on my CV, adding a touch of the exotic to give me the edge in the job market. Then return to the GP job I was good at, and be just another sausage off the sausage machine.

At least my Salonean experience should curb my moans about the state of the NHS. The main problem would be telling Alan and Jean that I was leaving. Oh poor Jean. In all decency I should at least give a month's notice, so they had chance to find a doctor who had the ability and the stamina that I lacked, but could I even survive another month?

"Come and see the baby Jesus, Dr. Gay."

"What?" I jumped. It was Fatmata.

"Come and see the baby Jesus." The young student nurse took my hand.

"I...." But I was already being led across the compound to a newly-built rafia shack. Moses and Tom were twining palm leaves and flowers to form an archway around it.

"Look at him, Dr. Gay," said Fatmata.

I peered into the shack to see baby Jesus and Company housed within. I smiled at the exquisitely carved figures framed by a halo of flowers.

"How sweet," I sniffed.

"Hey girl, what's wrong?" Tom gave me a hug.

"Nothing." Tom looked hard at me. "Oh Tom, its everything. Gasimu's going to die. His leg's crawling with maggots and it's all my fault. I'm going home."

"The diabetic man?" Tom asked.

"I sewed up an infected wound."

"You've given him your best."

"My best isn't good enough."

"Oh Gail, you're only a novice and you've already saved lives. Look at Jeneba, and Pa Bangura."

"You're being very kind, Tom." I looked into the gentle eyes of the American. "But it was such a basic mistake."

"Hey, I'll bet you've never saved so many lives in your career, and now you want to save them all." Tom looked at me square on. "You're not God. And don't you dare go home!"

"Oh Tom, what am I doing?"

"You're trying to help."

"It makes it so much worse that he's alone," I continued. "And I'm not helping, I'm just too ashamed to face him. All my other patients have a relative, why not Gasimu?"

"Diabetics are expensive," sighed Tom. "He's had two major operations and his chances were always real slim."

"But even MT can't charge a corpse!"

"She can withhold the body until the relatives pay."

"So poor Gasimu has to suffer alone."

"I'll help," Tom offered. "My Krio's real good now. And I'll get my students to spend more time with him too."

"Thanks, Tom. He badly needs a friend."

150

Friends are indeed wonderful things. Tom cheered me up enough to get me through Outpatients, and when I surfaced at four, I suddenly realised that the whole compound was in bloom. Flowers tumbled round every corner and threw their perfume into the air. A little wind fluffed their petals and I wondered if perhaps it was just a little cooler. Bolstered by the hospital's unexpected beauty, I looked in on Gasimu who was sitting up in bed laughing at a book of cartoons that Tom had lent him. And I had thought Tom only read the bible. Not wanting to spoil the magic Tom's human touch had worked on my patient, I closed the side room door quietly and went over to TB ward.

Standing in the doorway was Musu, with baby Laygby strapped to her back!

"Musu!" I gaped at the young woman. "You're walking!"

"Kushe kushe, Dr. Gay." She beamed and gave me a twirl. Her mother stood behind her, grinning from ear to ear.

"Well done Pa Kamara." The evidence before me hard to believe. "So. How's the chicken?" I had to ask.

"Very good. We don chop am."

"Poor chicken." That was gratitude for you.

I went home and fed Tikka an extra handful of rice, then lifted the blackened lid off Pa George's black pot. Instead of orange palm oil congealing on top of green sludge, I was astounded to see an omelette. Hallelujah!

Sleep came easily as I fell exhausted into bed. Unfortunately it left just as easily when Almamy banged on my door an hour later. He handed me a note. There was a very sick young woman on Surgical.

Christiana was dying. Her blood pressure was unrecordable, her skin was clammy and her belly was full of blood. AJ had already fetched Latif from the village and was putting up a saline drip.

151

"Well done, AJ." It pained me to have to praise one so cocky, but I was secretly most impressed. He was, after all, only a first year student nurse. "What's your diagnosis?"

"She get ectopic, Dr. Gay."

"Yes, I'm sure you're right. Tell me about ectopic pregnancy."

"The pregnancy try for grow in the fallopian tube instead of the womb-self. Then space is not there and it bursts, so everything bleed too much inside."

"I couldn't explain it better myself, AJ."

"I take her to theatre, Dr. Gay. You get for do surgery quick quick."

Unfortunately he was right about that too.

"Her blood count is less than four grams, Dr. Gay, and we get no blood." Latif shouted through the window. "Them relatives no get the right group."

"Can you look in the village?"

"I de try," Latif shrugged, and went off into the night to knock on doors of villagers who might be willing to donate.

This was hopeless. My confidence slumped back to the lows of that morning. What was I doing in the middle of Africa at two am faced with more impossible surgery for a patient who would probably bleed to death on the table long before I had time to look up the instructions in the book? Even Sister Hillary couldn't turn salt water into blood.

Well perhaps I could learn something from Gasimu. I should work within my limitations and accept that I couldn't save this poor young woman.

"I'm going to let Christiana die in peace, AJ."

"Too late, Dr. Gay," AJ piped in. "Peter don already give the anaesthetic."

"Damn!" I looked at the ashen girl, breathing shallow irregular breaths and was about to order Peter to withhold further

152

anaesthetic when Tiange held out my gloves.

"You get for do the work, Dr. Gay." she ordered.

"But…"

"Quick, quick." She shoved a scalpel in my hand.

I was sure that even Hillary had never been strong enough to disobey Tiange, so I made my incision. As soon as the knife cut through the distended abdominal wall, an oil well of blood burst out. Tiange jumped deftly aside but I was too slow. Christiana's warm blood spurted against my chest and ran between my thighs, down my shins and into my theatre wellies.

"Oh…" I howled, but Tiange was not sympathetic.

"Dr. Gay, you waste the blood!"

"What do you mean, waste it?" Instead of answering, Tiange grabbed a little jug from her tray and started scooping up the blood and pouring it through a sieve into a bottle.

"What are you *doing*?" I gasped. "You can't just…"

But Tiange had already handed the bottle to Peter who was running the blood into Christiana's drip. They couldn't seriously believe that you could recycle blood like that, but I was too stunned to argue. I lifted a second jug from the tray and started bailing in the blood until we had collected another two pints for Peter to transfuse.

Once we had cleared the blood, I found the tube containing the misplaced pregnancy and tied it off to stop further bleeding. Heaving a sigh of relief, I sneaked a look to the head of the table. Christiana was still breathing.

The operating theatre looked like a battleground with blood splattered over the patient, the drapes, the floor and me. But with the help of one more pint that Latif found from his nocturnal search, Christina's blood pressure finally stabilised. Peter helped me wheeled her back to Surgical whilst AJ and Tiange washed down the floors.

Once Christiana was settled on the ward, Tiange and Peter returned to their beds, spotless despite their toils, whilst I traipsed stickily back to my house.

It was now four thirty. Dismayed, I stared at the two cupfuls of water left over from my belated bath that afternoon. Lady Macbeth couldn't have cleaned herself with that, and she only had a spot of blood on her hands to worry about. I was covered from the waist down. Where could I find water? AJ had already pilfered from most of the wards to wash down Theatre's floors and I was too tired to walk to the village well in the dark with my bucket.

"Aw fo du." I said, rubbing off the worst of it with my towel, then dampening my flannel with a couple of cupfuls of water from the toilet cistern. Bloody hell!

Okay, I knew I had been toying with contracting a serious illness to buy me a free ticket home, but AIDS wasn't what I had in mind.

"Kushe kushe, Dr. Gay, Morning-oh." I lifted the sheet from my head and peered at my watch. Seven o'clock. What was Sesay sounding so cheerful about? Hadn't he been up in the middle of the night with the rest of us, on generator duty?

"Morning, Sesay. What is it?" I called from my bed.

"Dr. Gay, Tiange say you don make too much mess last night."

"Hmmph!"

"So I bring you water."

"WATER? Great!" I leapt up into a clean dress and dashed to the front door. Sesay stood, daisy fresh on the doorstep, a bucket of water on his head.

"Thanks, Sesay, that's great. Plenti tenki."

"But, Dr. Gay, I get no socks," Sesay pleaded.

"Sorry?"

"I get no socks."

"You get no *socks*?" I repeated like an idiot. Well I supposed socks and shoes were quite a status symbol. Perhaps I could give him a pair of mine in return for the water? "What size are you, Sesay?"

He looked at me blankly.

"Would mine fit you?" I persisted.

Sesay's brow furrowed. Obviously I wasn't breaking through the language barrier, so I stepped up to him and measured my foot against his. This was too much for Sesay.

"Dr. Gay!" he exploded. *"Durex!"*

"Ahhh....Socks!" I blushed. "Condoms!"

'NO ONE FOOT SUCKS, NO SEX.' The AIDS office sign finally made sense. Admittedly the wrong vowel for *socks*, but since so few could read, spelling mistakes were scarcely important.

Still, Sesay got his socks and I got my water. I rushed off to have a bucket bath in celebration.

15. Betty's Wedding

Betty and Ben were married on Christmas Eve. Baby Hindolu was to be christened on Christmas Day.

This laudable open-mindedness bumped Father Pete several notches up in my estimation. The fifty-something priest reserved a rather stilted bonhomie for we volunteers, but he always had a kind smile and even invited us round for the occasional beer and game of cribbage. The same formality infiltrated his sermons, which were delivered in a mechanical monotone, made almost comical by Patrick Kpukoma's animated line by line translation into Mende. But Pete was well loved by his community and his church was always full on Sundays and festivals.

And that Christmas Eve was no exception. The pews were overflowing with smiles and multicoloured well-wishers. Even the Muslim staff members and villagers were there. The men were all clad in their rich gara suits and the women wore their gowns and lappas and new hairdos. Most had tight braids twisted with beads or ribbons sweeping across the scalp to the sides or back or, like Fatmata, whirling round in elaborate swirls, but a few sported nests of little black snakes twisting Medusa-style around their heads. My ponytail and kirby grips were a bit of an embarrassment. At least Pa George had washed and ironed my own gown and lappa after the High Commissioner's party.

Betty outshone everyone; even the net veil dotted with little flowers couldn't disguise her radiance beneath. Ben, by her side, wore a slate grey three-piece suit, and wouldn't have looked out of place in the City of London had it not been for his matching smile. The service ended with Alan's beautiful voice filling the church.

Those smiles finally gave way to laughter as the bridal couple walked down the aisle together, ducking under each flowered archway until they reached the doorway and stepped into the sunshine. The congregation spilled out behind the happy pair, throwing flower petals, dancing, singing and banging drums. I even spotted MT smiling.

The party continued at Betty's house. The Bride and Groom changed into traditional white gara, yokes and sleeves embroidered in gold thread. Hindolu bounced on his grandma's lap, drooling happily over his own golden embroidery as the three sat like angels at God's table, surveying the rest of the throng as we danced.

What I lacked in style on the dance floor, I compensated with vigour. Laygby tried to teach me the secrets of the Mende bottom and hip gyrations but, even if I had had any natural rhythm, I was too busy struggling to keep control of my clothing. Legs were traditionally covered in Sierra Leone, and thighs were a definite no no. My thighs were a definite no no anywhere, so I battled to keep the lappa tied round my waist. How had I managed to Strip the Willow with Klaus? I flushed, remembering that I had just cast my lappa aside. Ah well. I didn't really care what the High Commissioner thought of me, but I couldn't snub Betty with such socially unacceptable behaviour. If only we had the High Commissioner's air conditioning system.

"Kushe, Dr. Gay." A beautiful young woman interrupted.

"Kushe," I replied, trying to place her.

"You look really fine in that gara, Dr. Gay,"

"Thank you." I looked down at my once smart outfit, now soggy with sweat.

"You want poyo?" She added.

"Tenki ya." It wasn't water, but I knew that the poyo was also compulsory drinking, and at least it was fluid. I held out my glass, smiling graciously while racking my memory banks.

"Poyo, Mr. Alan?"

"Tenki ya, Christiana."

"Chris...? Surely not. Christiana!" I couldn't believe it. "What are you doing out of bed?" I admonished.

"I notto dance Dr. Gay," replied the girl whose blood had covered my body only three days ago.

"But… but, your stitches!" But my patient had vanished into the crowd.

"Well now, doesn't she look just grand, Dr. Gail?" Alan gave me a friendly shove on the shoulder. "Perhaps you might stay with us a little longer after all?"

"What the hell does she think she's doing at a party?" I snorted, trying to cover up the little flush of pleasure that was creeping over my cheeks. "But she does look good, doesn't she?"

"Mighty," agreed Alan.

"So what's she doing here?"

"Latif invited her."

"Oh he did, did he?" I laughed. "I can see why, but he better not let MT find out he's been chatting up his patients."

By dusk the party was winding up. As I was making my way home I bumped into Fatmata, back in uniform.

"Oh, kushe Fatmata. You must be the only one working today."

"Kushe, Dr. Gay. It was a fine fine wedding notto so?"

"Lovely. Have you got a patient for me?"

"We get one woman who don labour for many days now. I think say, you get for do Caesarean."

"Can I change first? Otherwise I'll lose the baby in my dress." I waved my voluminous blue angel sleeves.

"But you must come quick. Onita get belly ten times but she no get pickin. They say she is a witch. If this pickin die, they no let her go back to her village."

"Oh Fatmata, that's awful! Let's go."

I jogged home as fast as my lappa allowed. Fifty metres from my door there was a crack of lightening and a rumble of thunder and suddenly I felt as if I'd jumped fully clothed into a swimming pool. An hour earlier, I would have revelled in the cooling rain, dancing beneath it getting deliciously soaked, but now I had work to do. Pulling the lappa off altogether I broke into a sprint, with the remainder with my gown flapping round my knees and the rain bouncing off my face.

Dropping my sodden clothes in the corner. I towelled myself down and listened to the rain hammering on my tin roof. Where had that come from? This was supposed to be the dry season. At least our water problem would be temporarily solved. I retrieved my umbrella, snapped it open and stepped through the curtain of water at my front door to slide and slither down the path that now rivered its way back to Maternity.

Fatmata was rolling out two large oil drums to collect the water flowing from the guttering of the ward as I arrived.

"Any sign of Tiange or Peter yet?" I shouted to be heard above the clattering on the roof, then paused. I hadn't heard the theatre bell, which meant it unlikely that anyone else would have either. "Fatmata, have you heard the bell?"

"No, Dr. Gay." She listened for a moment. "It's the rain."

"Then how will the theatre staff hear it?"

Fatmata shrugged.

"Damn," I muttered, following her back inside.

Onita was breathing heavily with the sweat clinging to her upper lip. We turned her now limp body onto its side. Fatmata strapped on an extra piece of tape to secure the drip as I listened to the baby's heartbeat - it was very faint.

There was a knock at the window. A drenched Moses stood outside with his face pressed to the mosquito mesh. He refused to come inside, so I had to join him in the dark and rain. Even an educated Mende man like Moses would not enter the labour room.

"Dr. Gay, I rang the bell many many times, but no person able hear it," he panted. "I don go to Tiange and Peter's houses, but all two are not there."

"Are they still at Betty's?" I asked, trying to squeeze myself further under Maternity's narrow eaves for shelter. The baby was going to die and Onita would be outcast, all because it was raining.

"No. I don check. Only Sesay and Almamy are there, drinking poyo."

"At least we have Sesay for the generator. Where else might the others be Moses?" I jumped uselessly from foot to foot. This baby should have been delivered two hours ago and Onita herself couldn't survive much longer in labour before she died of exhaustion or her womb ruptured.

"Perhaps the rain don catch them and they make shelter. Will I get Dr. Jon?" Moses suggested.

"Jean has gone to Mokanje for Christmas. Bloody hell," I cursed. "Yesterday there was no water, and today there is too much."

"I go and check every house."

"Thank you Moses. Fatmata, who's on Surgical?"

"Hawa."

"And Medical and C Ward?"

"AJ and Mohammed."

"First year students only, no trained staff?"

"It is Saturday. Aw fo do."

"Okay. We'll have to manage with students. See if Hawa can find any more."

Ten minutes later I had five eager first years, and Fatmata, in her second year. I gave the spinal and put Fatmata in charge of Onita's observations. Only AJ had actually done his two-month theatre

161

placement which, unfortunately, made him the only choice to be my assistant. AJ was delighted with his sudden promotion. My how he would boast to the other students now! He slapped the scalpel confidently in my hand, his eyes alive with excitement above his mask.

AJ's euphoria only served to accelerate my palpitations. I had never operated without Tiange, and we were surely too late for Onita's longed-for baby. Taking a deep breath I tried to focus on at least trying to save the mother.

Within five minutes I lifted a floppy dusky blue baby boy from Onita's womb.

"I can only just feel a heartbeat. Has anybody resuscitated a baby before?" I asked. A creeping silence gave me my answer. Could I risk leaving Onita with AJ whilst I tried to bring the baby round myself? I knew just how important this baby was. An alarming gush of blood spilt from Onita's womb and ran down the drapes to make my decision for me.

"Fatmata how is her blood pressure?"

"Too low to make a reading, Dr. Gay."

"Turn the drip full on, Fatmata. Hawa, take the baby quick. You must try to revive him," I called, turning my attention to the bleeding points.

"Dr. Gay I have never..." sobbed Hawa.

"TRY!" I shouted at the poor girl.

Just then the theatre doors swung open and a black angel dressed in theatre greens entered.

"Betty! What on earth...?"

"My mother told me Moses came looking for staff."

"But this is your wedd..."

"Where do you want me, Dr. Gay?" Betty interupted, snapping on rubber gloves.

"Help Hawa with the baby. Quick."

Hawa gladly relinquished her responsibility and I could hear Betty calmly asking for the ET tube as I tied off blood vessels to stem the flow of blood from Onita's womb. The theatre was so quiet that I could hear the gentle puffs of the ambu-bag as Betty filled the baby's little lungs with air. Only AJ seemed to be breathing, his masked face close to mine as he held clamps steadily or passed over suture material for me to sew up the layers. I focussed totally on Onita's abdominal cavity, too scared to ask how either of my patients were doing until I was finished.

"Thank you, AJ. Well done." I watched my fledgling assistant put a dressing on the wound. "How is Onita, Fatmata?" I asked, without daring to look up.

"Onita's blood pressure is one twenty over eighty."

"Really? Is she conscious?"

"Yes, Dr. Gay. She is watching Betty."

"Oh dear," I sighed. It couldn't be helped. There wasn't room to hide the resuscitation attempts from Onita. "And the baby?" I half whispered.

"We have a heartbeat of one hundred and forty," Betty announced.

"What? Do we?" I perked up. "That's great! Any attempts at breathing on his own?"

"Yes. He's straining on the tube. I get for take it out." Betty's last statement was punctuated by a loud cry, which was followed by cheers from the students.

"Betty, you're terrific!" I exclaimed, watching the new bride carry a screaming baby over to his mother. "Now for goodness' sake you'd better get back to that husband of yours. You can't spend your wedding night in an operating theatre."

"It was worth it," she beamed, nodding towards Onita, who was cuddling her first live child, with tears of joy splashing onto his wrinkled little face.

16. Where's My Christmas

At midnight, bolstered by my success, I joined the rest of Serabu round a huge bonfire that blazed at the back of the church. Thankfully the rain had relented in time for the Christmas festivities to go ahead. Everybody lit a candle from the flames then, singing, we formed a candlelit procession which snaked into the church and down the aisle, still arched with flower-entwined palm fronds.

Squeezing back into the pews poda-poda tight, we watched the mother Mary with baby Jesus bring up the rear of the procession. I looked again at the young woman. It was Jeneba walking tall and proud with two month old Problem in her arms! She lowered Problem into a basket crib before the altar where, surrounded by candles and flowers, he fell asleep.

Lucky Baby Jesus. Things went down hill after that, and by two thirty I was nearly crying with fatigue, so slipped off to bed. In my defence, oh Lord, this was the second time that day I'd been to church.

Six thirty am. My Christmas alarm call came from a group of children on my doorstep. I peered through my bedroom window to see Nurse Sankoh, junior entrepreneur, starting off the chorus.

"Dr. Gay, where's my Christmas?"

"Where me Christmas?" The others joined in.

"Dr. Gay, where me Christmas?"

"Dr. Gay?"

"Dr. Gay...."

Now much as I admire the adage 'Ask and it shall be given,' this direct approach rather clashed with my British upbringing of hanging around, being good and looking quietly hopeful.

I was going to have to get up anyway, if I was going to do a ward round before church, so I pulled on my dress and went to the door. They were only kids and they didn't have the vocabulary to be subtle. I gave them each a balloon from a bumper bag of fifty I'd bought from a Lebanese supermarket in Freetown specially for Christmas day.

Twenty sad pieces of multicoloured rubber drooped from uncertain fingers.

"Okay, let me show you what to do." I demonstrated how to blow up a balloon and tie off the end. My little audience watched with rapt faces. Nurse quickly got the hang of it and punched his balloon in the air to squeals of delight from the others. I helped some of the smaller children to blow up their own balloons and they skipped back down my path to show off their 'Christmas' to their friends.

Smiling to myself, I had breakfast of bananas and bread rolls. Gosh it was good to taste bread again, a rare treat in Salone. The village "baker" had managed to get a couple of sacks of flour in from Freetown and was doing a bumper trade for Christmas.

The path from my house was lined with expectant children and adults alike. I was out of balloons before I even reached the wards.

"Dr. Gay, where me Christmas?" chanted the patients as I came onto Surgical Ward. They had to make do with a "Happy Christmas" and a cheery smile. I struggled to swallow my irritation when even the nurses started demanding their own Christmas. Fortunately none took the huff when I shook my head.

The only patient not to ask me for anything was Gasimu. He just quietly wished me Happy Christmas. It was his leg that shouted out for further attention. It was a mess. I was going to have to take him back to theatre.

"Dauda can you ask the theatre staff to come in after church?"

"No problem, Dr. Gay."

Ten o'clock saw the church full for a further two and a half hours. Father Pete and the congregation carried on as enthusiastically as they had left off. I had theatre as an excuse for an early exit, but for

166

once I wasn't glad to leave before the end.

Gasimu's leg was even worse than I'd thought. Jean had gone to Mokanje for Christmas dinner and wouldn't be back for hours, so it was up to me.

After half an hour of cutting back the muscles, it took another twenty hard minutes with the Gigli saw, to cheese wire through four centimetres of thighbone. I handed the cross-sectioned stump to Tiange and wiped away the fine layer of bone dust to see what was left.

A long thin pocket of pus still ran up Gasimu's inner thigh to his groin. Shit. Other than taking his leg off at the hip (which even an orthopaedic specialist would balk at), I could only wash it out with sterile saline and pray.

This time I left the stump unsutured to allow the infection to drain. I watched Peter swaddle the raw end of Gasimu's stump in gauze and bandages. I knew I hadn't done enough, but I wasn't capable of more.

I climbed back into my dress and stepped out of theatre into the bright sunshine. My pupils constricted so emphatically that my vision blurred, but not enough to obliterate the crowd of children heaving towards me.

"Dr. Gay, where's my Christmas?" Came the battle cry.

I squeezed my eyes tightly shut, hoping to somehow magic the little army away. It didn't work. They started chanting, "Where's my Christmas, where's my Christmas." I wanted to scream. I wanted to go home. I wanted...... help.

Aisha provided a rescue of sorts, shouting behind the mob, waving a medical chart above their heads.

"Dr. Gay, you have a patient on C Ward. She get convulsions."

"I've got to go," I muttered, pushing my way through the crowd.

As I was calming the child's fits with diazepam, MT appeared on the ward.

"Peace and Goodwill to you all on this happy day," she

announced. "I bring your Christmas." MT held up a basket stuffed with little parcels.

The nurses and I gaped as the skinny, grey and white Santa made her rounds, giving a parcel to each nurse, each child and each mother and wishing them the blessings of the day.

"I don't believe it," I muttered, watching the children's faces light up as they unwrapped their little rubber balls whilst the mothers were equally delighted with their cake of soap and tin of sardines.

This sudden surge of goodwill from MT was almost too much to bear. I scribbled instructions on the child's chart, thrust it back to Aisha and stormed off the ward, my soul far, far from salvation.

It was late and Pa George had taken the day off, but maybe Alan would have some food left from the lunch he had promised me. I marched down to his house and banged on the door. No answer.

"Gone to the staff Christmas picnic, Mr. Party Animal? You selfish bastard!" I threw myself against Alan's locked door. "It's Christmas Day, what's my blooming Muslim cook doing with the day off?" I shouted into the nearly deserted hospital compound. "Where's my chop today? I….want….my….lunch." I punctuated my frustration with kicks at Alan's door, then slumped down on the doorstep, dropped my head in my hands and started to cry.

I wept because I had only slept for six hours across the past three nights, because my own incompetence had left a man rotting to death, because I was hungry and hot and all my family would be at home, stuffed with food and alcohol. I wept because there was nowhere to hide from nurses looking for me to sort out impossible problems, or from children wanting their Christmas present and because my once generous personality had sunk to a level lower than Scrooge himself. Then to top it all, bloody Klaus fancied someone else and Alan was not even in for me to talk to. I lifted my head and sniffed. Come on Gail, big strong girls don't cry. I dragged myself to my feet and headed home.

Pa Ali passed me, just as I reached my path.

"Bua, Dr. Gay."

"Bua bise, Pa Ali," I muttered into the ground without breaking stride, waiting for the inevitable demand for a Christmas present. It never came.

"Bi gahuyena," he answered as usual.

Surprised, I stopped and answered "Kayingoma," looking at him expectantly.

"Kayingoma. Malo-hua," he waved and headed off to his palm tree. Here was somebody who expected nothing from me.

I flung my door open, grabbed my carrier bag purse to fish out a handful of twenties and chased after the wiry figure. I thrust the notes in his palm.

"Happy Christmas, Pa Ali."

"Happy Christmas, Dr. Gay." He looked perplexed. "I bring poyo for you?"

"No, Pa Ali. No poyo. Happy Christmas."

"Plenti tenki, Dr. Gay," he beamed. "Malo-hua."

"Malo-hua."

My brief surge of Christmas cheer fizzled out five minutes later.

"Dr. Gay, Gasimu's brother is here." Dauda called through my mosquito mesh. " He wants to speak with you."

"Gasimu has a brother?" I said, surprised. "Well good! Finally, a relative. Okay, I'm coming, but let me finish my lunch."

"Only bananas, Dr. Gay?" Dauda pointed to the pile of skins lying on the table.

"I'm just a poor little poomui," I replied. "I've nothing else, so don't dare ask for your Christmas."

There was no private place to talk to relatives so I stood outside Surgical with Gasimu's brother, running my hands through my hair and telling him that Gasimu would surely die in the next few weeks.

"Aw fo do," he said quietly. He had just walked thirty miles

169

from Mokanje. My struggle to find some words of comfort was interrupted by an extremely drunken Latif, who threw his arms round me and wished me Happy Christmas in between declarations of my brilliance.

"Thank you, Latif. Can I have a few minutes with this gentleman now?"

"No problem, Dr. Gay. She a fine fine Doctor sir, fine, fine...."

"Latif, please!"

"No, no. A fine doctor. Dr. Gay, where's me Chri..."

"Latif!"

Thankfully Latif weaved off, and Gasimu's brother shook my hand warmly.

"Tenki ya, Dr. Gay, you have really tried." I tried to smile in reply as he left for his thirty-mile return journey.

"He's walked such a long way, why won't he stay awhile with his brother?" I whispered to Dauda who had appeared at my shoulder.

"He is too much scared that MT will make him pay for all the treatment."

"That's...oh....that's just...."

"Dr. Gay you really have tried for Gasimu. Do not feel bad."

"Thank you," I sniffed, feeling awful.

"Dr. Gay, I bring you your Christmas," Dauda smiled, proffering a sardine sandwich made with his morning's gift from Santa MT.

"Oh Dauda!" I sobbed, wolfing down his sandwich, salted with my tears, then glanced longingly at my watch, willing Jean back.

Right on cue, I spotted the back of Jean's truck heading towards my house. Twenty minutes early! With a yelp of glee, I ran towards them. My enthusiasm was soon tempered by a gang of children approaching from the wings, their sights fixed on fresh prey to torment for Christmas presents. I broke into a sprint.

"Quick, quick. Inside!" I rattled my key in the lock. Jean and Francoise exchanged glances. I pushed Jean into my living room and pulled Francoise through the door as she clutched Geraldine, slamming the door behind them, just as a wall of children's faces appeared at the window.

"Qu'est que c'est...?" started Jean. A plaintive wail came from behind my door.

"Maman!" It was Matthieu. I had shut him outside with the Christmas present seekers. Sheepishly I opened the door, but just enough to guide Matthieu in.

"Oh, I'm so sorry Matthieu."

"I think you have had a bad day, yes?" observed Jean, cuddling his sobbing two year old.

"They just want their Christmas," I sighed.

"Ah yes. And you want yours. The McGranes have a wonderful Christmas dinner waiting for you." Paul McGrane, the Mines MD, was treating all the Serabu expatriates to Christmas dinner at Mokanje. "No, don't tell me about the problems, I'll soon find out. Bon appetite." Jean bundled his family back into their truck like a bodyguard removing a celebrity from the paparazzi. He slammed the door and bounced off to their house with the bounty-seeking children skipping behind.

An hour later we were off to the Mines, Alan, Tom and I singing carols in the back seat of the Landrover. Father Pete clapped along and even MT was humming. Serabush fell behind us as I belted out the words, spoiling the harmony between Tom's rich voice and Alan's beautiful tenor, still piccolo clear, despite a heavy afternoon on the poyo at the staff picnic. No matter what he might have imbibed, he could not have felt as elated as I did at that moment. I was free!

Six miles down the road we passed a lone figure trudging slowly towards the sunset. Oh no, it was Gasimu's brother. "Moses, can we give him a lift?" I asked. Well, what else could I do? "He lives in Mokanje."

Moses pulled the Landrover up on the side of the road and Tom pulled him in by the arm. "Do ya. Come inside sir."

"Who is this man?" demanded MT. "Serabu hospital is not a taxi service." But Gasimu's brother had already sat himself next to me and was shaking everybody's hand.

"It's Christmas, Ignatius. We can give the man a lift, dear." Father Pete patted MT's arm.

"Drive on Moses," MT instructed, a kitten in the hands of the kindly priest.

"On....the....FIRST day of Christmas, my true love gave to me," Alan started, as soon as we were moving. I cringed. He couldn't know that only hours ago, I'd been telling this man that his brother was dying.

Selfishly starting to wish we had just driven straight past him, I gazed out of the window and dreamed of my family breaking open their Christmas champagne by my granny's roaring fire. They would be laughing and joking, surrounded by presents, new clothes, CDs, clever gadgets and computer games and boxes and boxes of chocolates.

"Seven swans-a-swimming. Come on Gail!" Tom nudged me out of my wallowings. I looked round to see Gasimu's brother singing along with the others, a huge smile on his face.

"Six geese-a-laying. FIVE GO-OLD RINGS!" I shouted. What the hell, it was Christmas.

17. Happy New Year

The New Year dawned with a teenage girl weeping on my doorstep.

"My father don die, Dr. Gay." The young stranger lifted her tearstained face.

"Oh. I'm sorry," I said hesitantly. What did she want with me? Once a patient died and the bill was paid, the relatives took the body away. We doctors were no longer wanted or needed.

"He's dead," the young girl sobbed again.

"Who is your father?" I asked gently.

"Gasimu Kallon."

"Oh." So there was a daughter too.

"I'm sorry," I repeated inadequately to the daughter. Why hadn't I spent a bit more time talking with him, instead of always finding excuses to leave? "How long have you been here?"

"Yesterday, Dr. Gay." At least Gasimu had not died alone. I was glad of that.

"They did not tell me my father was ill," she started to explain. "I don come quick but my village is near Kailahun."

"Kailahun! How did you get here?" Kailahun was where Sam and Tim were posted, a hundred and fifty miles to the East.

"I walked."

"You walked!" The girl had scarcely reached puberty. "Alone?"

"I get no mother and no brother." I was starting to understand why this girl was standing on my doorstep on New Year's morning - the responsibility for transporting her father's corpse back to their village now rested on her immature shoulders. And the bill - all those dressings, all those antibiotics and insulin, not to mention the surgery – God, it would be enormous. Remorse suddenly overwhelmed me. I had failed Gasimu in every way and my biggest failure was to treat him as a medical problem rather than as a person.

My horror at his condition and the language barrier were no excuse. I wished I had held his hand. Just once.

I felt quite sick at the thought of this girl, or anyone, having to pay for my failings. I had to help her now. I glanced at my watch. It was still early, and a hospital holiday. We had to get her father out of the compound before MT was back on duty and confiscated the body. We had twenty-four hours.

"Okay, come with me. Your uncle works at Mokanje notto-so?" She nodded as I slipped my feet into flip-flops and tied my unbrushed hair into a pony-tail.

By nightfall Gasimu's body was gone, thanks to Alan's Mines connections. We would face MT first thing in the morning.

We lied.

"Sister Ignatius, I'm afraid that the diabetic patient on Surgical Ward died yesterday. He'd been very ill and suffered greatly," I started to waffle, wringing my hands and shuffling my feet. "We tried to save him by amputating his leg, but it became infected and we had to amputate it higher, but that didn't work either and his diabetes got out of control and the infection took over his whole system and I managed to scrounge insulin in Freetown so at least we didn't have to pay for that. Anyway...."

"His body vanished in the night, Ignatius, before the bill was paid," Alan interrupted.

"Aw fo do," said MT, her head bent over her calculator. We stood and gaped.

"Aw fo do," I mouthed to Alan. "Is that all?" He shrugged.

"Now I'm sure you young people have work to do," MT added. "I must finish the annual report."

"Yes, yes, of course," said Alan, pulling me out of Admin office.

"I don't believe it," I exclaimed, as soon as we were out of earshot. "What's got into her? Aw fo do? I was expecting a lynching!"

"Well you know why don't you, Dr. Gail?" said Alan.

"No, I don't. Enlighten me."

"It's the annual report. Attendances are up nearly fifty per cent since you came."

"Really?" I exclaimed.

"Yes. You must be the first atheist to make it into MT's good books."

"Agnostic," I corrected, hastily reining in my enthusiasm. "It's just the curiosity factor. As soon as the patients discover I'm no Dr. Pat, attendances will slump back to normal."

"Maybe they have come to test you out," mused Alan. "But you try for them and you laugh a lot. Two things that go down very well here."

"Nonsense," I retorted, unused to a direct compliment from Alan.

"And you had quite a coup with Jeneba, you know."

"Jeneba?"

"She's the chief's niece."

"Never. She didn't seem rich enough!"

"That's Sierra Leone's economy for you. Even the chiefs are poor," Alan observed. "Still, they have plenty of influence. Problem did get to be Baby Jesus. Now there's a thing! You saved baby Jesus! Quite an achievement," he teased.

"Alan." I punched him in the arm, but I was pleased. Perhaps I could even achieve that first goal and help to save Serabu Hospital.

1991 assumed a nice little rhythm. The Harmattan came, blowing in cooler weather, which banished my prickly heat and lifted my mood considerably. At work, my surgical skills would never be the greatest, but they were good enough and attendances crept up steadily, taking my confidence with them. Pa George served his plassas and gradually my waistbands loosened. As for my love life, well, you couldn't have everything, but my social life was very pleasant: girly chats with Francoise, beers with Alan and Jean, cribbage with Tom and Pete, or Scrabble with Betty, Peter and AJ. Fellow volunteers popped in from time to time, and I even cycled to Sumbuya to spend a weekend with Tracey. When alone, I wrote long letters home with the World Service as my constant companion. The news from the big bad world outside scarcely touched me, even when I heard that we were at war with Iraq. But The Gulf seemed very far away, whilst I was safe in peaceful Sierra Leone, a country that had never known war.

"Dr. Gail! Why haven't you told us about Mr-Dr-Gay?"

"Mr-Dr-....What are you talking about, Tom?"

"Your man."

"I don't have a man," I snapped.

"Well, who was your visitor today?"

"Huh?"

"You know, the little German guy who fixes things."

"What?!!!" I exploded. "Klaus? He came to visit!"

"That was it! Hey you see. She's blushing. It must have been Mr-Dr-Gay."

"Rubbish," I retorted, trying to gather myself. Why did the staff assume he was my other half? Had he insinuated it somehow? That was very hopeful indeed. "He's just another VSO," I added hastily.

"Come, come, Dr. Gail. With a reaction like that, you can't tell us that there isn't something going on," teased Alan.

"So where is he?"

"Oh, he left long ago."

"You mean he's gone!"

"Sorry. Hey, Alan's right. You really like the guy!"

"Hmmmph!" I was doing my best not to burst into tears. "Didn't he..... why didn't he come and find me?"

"You were busy in theatre."

"But why didn't he wait?"

"He waited for nearly three hours, Gail. He came on his motorbike and wanted to get back before dark."

"Oh."

"Hey, his trip wasn't wasted," Tom continued. "Alan collared him and guess what?"

"What?" I asked in a flat voice.

"He fixed our water pumps!"

At least he had left me a note. I read it once I was safely free from my audience of Jean and Tom, who were enthralled by the thought of me having a fancy man.

'Dear Doc,-

How di body? Sorry to miss you. Aw fo do. I heard you were up to your knees in blood, and knowing how much you enjoy it, couldn't bear to disturb you. Next time. I've got this bike running like a pussy cat, so if I can scrounge some petrol, I'm on for that trip to Fiona's next month. Meet you in the Peace Corps rest house in Bo on Easter Saturday? Radio CARE to confirm. By the way, you owe me a big kiss for fixing your water pumps. We go see back!

Love,

Klaus xxxxx'

I cheered up a little. He'd signed his letter with love and five kisses and said I owed him a big kiss! I cheered up a little more.

And he still wanted to take me up to see Fiona at Easter. And he'd even fixed our water.

What a star! I had a shower and flushed my loo for the first time in six months.

18. Saffa And Scooby

Saffa was seven and he had rabies. He'd been bitten by a seemingly harmless dog three weeks earlier. We'd cleaned the wound and put him on antibiotics. We didn't give the rabies vaccine as his father couldn't afford it, and neither could we - one course would blow six months of the charity fund. Only those bites proven to be from infected dogs (and who would catch, cage and feed a potentially rabid dog for ten days when there was not enough food to feed their own families?) and those wealthy enough to pay, got the vaccine. Horrible though this was, even I could see that egalitarian principles were useless if the hospital bankrupted itself on one or two cases.

I had never seen rabies outside of the textbooks and I never want to see it again. Saffa could no longer swallow as even his own saliva started excruciating spasms in his throat. His young body twisted in pain, saliva frothing from his mouth.

"Saffa's father wants to take him home," Betty told me, as I stood, helplessly watching the child suffer, despite huge doses of sedative.

"Not like this," I exclaimed. "They live fifty miles away!"

"His father wants him to die with his family," Betty persisted.

"No!" I snapped. "No," I repeated more gently. I fully understood that his father should want Saffa to die at home, especially after we had failed him so badly, but how would he get him there? "Look, Saffa can't possibly go on a poda-poda." The memory of my own journey to Freetown in the glorified cattle truck was still fresh in my mind. "He has rabies. Please explain that apart from the extreme discomfort to the boy, we can't cram a child drooling infected saliva into a truck full of people."

Betty spoke at length to the father in Mende, then turned to me.

179

"He wants to take Saffa home while he still lives. Poda-poda drivers charge double to transport a dead body." Aghast, I had to gather myself for a calm reply. How could this man be so heartless when his own son was dying in agony?

"This child is suffering." I spoke to Betty without looking at the father. "The journey will be a nightmare – I doubt he'd even survive it. Let Saffa die here, at least we can sedate him."

Betty nodded and spoke again to the father.

"The father has agreed."

"Well done, Betty. How did you persuade him?"

"If Saffa died during the journey it would cost five times as much."

A fist of anger encircled my heart. How could that man be so mercenary? Was money more important to him than his son? I stood outside C Ward and took a few deep breaths to slow my pulse down before going to Outpatients.

My first patient was Pa Ndanema, an old man who'd lost a leg many years ago and now his stump was breaking down. It was probably a side effect of TB, I sent him to X-ray.

"Another patient is there in X-ray," said AJ.

"Really? Who?" I hadn't sent anybody and Jean was in bed with malaria.

"A patient sent by Dr. Momoh."

"Oh yes." We did have an agreement that Dr. Momoh, the Mines' official doctor, could use our X-ray facilities, even though we had little faith in Dr. Momoh's visual or medical faculties. We charged extra of course, and always sneaked a look at the pictures before they went back to exclude major problems. "So who is it?"

"I don't know. He get swelling on his jaw," AJ told me. "The patient's name is Scooby."

"Scooby? Not a Mende name, surely?" But with children called Nurse and Problem, I refrained from further comment.

"He black Dr. Gay, but he notto Mende man." AJ shook his head solemnly.

"AJ what are you trying to tell me?"

"Mr. Scooby Doo is not well." AJ was laughing now.

"Scooby Doo! A DOG?!"

"Dr. Gay what is going on? There's a dog in X-ray!" MT stormed into my office. "This is a gross misuse of precious facilities. I demand an explanation."

"Ask Dr. Momoh, Sister Ignatius." I threw my hands up defensively, "They've just told me."

"Dr. Gail, are you laughing?"

"No, Sister," I replied with great effort.

"This is no laughing matter. Are you not aware of the funding crisis that may force my hospital to close in a matter of months?"

"Of course, Sister. Shall we go and investigate?" I offered.

"I have work to do. Dr. Momoh will be hearing from me personally."

MT left abruptly, and suppressing a smile, I went down to the little X-ray room myself. An expatriate couple sat outside, stroking an old black Labrador with a large swelling on its cheek.

"Dr. Gay, look at this X-ray." Latif pushed a picture of the dog's jaw under my nose.

"Well there's a swelling, but you don't need an X-ray to see that." I gave Latif the film back.

"Doctor, Scooby has been unwell for a few weeks now and this swelling is just getting bigger. The vet's on holiday," a tearful middle-aged lady told me. Gosh, was there such a thing as a vet in Sierra Leone?

"How old is Scooby?" I asked looking into the cloudy brown eyes that gazed mournfully into mine.

"Nearly fourteen."

"Fourteen!" I exclaimed. "I doubt there's much even the best vet in the world could offer. It'd be kindest to put him to sleep." A double dose of out of date anaesthetic would probably do the trick. Perhaps triple to make sure.

"Oh please doctor, is there nothing you can do until the vet comes back?"

My knowledge of dogs was based entirely on James Herriot books, but surely Scooby wouldn't even survive until the vet's return. Poor old boy. I tentatively touched Scooby's swelling and he licked my hand.

"The swelling is soft, and there's a little pus dribbling into his mouth," I mused. "It might just be an abscess that needs draining."

"Could you do it?"

"Well I suppose so, but I've no idea how to safely anaesthetise a dog. You'll just have to hold him down." Dogs might be the only thing not covered in Maurice King's book, but the 'Where there's pus, let it out' doctrine probably still applied. It couldn't be much different from run-of-the-mill boil-lancing.

Except it wasn't an abscess. Not a drop of pus drained out of my incision. Scooby never released me from his placid brown eyes, flopping a paw onto my thigh as I knelt beside him. I put my gloved finger gently inside the swelling. All I could feel was a soft mush of rotting tissue.

"It's cancerous, I'm sure. Okay, Scooby, I've finished." I stroked the dog's head. "I should put him to sleep. I'm sorry."

"We'll wait for the vet," the woman gulped. Her husband mouthed thank-you, then scooped up Scooby and carried him to their truck.

"So Gail, what about Mr-Dr-Gay? Confess all to Father Alan."

"Just dish me out my chop." I shoved my plate over to the would-be-priest.

"A mighty choice."

"Hmmph!"

"Not as handsome as me, of course, but anyone who can fix our water pumps is a friend of mine."

"No wonder he was in such a hurry to leave, before you roped him into a hundred more jobs."

"Jaysus, is that all the thanks I get for providing running water!"

"Excuse me, who fixed them?"

"The mark of a good administrator, knowing the right person for the job," Alan sniffed. "I was after thinking he'd be a bit bigger though."

"Why?" I snapped. Was this a slur on my size, or Klaus's? Either way Alan realised our friendship was hitting rocky territory and rapidly changed the subject.

"So how much do you we charge the Mines for veterinary services?" he asked in his cheeriest voice.

"Double at least."

"Poor dog." Alan shook his head. "Just another little anecdote for Dr. Gail to write home about."

"Hmmph! There's more than enough to write home about."

"And we still haven't had confirmation of that American replacement for Jean."

"Don't I know it. I'm trying not to panic. This Dr. Fran might be waiting for the outcome of the July review. There's not much point coming if Serabu's going to close."

"We should be fine, what with the improved attendances. Er, I've, um, got something to tell you…"

I didn't like the way he was fiddling with his earlobe. Alan

183

was never hesitant. "Tell me."

"I'm leaving." He coughed. "Father Gregory has asked me to work at the seminary in Makeni from Easter."

"What?! But that's next month!"

"I know. I'm sorry. I've only just got confirmation."

"Well what can I say?"

"You can come and visit, it's less than a day's journey north."

"Yeah great. MT will never let me out if there's no one to replace Jean?"

"I'll visit Serabu."

"Hmmph. Well I'd better enjoy my trip to Segbwema, hadn't I? Looks like it'll be my last escape."

"Have a beer."

"Hmmph."

Three days later a smartly dressed young Salonean man interrupted our plassas.

"Kushe, Dr. Gail. Dr. Jalloh from Freetown."

"Pleased to meet you Dr. Jalloh." I shook the outstretched hand under my nose. Who on earth was he?

"I am most grateful for your assistance with my patient."

"No problem," I said, smiling politely. "Um. Who is your patient?"

"Scooby."

"Scooby." I glanced over to Alan who was raising his eyebrows as he put his flip-flopped feet on my table. "So you're the vet?"

"Indeed I am the only vet in Sierra Leone." Dr. Jalloh bowed. "I trained in America."

"Congratulations. I obviously don't have your training, but Scooby seemed very sick to me." Had this man really made a seven-hour journey to discuss a fourteen-year-old dying dog?

"Yes, very sick," agreed Dr. Jalloh. "I wanted to know if Serabu, the best hospital in the country, can do angiograms?"

"Angiograms?!!" I spluttered.

"What's an angiogram?" Alan asked sweetly from the corner.

"An angiogram is a specialist X-ray examination where radio-opaque dye is injected into the blood vessels to delineate the arteries," explained Dr Jalloh

"I see," Alan nodded in mock understanding. "Can I ask how this test would help Scooby?"

"Scooby's mass is undoubtedly a cancerous growth. An angiogram would outline the extent of the lesion more effectively than a plain X ray."

"I see." Alan rubbed his chin and nodded. He was enjoying this.

"I'm afraid we do not have enough resources to do only the very basic X-rays on our own patients," I said with forced politesse. Why were we even discussing hugely expensive treatments for a dog when we didn't have the money to give rabies vaccines to children? "This is a dog we're talking about." I snorted. "And a very old dog at that."

"I wish only to formulate an accurate treatment schedule," said Dr Jalloh. "Scooby's owners are very upset."

And Scooby's white middle-class owners were rich enough to pay his juicy veterinary bills too, no doubt.

"Yes, of course." I folded my arms. "It must be hard to see a loved pet suffer so." Admittedly Scooby was a nice dog.

"Yes. So you no able help me?"

"I'm afraid not. Aw fo do."

"Aw fo do. I better get back to work." Dr. Jalloh shook my hand. "It's been nice meeting you, Dr. Gail."

"Good-bye," I said.

"Nice to meet you too, Dr Jalloh." Alan waved from the sofa.

"Angiograms!" I snorted as soon as the door closed.

"Such is the advantage of a Western education," said Alan, before collapsing in a fit of helpless giggles.

It had all seemed very funny that evening but, by morning, the irony was no longer amusing. I stood twenty feet from C Ward, my feet frozen on the baked ground as Saffa's father left the ward. He was cuddling a white shrouded bundle close to his chest, making no attempt to wipe away the tears that rolled silently down his face.

Saffa's father loved his son – that much was painfully obvious and who was I to stand in judgement? We had sacrificed Saffa, for the survival of our hospital, just as this father had had to make impossible rationing decisions to ensure the survival of the rest of his family. We had failed Saffa but would try to save the next child who came to us. Saffa's father had lost his son, but he still had to struggle on to provide for his other children. God, what a life. I brushed away my own tears and did my rounds. Only four weeks to Segbwema. Oh Gail, don't start that again.

19. Creature Crawling In Abdomen

"Som ting de walka na me belly."

Dr. Fran raised a quizzical eyebrow at Patrick's rounded handwriting at the top of the outpatient card.

"Krio," I explained. "Have you had any lessons?"

"Hey, I only arrived yesterday. I know 'kushe', though," Fran volunteered. I still couldn't believe that he was here. His letters had gone astray, so the first we knew of his arrival had been a radio message the previous morning, leaving Moses a record breaking challenge to get to the airport in time.

"That'll get you further than you think," I smiled at my handsome new colleague. Married, unfortunately. His wife was coming in a couple of weeks.

"Well that's a relief." He said tapping a patient's card. "So, what's the system?"

"The senior nurses triage the outpatients and send those that need blood or stool tests straight to the lab." I told him. "They'll treat anything simple, then send the rest to us, after recording the medical histories."

"Well that's no damned help if they write it in Krio," Fran complained.

"Don't worry, they usually use English, but we see 'something walking in my belly' every day. Sometimes it's translated into 'creature crawling in abdomen'"

"D'ya mean worms? Hey! Isn't that just a great expression?"

"Everything abdominal from a little tummy ache to full-blown peritonitis is blamed on creatures crawling in abdomen," I agreed.

"I guess worms are so common here that most people don't even notice. Unless of course they cause secondary complications like anaemia with hookworm infestation," he mused.

That was the trouble with Fran. He hadn't been with us for

twenty-four hours, and already he knew it all.

The latest recruit to Serabu's medical staff was in his mid-thirties, an athletic all-American male. He wore little round glasses, just like mine but, where mine with their hint of verdigris shouted NHS, his gave him that serious but trendy look - like Harrison Ford in a Heroic Doctor role, putting me, more of a Dawn French sort of character, on the defensive.

"Kushe, Bockerie. How de body?" I asked the first patient on the ward round.

"Kushe, Dr. Gay. I no better Dr. Gay," Bockerie announced with a face-splitting grin.

"But I drained four pints of pus off your chest yesterday!" I exclaimed. Surely he could admit to feeling just a little bit better?

"I still de cough, I still no able blow fine, I still get fever...."

"Okay Bockerie, let me have a listen in."

AJ stood unhelpfully at the end of the bed as I struggled with Bockerie's chest drain to sit him forwards.

"AJ, are you just going to stand there or are you going to help me?"

"No problem Dr. Gay." He saluted and swaggered forward. I sighed. So much for the humble student nurse with undying admiration for the doctor.

"Probably TB," said Fran, examining Bockerie's X-ray. Sure enough, Latif arrived on cue with sputum results to confirm Fran's diagnosis.

"Aw fo do, Bockerie," chirped AJ. "You get for go na TB ward!"

Bockerie was not impressed. Nobody wanted to go to TB ward.

"Sorry-oh," I muttered inadequately. I could have hit AJ for

188

his insensitivity. Bockerie did hit him.

"Careful AJ, he's frail," I admonished as AJ shoved Bockerie back onto the bed.

"He done hit me Dr. Gay!"

"You asked for it AJ." But my words were lost in a Mende shouting match that had suddenly developed between student nurse and patient. Bockerie now had AJ's crisp white uniform by the lapels.

"Shall we continue?" I asked Fran, who stood gaping at the spectacle.

"Shouldn't we break it up?" He suggested.

"Have you seen the muscles on AJ? No. Sister Ignatius can sort it out."

"Who's Sister Ignatius then? Some sort of body-builder?"

"Er, not exactly. She's the hospital administrator. Seventy plus. About seven stones."

"I'm quivering in my shoes," laughed Fran.

"Believe me. Quiver."

Dr. Fran chewed gum and diagnosed all my patients promptly, decisively and confidently, suggesting treatment appropriate to a Third World situation. I cursed Jean for making me show him round - I just wasn't impressive enough.

"But you will soon be his boss, yes. Dr. Gail, the Medical Superintendent of Serabu 'ospital." Jean had teased, and trotted off to hold the fort at Outpatients. Fran and I continued on our rounds.

Isata, the first patient on Maternity, had a nasty wound infection from a tricky Caesarean and so did the first three cases on Surgical Ward. I knew they were all excusable given the poor condition they had all been in on arrival. I also knew the wounds would all heal eventually, but it just didn't look very good. Fran stayed tactfully quiet, until Ansumana.

189

"Ansumana fell out of a palm tree and had multiple intestinal perforations. Somehow he survived three days walk to the hospital," I told Fran. "When he reached us, his belly was grossly distended and he had septicaemia."

"Really? Well that's just amazing that he's still alive," Fran enthused.

"Yes, isn't it," I said, proudly. "It was tricky surgery, especially in a moribund patient."

I pulled off the dressing with a flourish to show off my handiwork. "Oh no!"

"Gee, what's that orange stuff and white flaky bits?"

The gauze dressing was soaked with thick orange palm oil, and grains of half digested rice were oozing between the stitches. Having the patient's dinner coming directly out of the wound was not a good way to advertise my surgical skills. I was speechless.

"Hey girl, even with proper equipment, anaesthetic and a real surgeon in the States he might never have made it." The newcomer slapped me encouragingly on the back and continued to chew his gum, no doubt privately wondering what sort of place he had come to.

Why couldn't I find a miracle recovery to show him? Jeneba for instance or Christiana? Like the rest of us, Fran hadn't had any surgical experience before coming to Africa, and with three cases scheduled that morning, I was going to have to teach him. Or rather Tiange was.

"This is Tiange, Fran. She'll teach you everything you ever wanted to know about surgery."

"Real pleased to meet you Tiange," Fran said, striding forward and firmly shaking her hand. Tiange actually smiled. How did Fran manage that?

"You don't mess with Tiange, our queen of theatre," I whispered to Fran as we scrubbed up.

"I'll remember that."

"Last week Tiange asked a patient five times if he was chewing gum before Peter gave him the anaesthetic. He denied it every time, despite her dire warnings of what could happen if he inhaled it whilst he was unconscious. When he woke up, he found the offending chewing gum stuck across his forehead."

"I'm real glad I spat mine out, " Fran laughed. "Do you really only use this ordinary bar of soap to scrub up?" he continued, looking round for proper antiseptic wash.

"It's all we have. Usually we don't have many post-operative wound infections…." I said defensively.

"Hmm." Fran was not convinced. "Tell me about our patient today."

"She's a lady with a large abdominal swelling. She's quite elderly, although no one really knows how old they are here. She also couldn't tell me how long it had been bothering her."

"So what do you think it is?"

"Probably an ovarian cyst. We've had a run of them lately. I removed cysts the size of basketballs from two separate patients last week."

"Gee! that's amazing."

Pleased that I had the chance to impress Fran, I made a confident incision in the abdominal wall. Separating the sides of the wound with my hands, we looked inside. The nature of the mass became quite, quite obvious.

"She get belly!" Tiange exclaimed.

"She must be nearly six months pregnant!" echoed Fran.

Gulping back tears of humiliation whilst Fran and the nurses gulped back tears of laughter, I closed the wound without disturbing the foetus any further. Tiange reassured the patient, who was still awake under a spinal, that her pregnancy would proceed quite normally. The patient, apparently unconcerned, asked why we didn't just remove it as she already had eight children.

Once we were finished, Fran picked up her Outpatient card and succumbed to helpless guffaws. Embarrassed, I snatched the card from him to see what had caused such amusement.

The presenting complaint read: Creature crawling in abdomen.

20. Raising The Roof

Serabu Hospital was one man down for the annual Hospital v Serabu Village football match.

"Wouldn't it be mighty if there was a doctor on the hospital team?" Alan suggested innocently.

"Well, Jean's off to theatre with Fran chewing at the bit to get stuck into his first Caesarean Section," I commented between mouthfuls of plassas.

"That leaves our favourite lady doctor. Even better!"

"Me? What about their favourite Administrator?" I prodded my terminally unsporty Irish friend.

"Ah, Gail, they'll be needing me to organise the supporters."

And so it was that the big strong girl became Serabu Hospital's left half. I jogged onto the field amidst much chuckling from the spectators. A poomui playing football was funny enough, but a woman?

Determined to do female caucasians justice, I ran doggedly round the lumpy threadbare pitch in futile pursuit. Every time I came within striking distance of the ball, our supporters, consisting of students, nurses, relatives and TB patients, roared with delight. The hysteria was palpable on the four occasions I actually made contact with the ball. Even Tiange was cheering.

Tom, malaria free, turned out to be quite a sportsman and achieved honorary black man status for his prowess, even if he did cheat by wearing trainers rather than playing barefoot like the rest of his team. With AJ and Tom on side, our boys managed to sneak a 3-3 draw.

With two minutes to go, Patrick Kpukoma, the ref, awarded the hospital a penalty kick. This was debated so ferociously by the village lads that the match could only continue when Patrick agreed to let them choose who out of our team would take the shot.

Since I could now barely stand, I assumed I would be the obvious choice to mess up a penalty kick. I was eternally relieved, and rather flattered, when they unanimously yelled out "Mr. Alan!"

Alan, never one to think of taking offence, high-stepped on to the pitch, his pasty arms held aloft to the cheers of encouragement from the supporters. He bowed, picked up the scuffed and patched ball, blessed it with the sign of the cross, kissed it and placed it gently on the ground. He took three deep breaths, crossed himself, then blasted it between the two bamboo stick goal posts.

Well, Scotland winning the world cup at Wembley couldn't have generated more jubilation. Alan was hoisted high on the victorious team's shoulders and paraded round the field. He gave me the royal wave before vanishing for his lap of honour, round the entire village. I managed a weak thumbs-up in reply before staggering home to drink my water filter dry.

"Bua bise, Pa Ali. Bi gahun yena?"
"Kayingoma. A bia be?"
"Kayingoma."
"Malo-hua."
"Malo-hua Pa Ali."

I waved at the wiry old man and watched him jog to the base of the palm tree. He placed his empty yellow two-gallon rubber container on the ground, slung his woven raffia halter round the trunk and shinned up. In the half light, he vanished into the umbrella of leaves, so I returned to thinking about Alan. We were going to have a last supper together in Bo on the Friday, before he travelled up north to Makeni, and I went east with Klaus to meet Fiona at Segbwema Hospital.

How would I survive without Alan? At least I had my consolation prizes – the surprise arrival of Dr. Fran, the whole of next week to turn Klaus into Mr-Dr-Gay, a chance to see Fiona and the opportunity to learn a bit more surgery of course.

"What for chop today?" My daily alarm call thundered through my bedroom door as the sun rose. Every wooden muscle in my body nailed me to my bed.

"Morning, Pa George," I sighed. "Plassas please."

"Cassava ten leones, bonga thirty leones....."

"Okay," I groaned. "I'm coming." I rolled my aching body off the bed, gave Pa George his money and waddled down to work.

"Kushe, Dr. Football!" Sesay called out.

"Look, Dr. Football de come!" AJ and Latif dribbled imaginary footballs round me. I stuck out my tongue and side-stepped into Maternity, where I thought interest in football would be minimal.

"Yo! Here's our soccer star!" Fran slapped me on the back.

"Fran," I coughed. "You're early."

"Come to check on my first Caesarean lady."

"And how is our new surgeon's patient?" I asked.

"She's real great." Indeed mother, baby and doctor were all radiant. "And this little fellow is called Dr-Fran," he added picking up his namesake.

"You're obviously a natural," I laughed, but stopped short when I caught the eye of a stony faced man standing, arms folded, by the bed opposite.

"Can I help, sir?"

"This is Isata's man," explained Laygby. He was surprisingly well dressed, his tailored shirt and trousers set off with shiny leather shoes and a gold watch.

"I done tell him Isata no able go home today, so he is angry."

"Kushe." I offered my hand but it was left hanging. I raised an eyebrow at Laygby.

"He say it he no able wait for that wound to heal," Laygby told me. "Isata get for work on the farm."

"I see." I folded my arms. "Let's see the wound then, Laygby. You removed the stitches yesterday, notto so?"

"Yes. Plenty pus came out, but I done clean it fine today." She pulled back the gauze to show a long gaping wound, exposing muscle underneath.

"You have to admit it doesn't look good," whispered Fran.

"It's clean," I retorted. "Laygby, can you reassure Isata that her wound will heal. It just needs time. And tell that man that leaving his wife to labour for three days, then making her walk to the hospital, will have exacerbated the infection."

"He speaks English."

"Good. Then he understands what I have just said?"

"Yes, but he say the infection is your fault, so he no go pay the bill."

"Isata is lucky to be alive at all after her ordeal," I snapped. "This wound will heal. It may take two more weeks, but it will heal."

"He say that this ward no get ceiling-self," Laygby continued. Fran and I looked up simultaneously. Sure enough, there was no ceiling. "And them bats drop their kaka in the wound."

"Her wound is covered with fresh dressings every day. I promise it will heal," I stammered, pulling Fran out of the ward behind me.

"Hey, girl," he grumbled, snatching his arm away as soon as we were outside.

"You obviously think I was rude to that man?"

"Mmm. He had a point, Gail. I did see some bats up there."

"Well, I can tell you I was struggling to be civil. That man refused to pay for transport, so Isata walked ten miles." I could feel my voice rising with anger. "She was exhausted and her baby nearly dead when she arrived. So now he's concerned for her welfare? This is his first appearance, you know - a week later."

196

"Hmm. He sure had a nice watch," Fran agreed.

"Bloody man!" I snorted. "This is one chap who deserves the full wrath of MT, bats or no bats."

That evening I returned to Maternity to find Laygby, now six month's pregnant, bending beside the baby's crib and beating a bat to death with her flip flop. Fortunately there was no sign of Isata's husband. Looking up, the rafters were alive with flapping shadows. How had I never noticed before? I had to admit a ceiling was probably a good idea, and went to confront MT the next morning. Maintenance was her area.

"Good Morning, Sister Ig.....er....hello?"

"Good morning," A sweet smiling lady, in a blue dress covered in tiny yellow flowers, looked up from MT's desk. Her hair was very black, cut fashionably short to frame a girlish face. I would have put her in her late thirties had it not been for the simple cross hanging on a gold chain that brought the eye to a cluster of age spots on the sun-damaged skin at her throat.

"Er, well, I was really looking for Sister Ignatius. Sorry. Er, I'm Gail." We shook hands.

"Hello Dr. Gail, I'm Bernadette," she introduced herself in a lovely Irish lilt. "I'm sorry we have not had chance to meet, but let me offer a belated welcome to Serabu."

"Oh. Er, thank you." Bernadette? Bernadette? I racked my memory. Ah, yes. Tom's boss at the nursing school, back from her sabbatical. Blooming Alan might have told me.

"I hear you're doing great work altogether, Dr. Gail," she smiled.

"Pleased to meet you too," I stuttered, unused to direct compliments. "Er, where's Sister Ignatius?"

"She's got malaria, I'm afraid. So since Tom's been doing

197

such a mighty job in the nursing school whilst I've been away, I've come to help in Admin."

"Oh. Is Ignatius all right? Should I take a look at her?" I felt obliged to ask, although I couldn't imagine what sort of doctor-patient relationship I would have with MT.

"Thank you, no," Bernadette shook her head. "Pete has driven her to convalesce at our convent in Bo. Hillary will look after her."

"Of course." Obviously I wasn't good enough.

"Now how can I help you, Dr. Gail?"

"What?" I'd forgotten why I'd come. "Oh yes. Did you know there's no ceiling on Maternity Ward."

"No... ceiling?" Bernadette raised an eyebrow. "Since when?"

"Well I don't really know, I've never seen one but I confess I've never looked. It's just that it's not very hygienic, with the rafters full of bats dropping their droppings into patient's wounds."

"Dr. Gail, are you telling me that in the six months you have been here there has been no ceiling in one of our wards?"

"Well, um, yes. I, er, don't usually look up."

"Didn't Ignatius ever notice?"

"Possibly," I shrugged. Most probably, I thought, but new ceilings cost money.

"Very well, I'll see what Sesay can do. Moses can take you and Alan to Bo in the Landrover tomorrow, if you don't mind picking buying the materials for him to bring back?"

"Of course," I said demurely. (Fantastic, a lift!) "Won't you be a bit pushed in Admin without Alan and Ignatius?"

"We'll manage," said Bernadette. "Tom's running the school and it's time we gave Moses more responsibility in Admin. He's wasted as a driver. Father Gregory's agreed to lend us Alan for a week to show Moses the ropes."

"So Alan's returning?" I brightened up.

"Yes, in three weeks." Bernadette smiled. "Meanwhile you

198

have a happy birthday and enjoy your break in Segbwema."

"You know about my birthday?"

"I always note down birthdays from the volunteer details."

Now this was how nuns were supposed to be. Didn't MT have the same God?

"Well there's good news and bad news," I announced at the weekly poomui gathering at Jean and Francoise's.

"So what eez this bad news?" asked Francoise.

"Alan's coming back!"

"Quelle horreur," joked Jean. "He has not even departed."

"I'm going to give Moses the low-down on Admin at the end of the month," said Alan. "He's going to take over my job."

"Moses will be very good, bien sur, but will MT accept a local working in Admin?" asked Jean.

"Who knows, but MT's out of action for a while," I explained. "She's got malaria."

"Hey, the poor old lady, shouldn't we go and check up on her?" asked Fran. Fran, as a handsome, confident, married, Catholic, male had received a remarkably warm welcome from MT.

"She's gone to get some proper medical attention from Sister Hillary in Bo."

"Ah Dr. Gail, she'll just not want to be displaying human frailty to her volunteers," soothed Alan. "Don't be getting sulky when you're coming for a night of bliss with me in Bo. And you've even wangled us a lift, you mighty girl!"

"I did well, didn't I?" I smirked.

"Alan will make very good birthday celebrations for you," said Jean. "To get the mood ready for Mr-Dr-Gay!"

"Ah, yes. Mr-Dr-Gay wiz the big motorbike," giggled Francoise.

"Hmmph!" I folded my arms. "Hey, I've just thought. We've got the Landrover so I could get beer for a big farewell party for Jean, Francoise and Alan."

"Mighty!" The word party was enough to distract Alan from further teasing about my tender bud of a potential relationship. "Can we have it when I come back at the end of the month?"

"Ah, yes," said Francoise. "A big goodbye party togezzer."

"Yeah, a party. My wife should have arrived by then."

"So Mrs-Dr-Fran is definitely coming? Have we passed the test?" I teased. Fran's wife was a lab-technician and was planning to join her husband, subject to the advance party finding the position favourable.

"Hey, this is a great place. Sharon will just love it," Fran enthused. "She's never been out of the States. But you guys will just have to be real nice to me over the next month in case I change my mind."

"You want anozzer beer, Fran?"

"Thanks, Jean. Cheers all." Fran lifted his bottle.

"To our party," added Alan, raising his bottle to Fran.

"Bon. So we make kitty, yes?" said Francoise on her way out to the kitchen. "Gail can send the beer back with Moses while she goes off with her luvver for the week."

"He's just a friend, and I'm going to learn some surgery!" I protested, but Francoise had gone.

"Bien sur," nodded Jean, knowingly. I stuck my tongue out.

Just then Francoise re-appeared bearing a charred, three-stone-fire baked banana cake with three eight-inch candles stuck in the top and everybody sang Happy Birthday to the sound of Star beer bottle lids being flipped off.

"Cheers!" I raised my foaming bottle. "One happy birthday coming up."

21. The Rebels Are Coming

"The rebels are coming!"

"Huh? What rebels?"

"The rebels have invaded from Liberia, and are heading towards Bo," announced a stern-faced, pony-tailed American. Alan and I looked at each other in disbelief. We were sitting at Ma Coker's bar, the favourite volunteer hang out in Bo, having just treated ourselves to a special birthday dinner of egg and chips (!!!)

"I'm evacuating everybody to Freetown. The Peace Corps trucks leave at dawn," our harbinger of doom continued.

"You're joking," said Alan.

"But I'm meeting Klaus tomorrow, we're going to Segbwema," I protested.

"Not now you're not," said the grim-faced man. "There are six thousand rebels invading the east and south. Kailahun and Segbwema are the worst affected. There are convoys of villagers coming west as we speak. Get back to the resthouse and pack your bags."

"Who was that?" I gasped, breaking the silence that followed the departure of the American.

"Our Field Officer," mumbled a Peace Corps.

"Was he for real?"

"I sure don't know, but I'm getting another Star."

"I'm with him," said Alan. "Two Stars please."

"Shouldn't we do as he says?" I asked, never one for disobeying authority.

"Don't be an eejit, you're already packed. Look, birthday girl, there's ice-cream on the menu!"

"Ice-cream!"

The next morning Alan and I joined an unruly gaggle outside the Peace Corps resthouse. Nobody had seen Klaus. The Peace

201

Corps Field Officer repeated his ominous sermon on how the rebels had come in from Liberia across the border south of Sumbuya, and from the eastern border through Kailahun and Segbwema. Oh God, Fiona was supposed to be in Segbwema, and Sam and Tim were in Kailahun. It had seemed like some sort of surreal adventure last night, but now I could feel the fear taking hold.

And so we were whisked down to Freetown with a crowd of Peace Corps, Alan entertaining them with his usual banter, whilst I looked anxiously out of the back window, in the unlikely event of spotting Klaus. Perhaps he was speeding towards the frontline on his motorbike, desperate to rescue me from the clutches of the rebels. Or more likely the CARE grapevine had kept him well informed, and he was sitting in Moyamba, drinking Star.

An hour down the road, we passed a Peace Corps trying to hitch a lift in the opposite direction. It was Tracey.

"Where do you think you're going?" The Peace Corps Field Officer yelled through the passenger window.

"Yo, what's your problem?" Tracey put her hands on her hips and eyed the full Landrover. "I'm headed back to Sumbuya, hard worker that I am. Where're you all going?"

"Kushe, Tracey! There's trouble," Alan called from the back. Alan knew just everyone.

"Hey, Alan. It's not like you to travel economy."

"Very funny," retorted Alan, but his face softened quickly. "I'm sorry Tracey but rebels have invaded."

"No way!"

"We're evacuating everybody east and south of Bo, and that includes you, girl." The Field Officer nodded to the back seat.

"But I just left the Freetown office! Nobody mentioned squat."

"We only got through on the radio to Freetown at nine," said the Field Officer wearily. "Don't argue. Jump in."

"Where? On the roof? It's worse than a poda-poda in there. God, there's even a couple of Brits in the back."

"Irish, please!" hummphed Alan.

"I could hardly leave them behind, though heavens knows, it's not my job to be evacuating VSOs," the Field Officer complained. "Just get in and be thankful."

"I'll ruin Tim's made-to-measure dress."

"Get in!"

"Okay, okay."

Five hours later, the Peace Corps field officer dropped me off at the corner of the road to the VSO office. Alan was going to stay at Santano house, the priest's Freetown hostel.

"See you at the Venue tomorrow, Alan."

"If we don't get shipped home," snorted Alan, then added with uncharacteristic concern. "Will you be okay?"

"No problem. I'll just report at the VSO office and let them know I'm safely here," I said. "I must say Freetown seems very much business as usual."

The VSO office was also business as usual, or rather business as usual for a Saturday. Closed. Even the Red Cross office downstairs was closed with no sign of the usual crowd of displaced Liberians hanging around outside.

Strange. Things couldn't be that bad. Well, I'd just have to try the VSO resthouse. Klaus might even be there with all the other evacuees. My step quickened in anticipation, quickly covering the mile to the resthouse. I skipped up the stairs, expecting to walk into an excited reunion with my fellow VSOs - comrades rallying together in the face of adversity, hugs all round, Klaus holding me tight and thanking God that I was safe.

The place was empty. There was not even a bag or a book or

an erected mosquito net to suggest that anyone was staying. I stood on the balcony, looking at life carrying on below. There was a tailor on the corner, pedalling furiously on his sewing machine, whilst a woman hung his finished products around him. Opposite was a stall that sold teabags, single triangles of processed cheese, miniature tins of condensed milk, bananas, cigarettes and matches. Children played in the potholed street and even in the big city, the women still had to carry water and firewood on their heads. There was no sense of any impending danger. Had it all been an April Fool?

What was I supposed to do now? No one had a telephone of course, so I supposed I'd just have to make my way to Nick's house. He was bound to know what was going on, and would probably feed me a couple of beers into the bargain. Now if only I could remember the way - it was over six months since we'd stayed, and he'd always taken us to town in his Landrover. It was a couple of miles uphill, I knew, just below the High Commissioner's Compound. Right, Gail, big strong girls don't just sit around, better make a move before it gets dark.

I headed out of town with my pack on my back, marching through two miles of corrugated rust, twisted with decaying wood and torn clothes drying in woodsmoke. A child squatted, passing liquid motions into a storm drain. Further along the same drain lay a dead dog, the gases of putrefaction distending its abdomen. I hurried past to reach the tarmacked road that wound up expatriate hill.

Slogging up the hill, the shanties gave way to larger white or pink-washed residences, with tiled roofs, verandas, walls and iron gates. This was where the Lebanese and other expatriates lived, and with Freetown bay stretching out to meet the sunset below me, it was obvious why they had made their choice.

After an hour's brisk walk, I stopped to catch my breath under a reassuringly familiar billboard advertising cigarettes. It stood, I remembered, half way between the British High Commission Compound on the top of the hill and Nick's house. Too relieved to spot the landmark to be disapproving of its content, I headed two hundred metres back down from the sign to the inconspicuous lane that led to Nick's door.

There was no sign of the VSO Landrover, and Nick's house stood suspiciously dark and quiet in the fading light. I banged on the door anyway. A young Krio lad appeared from round the back.

"Kushe. Where Mr. Nick?" I asked.

"He don go," the boy replied. To bravely go to evacuate his flock in the east and south, I assumed.

"Gone where?"

"He don go na Otamba Kilimbi for de weekend."

"Otamba Kilimbi! The National Park?" That was just great. Here I was evacuated to Freetown, the country riddled with rebels, and my fearless leader was off looking for hippos and chimpanzees.

"For look dem hippos."

"Yes, yes. Thank you," I said, flopping down on Nick's doorstep. At least it was a bit cooler up the hill.

"You want orange?" The lad offered.

"Oh, that would be lovely." He came back with four. I squeezed one after the other, into my mouth, not caring about the juice that dribbled onto my cotton dress, making big spots in the layer of dust that had collected on the material during my journey from Bo.

Now what? I knew our Field Director didn't live on the Des-Res expatriate hill, choosing instead to live by the sea so his wife could hear the ocean. However, he kept his actual address on a need to know basis (and believed we volunteers didn't need to know), so all I could do was head back down to the resthouse.

Night was falling and the expatriate houses started rumbling as their generators fired up. At least it meant there was light from their windows to illuminate my step. Once I hit the uneven streets of downtown Freetown, there was only the occasional kerosene lamp hung by the street-stalls to guide me between the treacherous potholes and away from the storm drains. Although streetlights lined the pavements, they had not been lit for years. After a few wrong turnings into very similar-looking streets, I got back to the resthouse. Surely somebody would have arrived by now.

The night watchman stirred as I banged on the door, and sleepily let me in. All was dark and silent.

"Where is everybody?" I asked the watchman.

"They don go na Otamba Kilimbi."

"Of course." Over half the VSOs were teachers and the schools and colleges were on their Easter break.

I dumped my bag, then went outside to buy a box of candles, matches, two teabags and a bunch of bananas from the little stall. Then sitting alone by candlelight, with a mug of black tea made on the kerosene stove, I flicked through someone's discarded book of Far Side cartoons and giggled at mean-spirited bugs, beasties and exploding mosquitoes which had all surely been drawn specifically for volunteers in Sierra Leone. Once I'd re-read the book from cover to cover, I stripped and washed first myself and then my travelling clothes in a bucket of water I'd carried upstairs from the outdoor tap. Somewhat cleaner, I curled up in my lappa and crashed out on the best bunk in the house.

It was Sunday and the lady at the stall actually had fresh bread rolls and processed cheese triangles! There were some benefits to be had in the big city. I sat on the resthouse balcony eating my cheese sandwich and wondering if Serabu knew where I was. Were they evacuating the hospital? Were there even any rebels? I always took my little short wave radio with me wherever I went, so I tuned in to the morning edition of Focus on Africa. There was no mention of Sierra Leone. The VSO office wouldn't open until Monday morning, so there was nothing for it but to go to the Venue.

The beach was two taxi journeys away. A Freetown taxi wasn't like your usual taxi. It went where it was going, and would squeeze you in if you wanted to go there too. Not even the driver was assured of his own seat. This time I was fortunate in only having two companions in the back seat of the old Ford Cortina, so I stretched back to enjoy the luxury of topping thirty miles an hour which stirred up a decent breeze through the window.

It was midday and the Venue was full, but with half of VSO off on safari, I couldn't see a single familiar face. To console myself, I guiltily bought myself a Star beer with the Maternity Ceiling fund. Hell, refugee status should confer some rights, I'd have another.

On my third bottle, I spotted Tracey, waving me over to a table of excited Peace Corps exchanging rebel stories.

Apparently all remaining Peace Corps from the east and south had been evacuated to Freetown that morning. Serabu was in the south, but since the closest Peace Corps had been Tracey, twelve miles away, nobody had any news about my friends or the hospital. Perhaps they were all en route to Freetown, or soldiering on, regardless of the threat? I prayed that everybody was safe.

"Oh Gail, I'm so glad someone else is here!" a breathless voice panted over my shoulder.

"Susan!" She was still wearing that lacy blouse. "Great to see you. I thought I was the only VSO left."

"Isn't it awful?" gasped Susan, close to tears. "They pushed me into a Peace-Corps vehicle. I had to leave everything behind in Kenema."

"Have you heard about any of the others? Klaus?" I asked hopefully. "Fiona? Sam and Tim?"

"Kailahun has been burnt down they tell me. I do hope... I

hope Sam and Tim..." she broke down.

"Let me get you a beer, Susan." What else was there to say?

"You know I don't drink, Gail."

"This sounds like a good time to start," I tried to joke, but Susan was not in the mood for joking. Neither was I really. We fell into awkward silence, surrounded by the remainder of the Venue's clientele who were swapping evacuation stories at the top of their voices. Susan stood, twisting the handles of her plastic bag, which contained all she had been able to grab of her worldly goods. "Okay, have my seat," I said. "I'll get you an orange juice."

I went to the bar, absorbing the heady mixture of adrenaline, smoke and alcohol. Finally our drinks were served and I barged my way back through to Susan.

"Look who's arrived," she said. I followed her gaze to see our Field Director ambling in, deep in conversation with his wife. They stopped in the open fronted wooden doorway, Suzanne tensing in front of the sea of bodies blocking their way to the bar. "I don't believe it, he's got no idea what's going on!"

"You're right, Susan, he's just come for his Sunday swim," I agreed and watched in fascination as the Peace Corps Field Officer pulled him aside. He was presumably whispering news of rebels in his ear. "Whoops!" Now, by the look of smug satisfaction on his face, he was doubtless following up with a detailed report of the Peace Corps efficient evacuation of their troops. Our Field Director started looking wildly round for any of his own volunteers. He spotted us and fought his way over.

"Kushe," I said. Susan just stared into her orange juice.

"Is this it? Only two of you?" our Field Director demanded.

"Looks like it," I replied. "It's the Easter holidays. All the teachers and Freetown volunteers have gone with Nick to Otamba Kilimbi."

"Bloody hell. We'll have to get them back."

"How? There's no mission radio anywhere near the park," I said.

"Damn."

"They might as well have their holiday, it's probably safer there than Freetown."

"How would you know if the north's safe, Gail?" he snapped. "Ten minutes ago I thought the whole country was safe. Hell, hell, hell. How can I evacuate anybody with one Landrover down? The Peace Corps Field Officer claims there are six thousand rebels bearing down on Bo. He tells me they've invaded Kailahun and Segbwema. God!" he sat down with a thud. "Sam, Tim and Fiona."

"Sorry," I said. "We've been trying to find out if any of the Peace Corps have heard any news of anyone, but..."

"I don't believe this! Right, you two, back in the resthouse by six. I'm going to speak to the British High Commissioner.

"Well if he wants information, he'd be better staying at the Venue," Susan broke her silence as soon as the Field Director had gone. "The British High Commissioner will be the last person to know anything."

She might be frightened, but she was sharp. I laughed uneasily. Her observation was not very comforting, if indeed we were caught in the midst of civil war.

22. The Refugee

Susan sat in the corner of the VSO office, pulling at her pearl earring as she read *Pride and Prejudice*. It was Monday morning and we were none the wiser about the rebels. About ten VSOs had turned up over the course of Sunday evening, but there was no sign of Klaus, Sam, Tim or Fiona. Moyamba was well clear of the borders, so the absence of Klaus was merely a disappointment, but the others were posted right in the trouble spots. All we could do for our friends was worry as we lolled around the VSO office, without jobs to do, or any idea if we were all to be sent home in the next few days. Suddenly the office door was flung open.

"Alan! What are you doing here? We can't be having Irish intruders in the VSO ranks," I exclaimed leaping out of my chair.

"Rubbish, the more the merrier. It looks like quite a party here."

"Yeah, all hanging around like idiots," I complained. "The Field Director is talking about sending us all home."

"Is it that bad?" Alan said dubiously. "Santano House had contact with everyone except Kailahun and Segbwema. Did you know they're transmitting in Gaelic, in case the rebels intercept messages? Isn't that great now?" I smiled weakly at the Boy's Own excitement written across his face. "Panguma's closest to the action and they're all fine," Alan gushed on. "Your friend Fiona is refusing to leave! A mighty woman!"

"Workaholic to the death," I muttered, irritated at how impressed Alan was at Fiona's heroic stance. "What about Serabu?"

"I spoke to Bernie herself this morning."

"Are they all still there? Are they okay?"

"I could hardly hear a word now, there was so much hissing and crackling."

"But they're all right?"

"As far as I could make out, it was business as usual."

"Good," I said dully, now feeling just plain guilty. "So what about you? Are you off up to your Seminary?"

"All's well in the Makeni," said Alan. "I've cadged a lift tomorrow with Father Gregory. Now, would I be seeing real instant coffee?"

"Help yourself, Alan," I said. "And make me one too. One spoonful of milk powder please."

"Will you lot go and buy your own coffee," snapped the Field Director, barging in and rescuing the last few grains for his own tenth cup. "Yes Susan, I promise to get you on the first flight home. Gail, go and make yourself useful and radio Klaus from CARE's Freetown office. Tell him to get himself and the other Moyamba volunteers down here ASAP."

"Well, that's put a smile on your face," teased Alan, following me down the stairs.

"What do you mean?" I asked, struggling to keep the excitement out of my voice. It looked like I'd be seeing Klaus by evening!

"Mr-Dr-Gay. Look at you! We're positively running to the CARE office."

"Can't you keep up?" I retorted.

"Of course. I will not delay love's true course."

"I hate you, Alan."

Preston, the CARE director, greeted us. Unlike the VSO HQ, CARE's office was an air-conditioned oasis in the heavy heat and grime of downtown Freetown. Its well-building operation was a huge project, run professionally across the whole country. They relied on their vehicles - all based at Moyamba - to get the equipment out to the remote villages. And thus they relied on Klaus to keep them on the road.

"So you're the famous Dr. Gail," said Preston. The famous Dr. Gail? Really? Gosh, what had Klaus said? This was most encouraging. I beamed back at Preston.

"Well then, Doc. I suppose VSO have sent you about this rebel business?"

"I'm afraid so. Our Field Director wants Klaus and the other three Moyamba VSOs back in Freetown today."

"I thought as much. Four of our Peace Corps have all taken an unscheduled rebel holiday and now you want Klaus, my greatest asset?" Preston sighed, but obligingly reached for his radio.

"Aw fo do." I smiled my most charming smile.

"Freetown to Moyamba. Do you receive me? Over." Preston spoke clearly into his radio.

"Loud and clear, Preston. Over." I smiled at the familiar Cockney voice.

"Ah Klaus. Rebels have apparently invaded the south and east. Over," said Preston.

"So we hear. The Peace Corps have all vanished. Any danger? Over."

"We don't know. Your Field Director wants all volunteers evacuated to Freetown by this afternoon. Take one of the CARE vehicles. Do you read me? Over."

"Loud and clear. I will have a vehicle ready by noon. Over."

Preston paused before continuing, "Very good, but if the rebels advance they may try to commandeer vehicles. Over."

"Quite likely. What's your point, Preston? Over."

"Will you stay behind to immobilise our vehicles if necessary? Over."

"Okay. The others will be on the truck at noon. Over."

"Thanks, Klaus. Over and out."

"Over and out."

Well thanks a lot Preston. Everybody else has to evacuate quick quick, big emergency, but Klaus has to stay and face hordes of rebels. So much for my romantic plans. On the other hand, I could not help being impressed. I had visions of Klaus trashing the vehicles with a sledgehammer then fleeing on his motorbike amidst a barrage of bullets. My hero!

Well it looked like it was back to the Venue with Alan, even if it meant swimming in my T-shirt and knickers. I hadn't come prepared for the beach.

So we sat there all afternoon, drinking our beers and catching up on gossip, whilst rebels were destroying entire villages. And all I could think about was that Klaus wasn't coming.

By Tuesday night the resthouse was getting decidedly cosy with VSOs pulled from upcountry. But there was still no Klaus, Fiona, or Nick's Easter holiday-makers from Otamba Kilimbi. However at midnight a dishevelled figure appeared.

"Tim!" we chorused, looking up from our candlelit game of poker. "You're here!"

"Er. Kushe, everybody."

"Where's Sam?"

"Are there thousands of rebels?"

"Are you all right?"

"What have you done with Sam?"

"Were you in Kailahun?"

"What happened? What about Sam?"

"What do the rebels look like?"

"Have the rebels got Sam?"

"Is she okay?"

"How did you get out?"

"Where's Sam?"

"Steady," laughed Tim, who despite his obvious exhaustion had lost none of his easygoing manner. "Sam has a friend, over on holiday. They're at Otamba Kilimbi with the others, presumably having a wonderful time."

"Thank God for that!" There was a collective sigh of relief.

"What about Tracey, has anyone heard about her? Sumbuya..." Tim's voice tailed off anxiously.

"She's fine. Down at the Peace Corps with the rest of them, waiting for flights home," I said.

"Thank God."

"Tell us about Kailahun. Is it as bad as they say?" asked Lindsey.

"Well, I don't know. I think it's pretty bad. Me and my students were drinking poyo when we heard gunfire. We all ran into the street. There were buildings in the town on fire and people streaming towards us. Then two Red Cross trucks appeared. They piled everybody in and drove us to Bo. That's it," he shrugged.

"That's it!"

"How many rebels?"

"Were they advancing?"

"Was anyone hurt?"

"I don't know," Tim sighed. "There were ten, maybe twelve, buildings on fire and several rounds of gunfire. I never actually saw a rebel. Everybody on our truck was fine though. Some people stayed of course, to find family, but Sam was out of town and I already had my squeeze-box, so I just hopped on with the others. It made a poda-poda feel positively deserted," he smiled. "Now is that a bread roll I see over there?"

"Of course," I jumped up. "Cheese triangle?" Tim obviously did not feel up to further embellishment.

"Cheers! A cheese sandwich and a glass of water, then I think I'll nip over to the Peace Corps resthouse...."

"Tim, its after midnight..." started Lindsey, but he had already bounded back down the stairs in his quest for Tracey.

By Wednesday afternoon the VSO office was in even more disarray than Monday. We were getting restless - our volunteer stipends insufficient to have a prolonged good time in the big city. Even Maternity's ceiling fund had been depleted. The Field Director was busy arranging flights home for those that wanted out. In fact he was positively encouraging it - everyone who flew home was one less for him to worry about.

"Gail, what about you?" he asked. "BA have put on an extra flight, there's a seat on Friday."

"What?" For some reason I was stunned by the question. Home! Chocolate in two days! This was my longed for escape route handed to me on a plate.

"But I don't want to go home!" I could hear myself saying.

"But Serabu is right in the official danger zone. And how would you get back?" exclaimed the Field Director.

"Moyamba's half way. CARE's bound to have a vehicle going up, so I'll get a lift and then Serabu can pick me up from Klaus's."

"I don't know..."

"But nobody else left Serabu," I complained. After months of dreaming up excuses to leave, here I was begging to stay. "Not even Jean and he's got a young family." I was warming to my theme, my head filled with visions of Klaus and I holding hands by candlelight. "And Fiona hasn't left and she's much closer to trouble."

"Believe me, if I could drag your friend down here by the scruff of her neck, I would!"

"But Serabu's so quiet! I'm more likely to die of boredom than rebel bullets."

"Bloody doctors!" The Field Director rose from his desk and went to look at his map on the wall. There remained a few red pins in the north, a cluster in Freetown, plus one in Moyamba and a lone pin out east in Panguma. The rest of the map was sprayed with miniature bullet-holes, where pins had once stood, including, to my dismay, only a pinprick left to show for Serabu.

"Serabu has a radio. And three vehicles." I persisted. "And four other volunteers. Even two Americans."

"Not Peace Corps surely!"

"No, admittedly not Peace Corps, but definitely Americans."

The Peace Corps had got their fingers burned in Liberia, finally evacuating their volunteers amidst artillery bombardment of the capital. This time they were steering well clear of flames and had already sent three-quarters of the Salonean volunteers back to the States.

"No Gail. We can't be sure it's safe, we just can't be sure," the Field Director mumbled.

"Oh please…"

Our argument was interrupted by the office door bursting open. "Kushe, kushe, everyone. How….?" Nick froze in the doorway. "What's everybody doing here? It's the middle of the week!" He flung his arms out in amazement. "Even you Gail! Are there no more lives to save in Serabu?"

"Right now, I'm saving my own skin," I said. "There's a slight problem."

"This is Sierra Leone," Nick gave his continental shrug. "There is always a problem."

"Rebels," said our Field Director wearily.

"Rebels?"

"Yes," he snapped. "While you were holidaying at the Park, Liberian rebels have crossed the borders into the south and east."

"Rebels? No! This is too hard to believe."

"Believe it," said the Field Director. "Sierra Leone has been invaded."

"But we heard nothing," Nick shook his head. "And I always listen to Focus on Africa."

"It all happened too quickly, even for the World Service. Fortunately the Red Cross got Tim out of Kailahun just in time."

"Kailahun!" Nick's colour leached out.

"All VSO's are in Freetown as a precautionary measure. Apart from Fiona and Klaus, who are just being difficult. Are you alright?" The ever-cool Nick had slumped into a chair and dropped his head in his hands.

"Sam and Diane!" he moaned.

"Who's Diane?" asked the Field Director.

"Sam's friend. She's here on holiday. I left them both at the roadside to hitch back to Kailahun four hours ago."

23. The Refugee Returns

Thursday. Still no further reports of rebel activity. The six thousand rebels could just as easily have been sixty, or perhaps even six. There was no Kate Adie or BBC film crew to update us. No one in Britain had even heard of Sierra Leone, never mind cared if there were a few rebels causing trouble. The World Service had started to report the rumours but, since their reporter never left Freetown, he was unlikely to have gleaned any more information than us.

Tim was our only eyewitness, but even he had only heard gunfire and seen some smoke before he was caught up in the clamour to escape Kailahun. Perhaps there had been only one rebel with a gun, but then perhaps that's all it took to decimate a defenceless village. The grapevine talked of homes plundered and people killed in the villages round Kailahun. The rebels may or may not have gone, but the villagers were too frightened to return and find out for certain.

We tried to convince ourselves that Charles Taylor, having depleted his forces in seizing power from his rival Prince Johnson, had sent his rebels over from Liberia on a food foray. Even a rebel needs sustenance and, now there was nobody left to kill and nothing left to burn in Liberia, they had come to plunder the homes and farms in placid, disorganised little Sierra Leone. We had no way of knowing, but the Liberian refugees that had flooded in over the past two years had told the Saloneans so many tales of the atrocities in their destroyed homeland that there was an understandable terror that such a thing should happen in Sierra Leone. We could all be forgiven for over-reacting.

On Friday morning, a familiar figure marched in to the VSO office. The roomful of thirty volunteers fell silent.

"MT! Good Lord, what is she doing here?" I gasped, slumping deep into my chair.

"I am Sister Ignatius and I want to know who is in charge here?" she demanded.

"I am," said Nick. "The Field Director has gone to the British High Commission this afternoon."

"And are you responsible for abandoning these girls to hitch back into the arms of the rebels?" she thundered. Sam and Diane appeared sheepishly at her shoulder. Sam gave us a little wave behind MT's back.

"Er. We had some difficulties with communication..." started an unfortunate Nick.

"Communication difficulties! We found them wandering the deserted streets of Bo alone at midnight. Come with me." MT dragged Nick into his own office by the elbow. The door clicked shut behind them.

"Whoops," said Sam, slinking behind Tim.

He grabbed her hand and squeezed it tight. "We were worried about you, Sam."

"We're fine," insisted Sam. "What about you though?"

"I tell God tenki," said Tim. "I tell God tenki."

"And Fatoma?" Sam added in a whisper. "Did he get out in time?"

"I don't know." Tim hugged her. "But Fatoma can take care of himself, I'm sure. That bloke of yours is a real Rambo."

"Yeah," Sam sniffed into Tim's bony shoulder.

"Sister Ignatius was such a sweetie last night and on the way down," Diane tried to distract attention from her friend's worries.

"A sweetie!" I spluttered on my coffee. "MT?!"

"All the nuns were," agreed Sam, tears wiped and brave face firmly applied. "Sister Ignatius is your boss isn't she Gail?"

"I'm afraid so."

"You're lucky to have such a nice boss," said Diane.

"Huh?"

220

"She said she had business in Freetown, so she'd give us a lift," Sam continued.

"Oh? Why?" MT didn't make unscheduled trips to Freetown. Diesel was too expensive.

"She said she had to collect the Easter drug order and fetch you back up to Serabu."

"I see." So I was her ulterior motive. The minute she was fit enough, she had to get that skiving doctor's nose back to the grindstone.

"The nuns fed us chicken and Star beer and everything," said Sam finishing her story with the ultimate accolade.

"Almost as good as Majorca," agreed Diane.

"Majorca?" enquired Tim.

"Diane usually goes to Majorca," explained Sam.

"Much more exciting here," said Tim

"She's moaned about conditions ever since, and that was before I got to show her our house in Kailahun. Oh." Sam's riposte died suddenly. "Oh Tim. Our house? Our friends? Fatoma?"

"Oh, Sam, I'm sorry." Tim hugged her again.

MT reappeared from the office half an hour later. I couldn't hide forever, so I stood up to face her.

"Ah, Dr. Gail. You are well?"

"Yes, thank you, Sister Ignatius." I thought I had better go through the motions of etiquette. "Are you feeling better?"

"I am well. I believe we have a hospital to run."

"Yes, sister."

"Very good. We leave tomorrow morning. I have cleared it with your Field Officer."

"Oh. Okay." Hmmph! Was my opinion not important here? Admittedly I had spent the morning pleading to go back, but that

221

was my decision, my bravado and under my terms. This way, MT made me feel like I'd been caught truanting from school. Why hadn't Nick vetoed her? Serabush was supposed to be in the danger zone for heaven's sake. But he wouldn't have stood a chance in battle with MT, especially not when she had the embarrassing episode of Sam and Diane to add to her weaponry.

"Seven o'clock at Santano house," MT interrupted my thoughts.

"Tomorrow then," I muttered. What about my trip to Moyamba to see Klaus? I didn't want to go with her.

"Don't be late. Good afternoon."

I closed my eyes. Oh why hadn't I just accepted the Field Director's plane ticket when I had the chance? Who wanted to be a bloody pin stuck in a map of some obscure war-torn country anyway?

"This Sister changes the tune very quickly," Nick grumbled loudly once MT was safely out of earshot. "I am the bad boy for the mistake of allowing Sam and Diane to go to Bo, but she does not worry about taking a young woman to Serabu, which is much closer to the rebels, just because she needs a doctor."

"Aw fo do." I chirped. The trendy Nick calling me a young woman cheered me up enormously.

"Well I suppose Serabu at least has a radio...." he added. "Promise me to be careful. Do not travel outside of Serabu and if we radio you to come back, you come immediately. Do not accept any arguments from your Sister Ignatius. Understood?"

"Okay," I agreed, happy to slip into this new heroic young woman role. "The least you can do for sending me back into the lion's den is to buy me a beer." It was worth a try. I couldn't afford any more beer otherwise.

"I sent you to the lion's den? You've been nagging the Field Director all morning to go back!" Nick snorted.

"That was this morning," I said, sweetly. "Aren't I allowed to change my mind?"

"No!" Nick folded his arms. "Serabu needs a doctor and I need you out of my office. You're a big strong girl, you can look after yourself."

"Hmmph!" So much for the heroic young woman. "Now you definitely owe me a beer."

"And us," Sam chipped in, camouflaging her anxieties with jollity. "I need to be very drunk until I hear that Fatoma's okay."

"Okay, okay," Nick sighed. "I will take you all to the Venue."

Windows down to clear my head of the after effects of Nick's generosity, I stretched out in the front seat of the truck. Sister Ignatius sat beside me at the wheel. So here I was going back to Serabush with MT, hungover, just like the last time, and without any progress with Klaus, just like the last time. Only this time the country was no longer a peaceful haven, but a victim of hostile rebel activity and, even worse from my egocentric perspective, there would be no Alan to cheer me up and soon there would be no Jean or Francoise either. I began to regret my impulsive rejection of the Field Director's no-strings, no-shame, free flight home.

Several volunteers had already gone home, including Susan, who left clutching her sole remaining plastic bag containing her Jane Austen and a change of underwear. The High Commissioner would not give clearance for any British subjects to go anywhere near Kailahun, so Tim was leaving too. With a glint in his eye, he had booked his flight for over a week's time, giving him that little bit longer to woo Tracey.

Sam, however, managed to persuade the Field Director that he needed a secretary at the VSO Office. She could not go looking for Fatoma (she certainly would not get any help from the British

High Commissioner), so she would just have to wait for him to find her. The Field Director's initial objections were soon silenced as she made herself indispensable by sorting out all the annoying administrative complications that the rebels had landed on his plate.

Meanwhile Klaus and Fiona bashed on at work.

I squirmed in my sweaty plastic seat. The journey was taking twice as long as usual. There were nearly twenty checkpoints set up by the soldiers between Freetown and Serabu. I had offered to share the driving for the long trip home but MT did not want to relinquish control. Her tactics, if not her motives, were sound, as dressed in full veil and habit and wearing her most determined expression, MT was enough to send the young soldiers scurrying to lift their wooden barriers with a tug of their forelocks. Since my services were obviously not needed, I settled down for a snooze.

As we approached Mokanje I stretched, yawned and peered out of the window. Two human skulls adorned the side of the road.

"Oh God," I whispered. Until that moment, this whole rebel business had seemed like a famous five adventure. Suddenly I realised it was all really happening.

The skulls were displayed on three-foot wooden poles like a pair of ghoulish lollipops, with bits of flesh still hanging from the cheekbones. MT hit the accelerator with a hint of unsisterly irritation. I gaped in horror at the skeletal mirage departing through the back window. If MT had seen them she wasn't going to let on.

Bernadette stood at the convent door to greet us.

"Welcome back, welcome back. We are so glad to see you both." Bernadette gave me a hug and smiled warmly at Ignatius. "I hope you are fully recovered from your malaria, Ignatius."

"I am ready to return to work, Bernadette," she answered. "There is much to be done in this troubled time."

Outside 'The Venue'   Downtown Freetown

The National AIDS Office

Francoise, Alan, Jean and Mattieu

Tom at The Mines

Von Hondabenda

Eelco, Zita and Karin

Hindolu and Betty

Serabu Village from TB Ward

Welcome To Serabu

Dancing Devil

Pa George

Poda poda

How to fix a broken leg 1.

How to fix a broken leg 2.

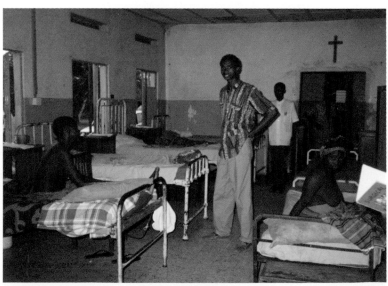

Surgical ward

"It's good to be back, Sister Bernadette," I said, as was expected of me.

"I will take a bath, if you will excuse me Bernadette," said MT.

"Very well, Ignatius. We will speak this evening." Bernadette touched her colleague's shoulder. "Now Gail, you must tell me all about it. Come in for tea."

"That would be lovely. How is everyone? Was there any trouble with the rebels? How are Jean, Francoise and the children? When are they going home? How are Betty and Hindolu? Is Laygby's pregnancy progressing safely? How's Fran doing? What about Tom? Has he had malaria again?"

"Everyone's just fine, Gail," laughed Bernadette. She motioned me to one of the wicker chairs in the convent sitting room. "After all you've only been gone ten days. Tom has managed to stay well and Dr. Jean and his family will be leaving next week. When Ignatius radioed to tell us the good news that you were returning, I asked her to book their flights." She patted my knee. "The break has done you good. I must say you look very well indeed, you've put on a bit of weight."

"Hmmph." Putting on weight was one of those inevitable consequences of a diet that blissfully did not include plassas, but Bernadette just meant to be nice. "So how is Fran settling in then?"

"We are all very impressed with Dr. Fran. He is doing extremely well."

He would be.

"Kushe, Dr. Gay, how di holiday? You don get body," Sesay called out as I walked up to my house with my weekend backpack.

"Dr. Gay welcome back. You get body." Betty hugged me with her free arm, holding Hindolu on her hip with her other. Hindolu gurgled and pulled my ever-growing ponytail.

"Kushe, Dr. Gay, you get body."

"Gail! Bonjour, bonjour. Ca va bien? You have been getting good food in Freetown, yes?"

"Kushe, Dr. Gay I see you don enjoy you holiday. You get body."

"Well hi Gail, you're looking well fed and contented, you lucky thing. I'm jealous. Ain't the food here just awful?" Fran must have lost at least ten kilos in as many days.

"Kushe, Dr. Gay, we gladdi for see you. You get body."

"What for chop today?"

Good old Pa George. At least he didn't tell me I was looking fat.

24. Post Evacuation Blues

"Bua, Dr. Gay."

"Mmm, bua bise, Pa Ali. Bi gahun yena."

"Kayingoma, a bia be?"

"Kayingoma."

"Malo-hua, Dr. Gay."

"Malo-hua, Pa Ali."

Well, it was life and death as usual at Serabu hospital, having obviously functioned very well without me. The only change was two new hospital signposts in proud red and blue. One was to point the way to Serabu from the Junction and the other to stand at the entrance to the compound.

The good news of the week was that Ansumana's dinner had stopped leaking from his abdominal wound and exited, duly processed, from the appropriate hole. He was hardly an example of slick surgical procedure - two months in hospital, three stones lighter with an angry crusted red scar bisecting his abdomen - but he would live. Isata's wound, however, healed even better than I had dared hope. Her husband paid the bill in full and arranged transport home for his wife and son. He even arranged for some men from his village to erect a basketweave ceiling on Maternity!

My glow of satisfaction from Ansumana, Isata and our swish new ceiling, was soon replaced by post-evacuation blues. Rebel fever kept admissions and outpatients down and with Jean having a last surge of workaholism before he departed and Fran whirling enthusiastically round the wards, I was feeling pretty redundant. The new boy was doing so well, already performing solo Caesareans, that there seemed little need for me to hold his hand while he settled in. Why had I bothered returning?

The staff all raved about Fran - even Tiange! He obviously

had a touch of Sister Hillary about him. It wasn't just Ansumana and Isata, all the patients seemed to be smiling their way to recovery.

So after only four days back in Serabush, I was bored, bored, bored. It was a Friday night and I sat alone on my velour sofa, *Tess of the d'Urbervilles* still only half finished on my lap. Tomorrow was Saturday and Fran was on call for the weekend, with Jean available to assist in the unlikely event of somebody arriving that Fran couldn't deal with. So what was I going to do?

I watched a mosquito fly round the stub of a candle that was dribbling its last down the sides of a beer bottle. "Come back, Alan. All is forgiven." I scratched my latest crop of bites until my shins bled. With all the trouble the priests at the seminary were never going to let him come down for the party next week.

"Oh no, the party! I forgot the beer," I cried. I'd confess to Jean and Fran in the morning. Chances were the party would be off anyway. It was all too depressing.

It was only going to get worse once Jean, Francoise and even Tom left, and since the Field Director had grounded any volunteers left in country, there was no chance of Klaus, Alan, or anyone else for that matter, dropping in for a visit. I blew the flame maliciously into the mosquito's wings.

"Ha! That'll teach you to mess with me," I gloated as the insect fell to its death in the pool of wax on the table. Oh dear, murdering God's creatures wasn't a good way to curry favour.

I had a banana and went to bed.

The next morning Jean and Francoise were surrounded by children playing tag outside their house. Geraldine came tottering towards me, chubby arms outstretched as my welcoming committee.

"Bonjour, ca va? You want a beer?" called Jean.

"Er, no thanks."

"No? You are unwell?" asked Francoise.

"It's ten o'clock in the morning!"

"Ah, but this was not a problem for Alan on his weekends off," Jean remarked.

"No. Probably not, but then we would be unlikely to see him before midday."

"Ah non. Not before lunch," Francoise laughed. "We were just going to have coffee. You will take a cup with us?"

"Thank you. You've got the best coffee in the country."

"Bien sur. My mother sends it from Belgium. You can have it when we leave."

"Ah yes, when you leave." That was the cue for my confession. "Well, um, you remember the kitty for your party?"

"Alan will not be allowed to come now, but we still have the party yes?" Jean asked.

"Well, yes, but it's just that I didn't get the beer. I'm sorry. And to make it worse, I spent the kitty. I was stuck in Freetown all week you see, and the only place we could go was the Venue.....
I'm sorry. Sister Bernadette says she'll lend it to me from next month's wages so I can pay it back before you go," I splurted.

"So. No beer. Quelle dommage," said Jean. "Aw fo do, we will ask Pa Ali to bring us poyo."

"Sorry." I hung my head.

"It is very good then that MT brought us beer from Freetown for our party. Yes?" said Francoise.

"She did?" I was flabbergasted. "MT brought us beer? MT!"

"Six crates," confirmed Jean.

"Goodness, was it cerebral malaria that she had?"

"She has the look of a healthy woman, I think." Francoise smiled.

"Do you think she expects an invite?" I asked in sudden horror.

"I think not," laughed Jean. "But we must pay for the beer."

"Phew! So when's the party?"

"Francoise and I leave for Freetown wiz the children next Sunday."

Next Sunday, so soon! I smiled weakly. "Saturday night, then?"

"It's a date." Francoise lifted her coffee cup.

"Let's drink to MT and her beer." I stood up.

"Never did I think I would say this, but sante MT." Jean knocked his chipped coffee cup against mine.

Normally I drank very little coffee: too hot, too dehydrating and the local stuff had to be filtered through your teeth. However, the reappearance of Sister Bernadette from her sabbatical had revived the tradition of the Saturday coffee morning at the convent for the sisters and volunteers. It was the one time that we met the sisters socially. So, after two cups of coffee with Francoise and Jean, we all went up to the convent to force down a third. Fran jogged over. "Hey you guys!"

"Fran, aren't you on call? Too efficient by half, you Americans," I teased.

"Outpatients is real quiet today. I guess the patients are all still worried about rebels."

"Welcome." Bernadette appeared at the door in another pretty flowered dress, looking as fresh as a young girl, "Nice that you could join us, Fran. God bless this beautiful day."

"Good morning, Sister Bernadette," we chanted. She ushered us into the front room, kept cool by the protective layer of guest-rooms above. Tom was already seated, sipping a glass of water, whilst MT poured out coffee from a flask.

"Did I hear you talking again about rebels, Dr. Fran?" MT

always addressed Fran as an equal. Must have been those all-American looks. "Did you hear some news from the outpatients?"

"No ma'am. I was just saying that the hospital is very quiet as though the people were still afraid to travel."

"Oh dear," said Bernadette.

"What is going to 'appen wiz your wife, Fran?" Jean asked, flopping into a wicker chair.

"Gee, I just don't know."

"Perhaps you can make a telephone call from Freetown?" Jean suggested.

"Can I? It would be just great if I could speak to Sharon. I don't want her to worry."

"At least it's unlikely that our minor skirmish will hit the news in America."

"I guess you're right," agreed Fran. "But the airline might say something when she tries to confirm her flight for next month."

"Coffee, Francoise?" asked MT. Francoise politely proffered her cup. "I'll be surprised if your Embassy will let her come now, Fran. I suppose that means you'll have to leave us?"

"I hope not, Sister Ignatius, but now you mention the Embassy, I never did register. Y'all whisked me straight here when I landed."

"Too keen to get you to work," I teased.

"Fran! We must get you registered," Bernadette exclaimed. "No wonder you weren't pulled back to Freetown with the rest of the Americans."

"Nor Tom," added Jean.

"No one contacted you either, Jean," said Tom. "And with Francoise and the children...."

"There is no Belgian Embassy," Francoise shrugged. "We are the only ones."

"I guess I've stayed longer than my year," mused Tom.

231

"Perhaps they think I've gone already."

"Fran, you must go to Freetown to telephone your wife and visit the Embassy," said Bernadette. "Perhaps while you are there, you can check that they still know about Tom?"

"Of course."

"Can you wait until the Landrover takes Jean to Lungi airport next Sunday?" asked MT, ever mindful of economy.

"Fine. By then it should be clear that things are safe and Sharon can start packing. That's if Gail can manage alone for a few days."

"Of course!" I bristled. "Nice and quiet, as you said, so I'm quite sure I'll cope without any male doctors around."

"She has just had her holiday in Freetown, yes," teased Jean. I gritted my teeth at him and he raised his coffee cup back to me.

"So what about this party then?" asked Fran.

With the details of the party duly sorted, Jean and Francoise went to relieve Ma Kpukoma from her childcare duties whilst Fran jogged back over to Outpatients and Tom took his final year students for a revision class.

With no pressing engagements and still three-quarters of a weekend to get through, I ventured into the convent library to find something I was more likely to read than Mr. Hardy.

The dusty shelves were devoid of Judith Krantz or Jilly Cooper – not being on your usual nun's reading list. So Agatha Christie looked like the best I could do. However, a battered box caught my eye on the top shelf - a jigsaw puzzle!

I was filled with an extraordinary sense of glee at the prospect of a thousand cardboard pieces depicting a bowl of fruit. Things were obviously getting bad. With the box under my arm, I dashed home in excitement.

"What for chop today?"

"Pa George, it's Saturday, you don't work weekends."

"You don take too much holiday," he said, as explanation. At least he had had the sense to defer his appearance to late morning. "Wetin dis?" He peered over my shoulder.

"A jigsaw puzzle. Look, you put the pieces together to make a picture. This piece, for instance, goes there." I popped a piece of banana in place.

"Hmmph." Pa George picked up a piece of red apple and rammed it into a hole in the middle of the grapes. "Why?" he asked.

"Well…." There was no good answer.

"Do they pay you?"

"What? Who?" I laughed. "No, they don't pay me."

"Hmmph. What for chop today?"

Pa George was lighting the three-stone fire when Betty appeared at the door. "Dr. Gay?"

"Do you do jigsaws, Betty?" I called to my friend, still focussed on the puzzle.

"It's Pa Ali," she said quietly. I looked up.

"What's happened?"

"He's fallen out of the palm tree."

"Is he all right?"

"They've carried him to Surgical," Betty answered.

I ran down to the small gathering round Pa Ali's bed on Surgical. He lay motionless.

"Bua, Pa Ali." I took his limp hand.

"Mmm. Bua bise, Dr. Gay," he replied, opening his eyes briefly.

"Bise. Bi gahun yena?" I asked, knowing he had broken his neck.

"Kayingoma. A bia be?"

"Kayingoma." Thanks be to God. I bit my lip.

"Malo-hua." He closed his eyes and died.

25. Jean's Party

The house was ready. Hawa and Fatmata had helped me paint a big Good Luck banner to string above the table we had pushed back against the wall. On it sat Pa George's massive pot of plassas, MT's crates of beer, two gallon rubbers of poyo and Fran's tape-recorder.

American volunteers weren't expected to survive on only 25 kilos, so where I had a short wave radio that could fit in a shirt pocket, Fran had a three foot ghetto-blaster plus two sets of spare batteries that would allow us to party long after our ten o'clock generator curfew.

Tom, Fran, Betty and I sat expectantly on the doorstep, drinking Star by moonlight.

"To Pa Ali." I raised my bottle.

"God bless," Tom replied.

"Poor old Pa Ali," said Fran.

"He was too old for climbing palm trees." I shook my head.

"It was his living," said Betty.

"He'd have made a real fortune tonight," sighed Fran.

"But he will be happy that AJ will make that money," Betty added. "I done see him up his father's tree this evening."

"AJ?" I asked, incredulous.

"Ali Junior, Pa Ali's son," confirmed Tom.

"Really. AJ? He seems so, well..." Cocky little devil, would-be-sophisticate, student leader, smartarse, suave dresser, pushy, clever, ambitious... "Assertive." I finally said, remembering the unassuming old gentleman who had given some serenity to my daily routine.

"AJ told me how his Dad worked so hard to provide his son with the chances he never had," Tom explained. Tom's knowledge of his students made me ashamed of my ignorance of the lives of the staff. We bantered at work or we exchanged greetings at the market or outside church, we played Scrabble or occasionally met for a cup of poyo in the village, or a cup of tea at Betty's, but still I lived in a different world.

"How will AJ fit tapping poyo in with his exams?" I asked.

"AJ can't afford to lose his father's patch to somebody else," said Tom. "He has to fund his training somehow." For someone who seemed to spend all his life with his nose in a bible, Tom had a firm grip on the realities of life.

"So hey, we'll have palm wine after all tonight." Fran tried to lift the mood. "I'm real excited about trying it."

"What a treat!" I teased.

"It is very fine," said Betty.

"Alan knocked it back like lemonade."

"But from my brief knowledge of Alan, any alcohol would do," Fran retorted. "Hey Tom, surely I can rely on you, my fellow American, to give me the lowdown on poyo."

"You know I don't drink."

"It's from God to Man, Tom. Can't I tempt you?"

"Thanks, Gail, but so is plain water."

"Perhaps I'll just hide some beers behind Gail's sofa," said Fran.

Several Stars later, there were still only four of us.

"Where is everybody?"

"Punctual doesn't translate into Mende, Fran," said Tom, looking at his watch.

"Still, it is late," I remarked, the anxious hostess.

Just then Moses came running up the path.

"The rebels done reach Buma!"

"Buma!" Betty paled.

"I thought those damned rebels had gone," said Fran.

"Buma, that's just twenty miles away. How do you know?" I asked.

236

"The soldiers done just return from Buma," Moses puffed.

"Returned from Buma?" Tom frowned. "Didn't you just say that's where the rebels were? Aren't they staying there to defend us?"

"Well, they never reached the place. They don go to Buma to make a checkpoint, but they don meet all the villagers running away."

"So....?"

"The soldiers say they get puncture. Now they don go to Mokanje....."

"But isn't Mokanje even further away?" asked Fran.

"Thirty miles at least," I agreed. "Couldn't Sesay fix their puncture? I'm sure Serabu Hospital would be more than happy to assist."

"I saw no puncture." Moses shrugged.

"Ah, our brave boys!" I exclaimed.

"You can't really blame them. They have guns but no ammunition, and the government always forgets to pay them," explained the ever-understanding Betty.

"Everybody in Serabu is very frightened," Moses continued. "Many are fleeing to the bush."

"Bonsoir, bonsoir tout le monde." Jean was striding cheerfully up the path, Matthieu perched on his shoulders. "Sorry I am late but Ma Kpukoma did not appear to look after the childrens. This is very unusual for her. Perhaps we bring them and they can sleep in your bedroom?"

"There seems to be a problem," I said, sorry to kill his good mood.

"Ah yes, there is always a problem."

"Moses tells us that the rebels are in Buma," said Tom.

"I think our party is off." I bit my tongue. As if anybody was worried about the party.

"Mon Dieu. Buma?" He lowered Matthieu to the ground and sat down next to us, pulling his son onto his lap. "Is this true Moses?"

Moses retold his story, then excused himself. "I must go to my family."

"Of course, Moses. Will you leave too?" I asked.

"Serabu is our home," Moses stated. "Aw fo do."

"And the rest of the staff?" Tom pressed on.

"The thiefmen will come even if the rebels-self do not. They will thief everything. I think-say most of the staff will stay. Perhaps I will come to your party later."

"Will you go to your man, Betty?" Tom asked. "He's with the Red Cross, isn't he?"

"Ben wrote that he get for go to Kailahun," said Betty in a trembling voice. "I must stay here so he can find me. Now I will go and check on Hindolu and my sisters."

"Let us pray it is another false alarm," Tom squeezed her hand.

"We will see you later." Betty smiled optimistically.

"Good," I nodded. "Bring your family too."

They left us, four pale faces sitting on the doorstep in stunned silence, with dance music playing on regardless from Fran's ghetto-blaster.

"Bloody rebels. First they mess up my birthday and now Jean's farewell. We were going to give you such a good party, Jean."

"Aw fo do." Jean adjusted Matthieu on his lap, and got to the point we were all avoiding. "Perhaps Gail and Tom should come to Freetown with us tomorrow?"

"We'll just panic everybody if we leave," said Tom without hesitation. "I'll stay, if you could let our Embassy know I still exist, Fran."

"Sure thing, Tom."

Bloody Tom, always putting others first. Now I would have

to stay too. "There's been no message from VSO, so it must be safe," I said in my bravest voice.

"God willing, the rebels will come no further, but perhaps we should pack essentials?" Tom suggested.

"Well I'm packed for my Freetown trip already," said Fran. "I'll guard the beer."

"Eh bien." Jean stood up. "Tom and Gail will go to pack and I will go and tell Francoise, then we start our party in one hour. You have plenty supplies, yes?"

"Plenty," I replied "Especially if there's only five of us."

"So, Gail," said Fran, once the others had gone. "Gin Rummy?"

"Give me ten minutes to get my bag together."

"Hey, what's the girl need, other than passport and clean underwear?"

"Three minutes tops, then I'll give you your biggest ever trouncing."

"Mon Dieu, I have a very bad head today. It was a party merveilleuse," said Jean as he loaded the last of his belongings into the Landrover.

"Yep, those guys sure know how to party," said Fran, climbing into the back seat. "I don't know how I managed to drink that awful poyo."

"Even the night staff came in shifts," Tom laughed. "Just as well the wards were quiet."

"I even spotted Pa Ndanema knocking back the poyo with Bockerie in my kitchen."

"What? My new patients!" Fran exclaimed. I had handed TB ward over to Fran at the earliest opportunity. "They'll soon learn who's boss when I get back from Freetown."

"Eh bien, bonne chance Fran. Those TB patients get bored too much and look for trouble. This is why I handed them over to Gail the day after she arrived."

"Oh, so the truth comes out now you are leaving." My words were lost as Jean, Francoise and the children were smothered in hugs, kisses and back slaps by the assembled crowd of well-wishers. Ma Kpukoma was in floods of tears, clinging onto Geraldine and Matthieu.

"They're really letting it all hang out," Fran whispered to me through the open window. "Probably high on fear."

"I suspect farewells are always like this, especially for those as loved as Jean and his family."

"Yeah, you're right. Take care now. I'll see you in a few days." Fran kissed me on the cheek.

"Give AJ my compliments on his poyo, Tom." Fran and Tom shook hands.

"Don't worry. I'll tell him he is a worthy successor to his Dad."

"Have a nice time in the big city, Fran," I added, with a hint of jealousy.

"Sure will. I've got my swimming trunks packed."

I smiled and fought through to get my turn at hugging Jean and Francoise. "How will I manage without you?" I clung to Jean.

"Pas de probleme." Jean ruffled my hair before lifting Matthieu into the seat next to Fran. I swallowed back a sob.

"I'll miss you," I sniffed.

"We all will," added Betty. Her feelings were chorused by the throng.

There were more hugs and tears before the Landrover finally pulled away, followed by a crowd of children, skipping and waving.

"Au revoir tout le monde. Malo-hua Serabush!" Jean called

as they turned out of the gates and past Sesay's shiny new sign. "And au revoir to the new Medical Superintendent." A bony thumbs-up stuck out of the front window and they were gone.

Medical Superintendent. That was me. Oh shit.

26. Guarding The Hospital

Just as the dust settled from the departing Landrover, another truck lurched into the compound. It screeched to a halt, scattering the residual well-wishers outside the convent. Father Andrew from Sumbuya burst out of the passenger seat and stumbled into the arms of Sister Bernadette.

"The rebels have come to Sumbuya," Andrew gasped. "Everybody has fled. The Lebanese family who run the store have all been killed. I don't know who else."

"Oh no! May God be with them." Bernadette crossed herself. "Are you all right, Andrew?"

"Yes, yes. I had to leave everything. I just…." He sucked in a lungful of air "…came to warn you."

"Are the hospital staff and patients in danger?" MT got straight to the point. "Should we make evacuation plans?"

"No. No, I think that would be over-reacting. There were only five maybe six rebels. We think they just came for a…a… day trip," Andrew snorted. "Serabu is still twelve miles away."

Twelve miles didn't sound very much to me. Hell I'd cycled to Sumbuya just five weeks ago. And Tracey had bought milk powder and stock cubes from that Lebanese store. We'd even shared a Star beer with the owner.

"What do you think Gail?" asked Bernadette "As our only doctor and Medical Superintendent, will you stay?"

"Me? Er, yes. Of course," I replied. It was hard to refuse when she put it like that.

"Very good. We'll have a senior staff meeting in one hour to discuss the situation," announced MT.

"Will that give you time for rounds, Gail?" asked Bernadette.

"No problem," a voice answered. Meanwhile my mind raced over visions of skulls on sticks perched all round the hospital. The voice carried on talking. "A few patients left to see but we're quiet just now."

"Betty, call the senior staff from the village."

"Of course, Sister Ignatius."

"Moses, fetch Father Pete."

"No problem, Sister Ignatius."

"Good. We'll meet in one hour," MT turned and went back into the convent.

"Come inside for a cup of tea and a wash, Father Andrew," Bernadette guided the traumatised African priest into her sanctuary.

Ten of us sat in the convent. There had been no mention of any further trouble on the World Service, but then we would probably be the ones to report it. MT had managed to radio Mokanje, but they knew no more than us. There was only one Sunday transmission on the Catholic mission radio network, and it had long since finished. We couldn't receive any more news until the morning.

"How does everybody feel about staying?" asked Bernadette.

"We should stay," said Pete. "Serabu hospital will be needed more than ever."

"Hear hear," added Tom. I forced a smile. I didn't really fancy the thought of rebels running around waving their guns, but didn't want to be the only wimp.

"Most of the staff have no place to go. We will stay." Betty was announcing. "But we understand if the volunteers and sisters get for go to safety in Freetown. You no able take eighty staff with you in a Landrover and a truck." Her matter-of-fact words suddenly made me realise all my idealistic VSO principles of equals working together without any us and them was all rubbish. When the crunch came we could jump on a plane home, but they couldn't escape. This was their home. Betty might be as educated and able as I, but she just did not have my choices. And my choice right now would

244

be to get the hell out.

"God willing there will be no need for any of us to leave." MT's voice broke through my thoughts.

"There's no need to panic," agreed Pete. "Our brother Andrew, suspects the few cowardly rebels that attacked Sumbuya have already gone."

"Good," added Moses. "If the poomuis stay, then we get for feel safe."

"So business as usual," MT said briskly.

"Business as usual," Tom, Bernadette and Pete echoed.

"And our Medical Superintendent?" MT prompted me.

"What?" There were those skulls again. Oh God, how bad did really bad need to be? "Yes, yes. Of course."

We came out of the convent into the midday heat. A rare little breeze gave momentary relief and ruffled the beautiful blossom-laden trees in the courtyard, releasing its perfume and carrying a few petals to the ground. I stopped and listened for shouts and screams or distant gunfire, but heard only a solitary bird sing. Silly me, there couldn't possibly be any rebels here.

My ward rounds finished, I went home and opened the door to the forgotten debris of the previous night. Empty beer bottles lay round the room and the floor was sticky with spilt poyo. The same gentle breeze that had blessed the convent blew through my mosquito mesh, carrying a waft of stale beer and bodily fluids.

What was I doing here, with a crashing hangover, clearing up a house rank with unspeakable odours, in a strange country with rebels only twelve miles down the road? I was not made of the stuff of heroes. Why hadn't I just jumped onto the Landrover with Jean and Fran and gone down to Freetown? I could easily have justified myself to the sisters and staff, perhaps by blaming VSO.

At least it would have got me out of the tidying up.

"Aw fo do," I sighed, picked up a few empties and plopped them into their crate. Three smiling faces appeared in the doorway as I straightened to wipe the sweat from my specs.

"Kushe, kushe, Dr. Gay. We come to help," called Aisha, accompanied by Dauda and Fatmata.

"Tenki ya," I smiled back. Within thirty minutes the place was sparkling cleaner than it had ever been since my arrival. Cleaning was neither my, nor Pa George's, forté.

By Monday morning I seemed to be missing several patients.

"Have they gone to fetch water?" I asked Betty.

"No. They have run away from the rebels," she replied.

"Oh."

One of my few new arrivals was Rose, who would have been a sturdy picture of health had it not been for the cancer that had taken over her whole breast. It was too late for a mastectomy, not that I had ever done one, and of course there was no radiotherapy or chemotherapy. The tumour was in overdrive, pushing up mounds of pink tissue round a creviced and smelly central crater. Fatmata had cleaned it up nicely so at least the odour had gone. This was as good as it was ever going to get.

"There is no more I can do, I'm very sorry," I explained to Rose and her mother as gently as possible. "You can do her dressings at home."

"But we get money, we able pay," her mother objected. "We able pay for surgery-self."

"I'm sorry, it's just not possible to do surgery," I repeated. "It has spread too far."

"We get for pay extra for you to do surgery," she offered. "Please Dr. Gay. Help my daughter."

"I'm sorry, it's not the money," I sighed. "I'm not able to do any surgery. We can only keep it clean. It's better that you take your daughter home and care for her in the family."

"Do ya, Dr. Gay. Please," she begged. I couldn't argue that we didn't have enough beds, as the rebels had left the ward as empty as I'd ever seen it. Taking the easy option, I agreed to let Rose stay for daily dressings.

The rest of my rounds were rather subdued. I even wished that the TB patients would torment me with their usual teases and complaints, but even Pa Ndanema placidly accepted his medication while Patrick dressed the TB abscess that had made such a mess of the stump of his leg. Only Bockerie seemed oblivious to the rebel threat, setting up his draughts board outside the ward.

"You want play, Dr. Gay?"

"I'm working Bockerie!"

"Noboby will come today, they are too scared," he shrugged and moved the first black man a square. "You are the white man."

"Thanks Bockerie, but I must get to Outpatients," I insisted.

"Look at the bench Dr. Gay. Those rebels don make your job easy."

I glanced over to the empty bench and sighed. "Okay." I moved my man one square and sat down.

Five minutes later Bockerie was grinning beside a tower of white discs and the black plague on the board. Fortunately, Pa Ndanema gallantly rescued me by throwing down his crutches in challenge to Bockerie. I left them to it and went home.

Pa George was surprised to see me back so early. "You na the only doctor, Dr. Gay. You don finish already?"

"Very quiet today, Pa George."

"Hmmph. Chop not ready."

"No problem. Can I help?" Pa George looked horrified. "Okay, I'll read." I held up my book and Pa George grunted. He

247

slammed the door behind him, and I half expected him to reappear to nail a No Trespassing sign on my kitchen door. Smiling, I stuck my nose back in *Tess of the d'Urbervilles*, but she was not seductive enough to keep it there. My eye kept wandering to the jigsaw, which lay hidden under a piece of gara so I would not have to tolerate disapproving looks from Pa George.

As soon as Pa George had dished up and gone, I cast Tess aside, whipped off the gara, and settled down to a tricky bit around the apples listening to *Hitch-hikers Guide to the Galaxy* on the World Service.

A rare forty minutes of pop tunes followed, and I sang along, popping piece after piece into place in time to the music, pausing only to spoon in mouthfuls of plassas. Just as I was thinking life was not so bad, Tom burst in.

"What is it?" I looked up, alarmed. "Rebels?"

"No, I think Pete is having a stroke."

"Not rebels then," I sighed, forgetting to hide the relief in my voice. Tom frowned and I cringed at my selfishness. "Right." I leapt to my feet. "I'm coming."

"Can you squeeze my hand?" I asked, squatting in front of father Pete. "Good. Now push me away."

"Yes. There's only a bit of tingling in my fingers now," Pete said with obvious relief. "I dropped my coffee cup you know, look, it's everywhere."

"I'll soon sort that." Tom touched the priest's arm.

"And I was slurring my words like some eejit, wasn't I Tom?"

"You sound real normal now."

"How's your vision?"

"That was the most frightening thing, everything blacked out down one side."

"Okay. Can you see my finger here? Good and here? Fine. And cover the left eye.. and the right…Great." I smiled at the anxious middle-aged man. "I think you've just had a Transient Ishaemic Attack – a self-correcting mini-stroke. Nothing like it before?"

"No, no, thank the Lord. I've been well since I gave up the cigarettes last year. I do drink the beer now," Pete smiled.

"Well smoking's the worst thing for TIAs and a bit of beer might even be beneficial."

"Well that's mighty news."

"Yes, alcohol opens up those blood vessels to the brain. Keeps everything flowing,"

"So am I going to have a stroke?"

"No. Take this as a little warning. Your blood pressure is up a bit." His blood pressure was up quite a lot, none too surprisingly. "But half an aspirin is great at preventing strokes. Nice and simple and even we have it in stock! You'd better take things easy, though. Could you stay with Father Brendan in Mokanje?"

"Yeah," agreed Tom. "Things are getting real stressful round here."

"Oh no. I can't leave my people."

"Just for a few days' rest."

"Absolutely not, I must see Serabu through this unsettled time."

"Hmmm." A full-blown argument wasn't going to help anybody's blood pressure, so I got up to go and search our drug stores to see if we had any suitable, in date, anti-hypertensives. "I'll bring back the aspirin and redo your blood pressure once Tom's fed you a few cups of tea."

"Sure thing, doc," said Tom. "The best cure for blood pressure!"

"Hmm." I suspected I wasn't going to find anything much better from our limited supplies.

The village lay peaceful, with the occasional wisp of smoke spiralling up from between the houses as I wandered back home from the mission house. The only person out and about, was Nurse, who collared me outside Pete's to sell me a bunch of bananas. The rest of Serabu were probably having a siesta, the only sensible option for the hottest part of the day. I stopped under a palm tree to peel myself one of Nurse's bananas.

A roaring engine suddenly invaded the tranquillity. Coughing out a piece of banana, I gaped at the truckful of soldiers bouncing over the hill. It screeched round the corner into the hospital compound, nearly knocking down the new sign.

"What on earth.....?" I broke into a run, arriving in time to see ten soldiers jump out of the truck, circling their guns Rambo-style, right outside Maternity. Screams suddenly filled the air as staff and patients flooded out of doors and windows to flee into the surrounding bushes. "Oh God."

Remaining rooted to a spot behind TB Ward latrines, I stared at the suddenly deserted Compound. What was this all about? What was I going to do? I looked frantically around for help and saw a lone figure striding towards the soldiers. It was MT.

"What do you think you are doing?" she exploded, a tiny seventy-year-old woman against ten men with guns. Good Lord, she was magnificent.

"I go protect you sister," a soldier announced, pulling himself straight. "We come to guard the hospital," he added proudly.

"Guard the hospital!" MT spluttered.

"Yes sister. Guard the hospital."

"You call terrifying my staff and patients guarding the hospital?"

"Sorry, sister."

"None of you children should have a peashooter, never mind these monstrous weapons," MT continued, her passions more inflamed than I ever thought possible. "We don't want you here. Now stop playing soldiers and fok-off!"

"Yes sister, sorry sister," said the soldier. And that was that. They left.

"Sister Ignatius, you were fabulous!" I laughed, bravely showing my face now the danger had passed.

"Well, sweet Jesus, have you ever seen such a display?" MT was addressing me almost as an equal. "But more importantly, how is Pete?"

"He's better. I suggested he should rest awhile outside Serabu."

"Oh, he won't be leaving us now."

"No, you're right, he won't."

"Well Gail, you will look after him very well here, I'm sure."

Goodness, was that a compliment? But MT had already turned to call to the frightened faces in the bushes. "They have gone. Please come back. It was only soldiers, not the rebels. They have gone now. You are safe."

One person who hadn't hidden was Betty. She came running from the direction of Maternity.

"Zainab fled Sumbuya on Sunday. She had her baby in the bush yesterday, but she cannot deliver the placenta."

"Oh. Since when were you our midwife, Betty?"

"I am covering Laygby until she has her baby."

"Of course. Okay, let's go."

I was scrubbed and ready to start when a poomui appeared at the theatre window.

"Dr. Gail?" The white face peered uncertainly at my generous figure clad in theatre greens. "It's Preston, from CARE."

"Preston?" I pulled my mask off. "Goodness, what are you

doing here?"

"CARE has several projects in this area, so I came to assess the rebel situation for myself," he told me. "And Klaus asked me to check up on you. I sure don't like it. You should evacuate."

"Huh?"

"Klaus sent this." Preston handed me a letter. Klaus's writing covered two sides of an oil-stained page pulled from a school jotter, which roughly translated to GET OUT.

I read it, a twinge of fear entwined with a surge of excitement. Klaus was worried about me! He cared! "Well, this is mostly about Sumbuya, which we knew already," I said, in my most offhand manner. "The British High Commissioner and VSO will surely let us know if it's not safe."

"Don't rely on them," Preston snapped. "We think you should leave."

"I can't think about it now," I said. "I have an emergency operation to do."

"Well, we can't force you," shrugged Preston. "Think about it. I have to go."

"I will. Thanks. Send Klaus my love." Gosh, I was getting to be a cool customer.

Zainab's afterbirth was well and truly stuck. At least we had scarcely used the Easter drug shipment over the last couple of weeks, so could afford to give her a decent anaesthetic. Once numbed, I plunged my hand deep into Zainab's bleeding womb and scraped the placenta out with my fingers.

"That was hard, look at it, it's in shreds. Currette please Tiange. What was her blood count, Betty?"

"Six grams."

"Right. Get Latif to arrange a transfusion. Her clottings likely

252

to be deranged after that long delay getting to the hospital, she may well bleed again."

"Latif don aks already. Her mother no get the right group, and he cannot find a donor in the village."

"Tell him I'll pay." I'd do battle with MT in the morning.

"Nobody go give blood, Dr. Gay," said Tiange. "Better person keep it to fight the rebels."

"Uh? Well….the bleeding seems to have stopped for now. Let's put her on iron and cross our fingers." We lowered Zainab's legs back onto the operating table. "That's us don don."

The next morning the sun streamed through my mosquito net. Nine o'clock! Where was Pa George? Never had I slept in beyond seven-thirty without him virtually breaking down my bedroom door. Not that it would matter if I were late, the hospital had been so quiet the past week.

Yawning, I admired my finished jigsaw, displayed in its full glory on the table in the morning sun. I ate some cold plassas for breakfast, before ambling down my path to the wards. Tom was striding up the path towards me.

"Morning oh Tom, come to drag me out of my bed?......what's up?" Once we were face to face, I saw his expression.

"More problems, Gail."

"Oh no, now what?"

"Pa George has been arrested."

27. Rebels This Way

"Pa George arrested! What's he done?"

"Nothing. The soldiers are just arresting people," Tom told me. "Including my students."

"What? These same soldiers who were in the compound yesterday?"

"I presume so."

"Why?"

"Because they've got guns."

"Does that mean they're in charge now? I suppose nobody's going to argue with a gun."

"Nobody except Pa George, who was last seen vanishing up the hill on the back of their truck shouting, 'You no able take me, I get for make chop for Dr. Gay!'"

"Good old Pa George!" I smiled, despite the tightening in my chest.

"Anyway, the rescue party has gone storming after them."

"The rescue party?"

"Moses and Ignatius."

"Good Lord." Did the woman know no fear? "Should we, er....go and help?" I offered unconvincingly.

"You stay out of it, Gail. We need our only doctor here to save lives." Tom squeezed my arm. "Bernadette and I will go if they haven't returned by ten."

"Oh dear," I said weakly, impressed by everyone else's bravery. "The soldiers probably want the extra men as front-line rebel fodder."

"I hate to think. Anyway, to change the subject, Pete was looking much better at Mass."

"He took mass this morning?" I exclaimed.

"Six thirty, as usual. We had just come out of the church

when we heard about Pa George and our students. Pete has invited you for lunch, in case you were worrying that you might starve."

"Hmmph." Tom of all people, was beginning to sound like Alan, but flippancy was much easier than frightening rebel talk. "So much for taking it easy," I sniffed. "Mass at dawn and making lunch for guests?"

"Well, I guess he'd enjoy some company just now. I'm invited too."

"Fair enough. No more symptoms then?"

"A bit more tingling in his fingers, but he told me not to tell you."

"I see. I'll stick my nose in before rounds."

"Thought you might. See you later, Doc. I promised to take Bernadette's classes this morning. "

I spent an inevitably fruitless half-hour with Pete, suggesting rest and relaxation somewhere far away from rebels and teenage soldiers with their lethal toys. He did at least look better so, after two cups of tea, I headed back to the wards. En route, I spotted Moses, with a figure that looked distinctly like Pa George, coming through the market-square.

"Pa George! Kushe, Pa George!" I dashed towards them.

"What for chop today?"

"For heavens sake, Pa George," I guffawed. "Have the day off!"

"Dem soldiers don arrest me!" Pa George sounded suitably outraged.

"I heard. How di body?"

"Look." He pointed at his forearm and I searched in vain for some slight graze or bruise beneath his finger. He was obviously going to play this for all it was worth.

"No harm done, Pa George."

"Hmmph."

"So what was it all about?"

"Dem soldiers want men to build a checkpoint at the Junction," Moses told me.

"So why not just ask nicely?"

"They get guns," Moses shrugged.

"So how did you get Pa George released?"

"MT say he is the only cook of the only doctor, and the only doctor get for eat," Moses grinned.

"Hear hear!" I clapped. Pa George nodded gravely. "I'm surprised that the soldiers have such concern for my welfare."

"MT say they get for need a doctor if the rebels shoot them," Moses continued. "Dem soldiers are frightened."

"Of the rebels or of MT?"

"All two."

"Well plenty tenki, Moses. You were very brave."

"No problem."

"What for chop today?"

"Please, take the day off, Pa George," I insisted. "Father Pete has invited me to lunch." Pa George looked crestfallen.

"Dr. Gay," Moses whispered. "The only cook of the only doctor no able take the day off."

"Of course not," I chastised myself silently. "Plassas please, Pa George."

Pete produced an enormous tin of tomato soup, courtesy of Desert Storm.

"Tomato soup!" I enthused. "Making me sweat a bit though."

"Yeah. No wonder the US Army had spare to send to Africa," laughed Tom, rubbing his sweaty brow against his shoulder. "It sure can't have been the number one choice in the middle of the desert."

"Bananas and tea for afters?" asked Pete. "Then cribbage perhaps?"

"Sorry, I've got a class in ten minutes. My students have their finals coming up." Tom stood up and wiped the tomato soup from his beard.

"Bit left on your moustache."

"Thanks, doc. And thanks for lunch Pete."

"And for your company, Tom. Well Gail, cribbage?"

"Okay, there's not much doing on the wards and it's better than sitting at home alone, waiting for the rebels." Yesterday's little surge of courage that had sent Preston back to CARE and me back to the operating theatre was definitely waning.

"Mighty." Pete enthusiastically shuffled an old pack of cards that looked as much of a hepatitis hazard as the twenty-leone notes.

"Let's hope losing doesn't put your blood pressure up."

"Ah doctor, you'll not be beating me now."

Two hours later, Betty rescued me. "I sorry to disturb, Dr. Gay."

"No problem. Father don beat me bad one."

Princess, our Liberian refugee with TB, had started labour.

"I think the baby is lying transverse, Dr. Gay."

"Yes, you're right," I confirmed Betty's findings with an internal examination. "The shoulder has slipped down. It's completely jammed. We'll have to do a Caesarean."

"Princess." Betty took her patient's hand. "Sorry-oh, but you no go able born this pickin, pass Dr. Gay do surgery."

"How di pickin?" she cried. "I don loss two pickin."

"The baby is fine at the moment," I reassured her.

"But we get for do the work quick quick," Betty added, squeezing her hand. The two stillbirths made it doubly important to deliver Princess as soon as possible, if we were to give her her

258

first live child.

Twenty minutes later I handed Princess a particularly beautiful daughter, Dr-Gay. The ego boost from saving a life, two lives in fact, gave such a feeling of invincibility that such minor emotions as fear and love were momentarily wiped.

We cleared up theatre, joking about the rebels. "Sesay don just put that new hospital sign at the Junction," said Tiange, washing the blood off her rubber gloves and tossing them in the bucket for resterilisation. "Rebels this way."

"No problem," Betty giggled. "If Pa George cook for the rebels, then we are safe." Pa George was not considered a good cook. He was a man after all.

"And Bernadette get for forbid the dirty rebels to attack the hospital because they will bring in germs," added Peter, once one of Bernadette's students, well drilled in cleanliness, godliness and the troubles caused by germs.

"After their baths, Bernadette would ask if they would mind attacking quietly, so as not to disturb the convalescing patients," I joined in.

"Please Mr. Rebel, I would be most grateful if you could kindly leave your guns at the entrance to the hospital. They are too noisy." Peter gave a regal imitation of Bernadette. "But do come inside for a cup of tea."

"When Bernadette get all dem rebels in the convent, she get for lock the door." Tiange continued "Then MT go thief their guns."

"Then what would MT do?" I asked, enjoying seeing Tiange in such a jovial mood.

"MT get for make her own checkpoint and she go charge each rebel a thousand leones for their own gun."

We were still laughing as we left theatre.

"We go see back, Tiange, we go see back, Peter," I called happily.

"Tomorra, Dr. Gay. Malo-hua." Peter and Tiange waved and I listened to their giggles vanish into the dark. God, I loved this job.

"Dr. Gay," a voice whispered from the shadows.

"Moses," I jumped. "What are you doing there?"

"Dr. Gay, Sister Bernadette and MT are at Mr. Tom's waiting for you."

"Oh?" It was most unusual for the sisters to come to the volunteers' houses. Moses knew it too. "Why?"

"I no know." He shrugged and waved good-bye without his usual smile. Left alone outside theatre I shone my torch on my watch. Eight o'clock. I didn't like the sound of this.

28. Last Orders

MT was crying.

"What is it?" I clutched Tom's doorknob in alarm at this extraordinary sight.

"Have a seat, Gail." Tom stood up to make space for me. Bernadette and MT sat in silence opposite. The room was cramped and the thermometer must have been reading thirty six degrees, but it still gave me the same shiver one gets when entering a morgue.

"We've had a radio message," sobbed Bernadette. "The Archbishop strongly advises Serabu hospital to close and the British High Commissioner requests the immediate departure of all British subjects."

"Oh." I slumped down into Tom's seat. "More rebel attacks?"

"No...well...I don't know." Bernadette shook her head. "Perhaps they have news that we don't. We may be under threat."

"Didn't they say?"

"Santano House only transmitted the message."

"You need to decide what to do, Gail, as Medical Superintendent," Bernadette continued.

"Decide what to do?" Me? My mind raced.

What did she mean decide what to do? Good Lord. Surely it wasn't going up to me on my second day in the job to decide whether or not to close the hospital. Hadn't we just been told what to do? We couldn't just disobey the British High Commissioner and the Archbishop, and why was Bernadette doing all the talking instead of MT, anyway?

"It might be useful to know whether or not there are actual rebels storming towards Serabu as we speak." My old friend flippancy put the words in my mouth.

"We don't know. We just don't know." MT shook her head, looking for the first time like the little old lady that she was.

"This'll just be a belated response to Sumbuya," Tom snorted. "Let's face it, Freetown hardly has its finger on the pulse where up country is concerned and I'm sure not accountable to the British High Commissioner. It's been quiet for three days now. I'm staying."

"Apart from the soldiers," I muttered.

"They're just little boys," said MT.

"With big guns."

"Oh Tom, I agree." MT said, ignoring me. "We cannot abandon our hospital. After all the only British here is Gail, and she's a doctor."

I shuffled my feet at her words. What had being a doctor got to do with it? Did that mean I was expected to stay? MT was more upset at her beloved hospital being forced to close rather than the prospect of personal danger. It was the personal danger bit that bothered me. This didn't seem to be a good time to get on the wrong side of the High Commissioner. On the other hand I didn't want to appear cowardly. I knew I'd probably stay if the others insisted.

"The Archbishop has also advised us to leave, and ultimately he is in charge of this hospital," Bernadette reminded us.

"And when did he last assist us in our recent difficult times? Or even pay a visit?" MT snapped. "He's washing his hands of us because we no longer provide enough glory for him to reflect in!" We looked in amazement at the nun's blasphemy.

"Ignatius," Bernadette said gently. "It's about safety. I'm sorry, we must leave." I exhaled silently at the words that relieved me from the decision making. "We may actually be in danger," she continued. "We are the first sizeable target between the rebels and the rest of the country. We have equipment, vehicles, diesel, drugs, food and a couple of young Western volunteers."

"And why are we any more special than the rest of the staff?" Tom interjected.

"You and Gail would be worth a large ransom. And the rebels

themselves may well be in need of medical attention."

"So we are to close. Poor Serabu." MT shook her head. Tom rubbed her bent shoulders.

"I'm afraid so. Ignatius, you and I are responsible for the safety of these volunteers and over a hundred and fifty staff and patients." Good old Bernadette. At least I wasn't supposed to be responsible for them.

"What does immediate departure mean?" I asked. "Tonight?"

"I think if we were in immediate danger we would know about it from the soldiers," Bernadette suggested.

"I wouldn't rely on the soldiers," said Tom with uncharacteristic cynicism.

"Well as long as they're here, we're safe. They'll be off at the first sniff of trouble," I snorted.

"That's as may be."

"I'm sorry, Bernadette," I sighed. Sarcy comments were no help to anyone.

"We sure can't just sneak off in the dark and leave our friends," said Tom. "Not without an explanation."

"Tom's right," agreed Bernadette. "We can't be starting a mass panic in the middle of the night. I suggest we have a staff meeting first thing in the morning and try to do this awful thing in a controlled manner. Gail?"

"What?" They were right, of course they were right, but if we were going, couldn't we just go now? Why hang around to be embroiled in the chaos? I closed my eyes. "Of course, Bernadette. I'll arrange medication for all the patients for the next.... I don't know." I stopped. "This isn't going to be forever is it?"

"Let us pray it is not."

"How can we just walk out?" MT nearly howled.

"I don't think we have a choice, Ignatius." Bernadette put an arm round her colleague.

"Serabu's doors haven't been closed for a single day in thirty years," MT sobbed. "I never thought it would come to this."

"Neither did I, Ignatius. Neither did I." Bernadette shook her head. "I'd better go and tell Pete. Oh dear."

"I'll come too." I stood up.

"We'll all go," said Tom.

"Oh dear. Oh dear, oh dear." Pete sat down heavily. "I will stay of course."

"But you've just had a TIA," I exclaimed. "Braving it out alone is hardly going to bring your blood pressure down."

"I won't be alone. I have my God and my friends of twenty-five years."

"Pete, many villagers will flee when they hear the poomuis are pulling out," Tom suggested gently.

"Of course, but those that stay will need my support. My place is here."

"I know but..." I started.

"Oh Pete, you know Bernadette and I feel the same way," MT interrupted. "We will stay too."

"No. No, it's not the same for you at all. If the rebels did come, you couldn't safely evacuate everybody at a moment's notice, but I could just drive off in my truck."

"Not if you have a stroke, you couldn't!"

"Okay, Gail." Pete spread his hands on the table. "Here's the deal. My sabbatical's already booked next month. I will go home as arranged, and as soon as I get back to Ireland, I promise to see my doctor. Okay?"

"Let me stay with you until then," Tom offered.

"No Tom. You are young, you are just a volunteer. I am telling you, you will go to Freetown with the others. Who knows? It may only be for a few days."

"But..."

"No."

We all fell silent until Bernadette spoke calmly.

"We'll have an emergency staff meeting at eight. Tonight we should pack and try to get some sleep. Lord knows we will need it for what will be a most difficult day tomorrow."

"I'll do my bedtime rounds as usual," I said. "Let the patients sleep easy for their last night. They'll have long journeys in the morning."

"Tom, will you help us with the staff pay packages?" asked Bernadette. "I think we have enough for two months advance each. They're all going to need money."

"What about the students?" Tom asked. "Transport is expensive."

"And the patients," I added.

"There simply isn't enough," sighed MT. "All we can do is waive fees."

"At least most patients and staff are local, but my students have come from all over the country," Tom continued

"How much is a poda-poda to Freetown?" asked Bernadette.

"Six hundred leones," I said. "But with demand so high they could charge anything."

"And the Junction is towards rebel territory, so they'll have to go to Mokanje," added Tom. "That's thirty miles. Can't we give lifts in the hospital vehicles?"

"Forty students, seventy staff, eighty patients and Lord knows how many relatives. No Tom!" said Bernadette.

"Perhaps Moses could make a few trips to ferry the students as far as Mokanje," said MT. I gaped at her. "And if we gave each student a thousand leones, it would help. It's no use, I'll have to work out exactly how much we can afford. Please excuse me." She stood up and stumbled towards the door.

"Ignatius, wait for us," Bernadette said. "With Tom's help, we'll have all the money counted out in a couple of hours."

"I'll come too." Pete pushed himself out of his chair.

"No." Tom and I chorused.

"You'll have a lot of distressed villagers seeking reassurance tomorrow. Tonight will be your last chance to relax." Tom pushed the older man's shoulders back into his seat.

"Oh dear. Well, would my doctor allow me a beer?"

"Good idea. I'll come and join you after my rounds."

An hour later I was sitting down with one of Pete's beers. "That must be the shortest reign as Medical Superintendent in Serabu's history." Weak jokes were my only remaining weapons. "Not even two days and the hospital closes." I took a long drink.

"She's just taking that for your own health you understand, Pete," said Tom, an unlikely conspirator to my fake cheer. "So you don't yield to temptation when we aren't here to keep an eye on you."

"Thank you for your kind concern," said Pete, eyeing his near empty beer crate as Bernadette reached for her second bottle. Tom drank his water.

"Oh, I'm just after remembering, I have a bottle of Bailey's!" said Pete once the last beer had gone.

"Goodness, Father. How can you forget such a thing?" I teased.

"It was a present I've been saving for a rainy day. This, the Lord have mercy, must qualify as a rainy day." Pete stood up. "We can't be letting it fall to the rebels."

"Certainly not," I exclaimed. "Whatever you do don't let them get the Bailey's."

Pete returned three minutes later with a tea towel over his arm, two teacups, a tumbler, a chipped Charles and Di mug and a litre bottle of Bailey's poking seductively out of a brown paper bag. I had never seen him so animated. Danger obviously suited him. He poured out hefty measures into four of the inelegant but voluminous vessels and stopped over the fifth looking at Tom.

"Tom?"

"No, not for me. You know I don't....oh what the heck, yes!"

"Oh Pete, this is just heavenly." I smacked my lips.

"Hey, this is real nice."

"You've made an alcoholic out of him, Pete," Bernadette exclaimed.

"Tom that's 17%," I pointed out. "You're drinking it like a milkshake!"

"To you all for all the hard work you have put into Serabu Hospital. Thank you." Bernadette raised her teacup. "Slainte."

"Slainte," I replied. "We'll be back!" Bernadette gulped down half the sickly warm cream liqueur without responding.

"I never thought I'd leave Serabu." MT was toying with her tumbler. She sat slumped into the chair with her skin folding into its greyness and tears riding over the ridges from her puffy red eyes. I instantly regretted all our clever-clever comments and could feel all the frivolity in the room dissolve as the others' eyes were drawn simultaneously to the old lady.

"Perhaps we all ought to try and get some sleep," Bernadette said gently, breaking the sudden awkward silence. "It's past midnight and tomorrow's going to be very stressful."

"I never thought I'd walk out of Serabu," MT repeated, struggling up from her chair.

"Come on Ignatius, we'll walk you home," Tom took her arm and gently guided her out of the door and into the warm, peaceful night.

29. Discharged

"Dr. Gay, come quick to Maternity!" Laygby banged on my door. So much for getting some sleep.

"Laygby! Aren't you on Maternity leave'?"

"But there is nobody left. Betty don already do a double shift."

"You can't run around at two in the morning when you are eight months pregnant! Where's Almamy?"

"He don go," she shrugged. "Many are too much frightened and have run to the bush."

"Oh." Had they guessed that we were leaving? Was it the soldiers who had scared them? Or had they got more news of rebels approaching?

But there was no time to worry about rebels. "This doesn't look good," I whispered as we reached Maternity.

Zainab had started bleeding again, her life pumping over the mattress, her face ashen and sweaty, while her newborn baby slept alongside her. Her mother sat quietly stroking her daughter's hand. Fatmata had come from Surgical to put up an intravenous line, whilst Princess, a day after surgery, held Zainab's arm steady.

"Run that saline in as fast as it will go, Fatmata," I instructed. "Have you got another bag, Laygby? Laygby, are you okay? Sit down for a few minutes and get your breath. God, I can't get a blood pressure. Fatmata, turn that on full and find another bag and syntocinon. Laygby can draw it up sitting down. We need blood NOW. Call Alamamy to fetch Latif."

"Almamy is not there," said Laygby.

"Pah, I forgot, Fatmata, you'll have to find Latif, and Tiange too."

"No problem."

The blood just kept coming. "Another bag of saline Laygby,"

I shouted. "..and the ergometrine. Come on Latif, where are you? I need to transfuse her now." My orders dwindled to a mutter as I knew I could not realistically expect Latif for another fifteen minutes, and that was if he had not fled to the bush himself. "We are losing her. More saline, Laygby."

"Saline don don, Dr. Gay."

"Then thief some from Surgical. Quick. We'll have to take her to theatre. I'll give another dose of ergometrine."

After two hours in theatre we finally stopped the bleeding, but she was slipping away. There was virtually no blood left circulating in her veins. Latif was knocking on doors in the village looking for a donor with the promise of double or treble pay, but the villagers had already fled, or were too frightened to answer their door.

"This is hopeless. She needs blood, not salty water."

"Latif is trying."

"I know Tiange, I know."

Zainab died at eight, just as the emergency staff meeting was starting. Her baby's cry rang in my ears as I hurried over to the convent. I opened the door to silence. Had the meeting been cancelled? But no, twenty people sat clustered in a circle, shoulders bowed and scarcely breathing. None of the swollen red eyes acknowledged my arrival. Why should they? Their Medical Superintendent hadn't even tried to save their hospital nor had she been present to deliver the bad news. I couldn't say I'd been delayed saving lives, because I'd just failed at that too.

"While the Poomuis stayed, we were safe." Patrick Kpukoma finally broke the silence. "But you must go to your own homes, and we must stay with our families."

"There will be a panic," said Betty. "We get for keep calm

ourselves and do the best for our patients."

"I'll, er…" I cleared my throat. "…make sure everybody is discharged with plenty of medication." Big deal.

"We are waiving fees, but the dispensary nurses must fill in the charts." added Bernadette. "We'll need to do a stock take when we return."

"Are you coming back?" asked Patrick. He knew, like all the others, about July's financial review. If Serabu was already closed, then what better excuse for the Catholic Mission to send their funds elsewhere? The very act of evacuating, even if no rebel came a step closer, might be Serabu's death knell.

"We will return." MT's first contribution to the meeting was not a promise that she could make. The rebels and her superiors in Bo, Freetown and Ireland would determine Serabu's future.

"As soon as possible." Bernadette was vague.

"Days? Weeks? Months?" pressed Patrick. "We get for know. If Serabu don finish completely then we get for leave and look for other jobs. If Serabu go open back, we get for stay." Patrick looked around the room for the nods of confirmation.

"I can only pray that our funds will still be there and that the rebels will come no further," Bernadette said. "And that the staff will reopen our hospital. But I cannot say when it will be safe."

"We understand," said Betty kindly. "But we get plenti work today. The two nurses in dispensary go need help. We get for bring more drugs from the stores. Dauda, will you help me?"

"No problem."

"Tenki ya. The other charge nurses must stop palava on their wards," Betty continued. She was being marvellous. I closed my eyes to shut out the thought of the chaos that was about to break out.

"What about the equipment?" asked Dauda very practically. "And the drugs? The rebels will thief it. If notto the rebels, the thiefmen-self go come."

"And the books and chairs and desks in the nursing school," added Tom.

"And the beds and mattresses." Peter took up the theme. "They will all be thiefed." Peter directed his comments to Bernadette, rather than MT. Everyone sensed that Bernadette was now in charge. MT sat outside the circle of conversation, moist eyes gazing out of the window.

"You all make very good points," agreed Bernadette. "We must ensure that we have a hospital to come back to. Mr McGrane sent a message from Mokanje this morning offering to help secure the buildings."

"Them theatre doors get metal frames," said Sesay. "And Surgical-self. Them Mines' people get for weld them shut."

"Excellent idea, Sesay," said Bernadette. "Then we'll have a safe store for our equipment. Moses can you get back on to Mokanje to ask if they have welding facilities?"

"No problem, Sister Bernadette."

"Good. Sesay, you're in charge of moving beds and equipment to Theatre and Surgical."

"I'll start discharging patients from Surgical, to get it emptied," I suggested. "Then Maternity, Children's, Medical and finish on TB Ward."

"Why are my TB patients always last?" complained Patrick. "Many come from far. There will be plenti palava."

"Oh Patrick, I know," I sighed. "They're rebellious at the best of times. But they're on so many tablets they'll just jam up dispensary. Also they're fitter than most other patients."

"The two new ones are very weak," he retorted. Patrick was very paternal about his TB patients.

"Okay, bring me those two charts for discharge straight away."

"What about their daily injections?"

"You must teach them how to give their own injections, starting with today's dose. We'll supply the needles and syringes, if you can teach them how to sterilise them," I said. "That should fill some time until I arrive."

"No problem."

"Right, we must get started." Bernadette stood up after our brief plan was agreed. "I'll pay staff salaries at eleven in Admin and Tom will pay his students a travel allowance at the school. Everybody will be paid, so please be patient. I don't want a big palava outside Admin. Peter, will you be responsible for getting the message to those currently off duty?"

"No problem, but they will know the news already, Sister."

"Probably yes," Bernadette sighed. All senior staff did not vanish into the convent at the busiest time of day for no reason. She took a breath and continued with a wavering voice. "Thank you. Thank-you for all the hard work you have given to Serabu over the years. We are very sorry." Bernadette hastily wiped her eyes with the back of her hand.

"We are very, very sorry." MT spoke for the first time that morning. All the heads turned to the tiny old figure shaking her head in the corner.

"Aw fo do," said Patrick, gently. "Aw fo do."

We came out of the convent to a compound alive with sobs and screams. Within seconds I was at the hub of a whirlpool of patients and staff, grabbing my arm or my skirt and begging me not to leave. I tugged myself away from the distress and ran over to Surgical to begin my role call of discharges. Mechanically, I signed off every patient, looking at their charts rather than their eyes, writing them up for as many dressings and tablets as might help them over the coming weeks. I discharged Rose, the young woman with terminal breast cancer, absolving myself from any further responsibility, before moving on to wash my hands of the next patient in line.

After only an hour's sleep, I walked from Surgical to Children's, from Children's to Maternity and from Maternity to Medical in an exhausted daze, only vaguely aware of the chaos surrounding me. There were relatives filing up to the dispensary, clutching their loved one's charts, nurses queuing up at Admin for their wages and people streaming out of the hospital with rolled-up belongings on their heads. Even the unflappable Betty was running backwards and forwards, between wards, stores and dispensary, stopping to shout instructions, point directions or hug patients and nurses. The only island of sanity was the "Kushe Dr. Gay," shouted across the compound by Bockerie from TB ward, who was helping Sesay carry the mattresses over to Surgical. My smile soon faded when a woman fell to her knees and threw her arms around my waist. It was Rose's mother.

"Dr. Gay, don't go. You get for save my daughter!" she cried, tightening her grip on my middle. I froze. I couldn't cope with this mother's anguish and my impotence. Not today. There was no more I could do for Rose, just as there had been nothing I could do for her last week, but I had to escape from her mother's grasp. The rest of my patients had to be sent home, and then there was Outpatients. Prising Rose's chart from the elderly fingers that encircled my waist, I prescribed another type of different coloured vitamin pill that could never save her daughter from the cancer of the breast even if there had never been a single rebel in Sierra Leone.

At Outpatients, I closed the office door on Friday rush hour at Piccadilly tube station. Two hours later, once I had sorted out staff, students and their families who wanted medication for ongoing problems, or just-in-case supplies, the compound had become a Sunday morning Highland branchline. I shouldn't have been

274

surprised; after all, I was the one to throw everybody out, but the sight of Serabu Hospital populated only by goats, sent a shudder down my spine. Then, just as a reminder of how desperately I needed sleep, Zainab floated across the empty compound, a funny little smile across her deathly white face. "Stop it, stop it, stop it," I shouted, shaking the ominous vision out of my head.

Perhaps Zainab had taken the easier escape. What about everybody else? Her mother, for instance? Last week she had lived in peaceful Sumbuya with a beautiful daughter, happily awaiting her grandchild's arrival. Now she had no home, a newborn baby she could not feed, and her daughter's corpse which she could not carry or bury alone. Normally there would be plenty of people to help her, but not today, when everyone was so scared for their own family's lives. What would happen to Zainab's body?

I never found out.

Bed was not going to be on the agenda for a long, long time - Freetown was at least a seven-hour journey and I still had thirty-six TB patients to discharge. Working out six week's supply of four or five different types of medicine apiece, each individually weight adjusted, would defy my arithmetic skills at the best of times. But worse than forcing my sleep deprived brain into number crunching was the prospect of facing the TB patients, who would surely be furious that I had left them till last. And they would have a point.

They already felt like second class citizens, frequently cast out of their communities, certainly avoided by the rest of the patients and, since they were not acutely unwell, always left to the end (or like Christmas, left out altogether) of my priority list. Consequently they had bonded together against the common foe, the poomui doctors, who wouldn't trust them to take their tablets at home and forced them into an unwanted three months admission away from their homes and farms. We didn't even feed them in return. Now here I was, blithely turning them out into the void. God, I wasn't going to be popular. I took a few deep breaths and forced myself to stride across the compound towards TB block.

I stood at their doorway and listened. Why was it so quiet? Had they decided I wasn't worth waiting for and fled already?

"Patrick?" I called tentatively. "Are you still here?"

"We de inside," he replied. And there was Patrick sitting cross-legged in the middle of the floor with two neat piles of charts piled on beside him. All the mattresses had gone, leaving only rusty bed frames and thirty-six TB patients sitting or squatting on the floor, with bundles of possessions at their feet.

"Kushe, Dr. Gay," they choroused. My mind flashed back twenty years to primary school when two hundred little voices chanted 'Good mo-oorning Mr. Stones' when the headmaster entered morning assembly.

"Er... yes...kushe." Flustered by this unexpectedly warm welcome, I hid my face behind the first of the charts and whispered to Patrick. "Where shall I start?"

"I don write one month's medication for all. Them nurses in dispensary are too much tired to do the sums so I write the totals at the bottom of the chart-self. You want check, Dr. Gay?"

"Patrick, you are marvellous." I felt like hugging him. Oh what the hell, I did hug him. The patients cheered.

"The charts, Dr. Gay," he chastised, blushing. I glanced at the first one, the drugs clearly marked with a little circle round each total.

"I can't do better than that. Why did you never go to medical school, Patrick?"

"There is no medical school," he shrugged. "Look at the charts."

"Okay." I dashed off thirty-six autographs and Patrick

distributed the charts. Their patience exhausted, Serabu's last thirty-six patients welled out of the ward and headed towards dispensary.

"That's an awful lot of tablets for those poor girls to count, Patrick." We had no automatic tablet counter in Serabu.

"Too many," he sighed, leaning against the wall beside me. "Can I go home now, Dr. Gay?"

"Of course Patrick. You've stayed longer than anyone, thank you." I hugged him once more. "Look after Ma Kpukoma and Patricia."

"We go see back, Dr. Gay."

"We go see back, Patrick," I replied automatically. We would probably never meet again.

"Well, Dr. Gail, you have earned your lunch," I said to myself, stretching out my back and neck in the doorway. "Oh, no. Now what?"

Bockerie was running back towards me, waving his chart. "Dr. Gay, Dr. Gay, they have gone home."

"Who?" But I knew. I had sent over two hundred prescriptions to the dispensary nurses that morning. That was an awful lot of tablets to count and wrap and label in little paper sachets. I couldn't really blame them, especially now that everybody else had long gone. They had families too.

"Them nurses in dispensary don go," wailed Bockerie. "The door is locked."

"Okay Bockerie, don't panic. Tell the others I'm coming. I'll try and find the key." Betty would probably have it, if she was still here. At least I knew where she lived.

I tried the wards first, but met only two Mines' security men wandering across the compound.

"Kushe. Have you seen our matron, Betty?" I asked.

"Yes. She is collecting more drugs from stores before we seal it up."

Good old Betty. Why had I doubted her? I ran over to the storeroom.

"Betty?"

"Dr. Gay?" Betty turned round from the boxes of tablets. "You are finished? I just get them TB drugs to take to dispensary, but I no able carry all at once. This is my second trip. We need plenti, notto so?"

"Isn't there anybody helping you?"

"Everybody don go," she sighed. "I don forget about those TB drugs this morning."

"So did I, Betty, it's been chaos. If only the dispensary nurses had stayed one more hour."

"They don stay longer than any others already. I will dispense the tablets myself."

"Betty, there'll be hundreds. Come on, I'll help. The TB patients won't be able to control themselves for much longer."

We half-ran, half-walked with box loads of tablets and injections, past the two security men hovering at Pharmacy's doorway with their welders.

"We're lucky they didn't seal us in there forever," I joked.

"We get for give them rebels a big fright, notto so, if they tried to thief the drugs?"

We sneaked into the back of Dispensary, a windowless room little bigger than a public loo, and flicked the light switch. Nothing. Sesay had shut the generator down hours ago.

"I can't see a damned thing." I felt around on the table for a place to put my box of medication, but it was cluttered with empty containers and spilt tablets. "Oh, to hell with it." I cleared the surface with a sweep of my arm.

"I put all the kerosene lamps in Theatre," shouted Betty above the noise of fists banging on the wooden shutters outside. "The Mines' men don seal it already. Shall I fetch one from home?"

"Listen to them Betty, they'll lynch you if you try to leave. They're all terrified that the rebels will come marching down the road at any moment. Dah! I can't open these damned shutters."

"Let me do it, Dr Gay." Shaking, Betty released the catch and begging hands clamoured through the metal grille more suited to a Wild West bank than a hospital.

So we counted and counted and counted until tablets swam before our eyes and stuck to the sweat on our fingers. We had no water, so rubbed our hands on our skirts and counted some more. We took one chart at a time as it was thrust through the grille, concentrating only on Patrick's neatly circled numbers at the bottom, rather than the name at the top.

Betty explained which tablet was which in the patient's little packages and how many should be taken each day, but whether the patients took any of it in, if indeed they could hear a word she was saying in the uproar, I'll never know. At least most of them had been on the ward for long enough to know their own daily dosages, so I was reasonably happy they wouldn't poison themselves.

We came to the last two charts. They belonged to Pa Ndanema and Bockerie, who had spent the past ninety minutes trying their best to control the unruly crowd as it surged forward onto Dispensary.

"There's no thiazina left, Dr. Gay."

"Oh no, they've been so helpful, we can't leave them short."

"You get any of the children's thiazina on the shelves?"

"Betty, you're a genius. We'll just have to triple the dose."

So Pa Ndanema and Bockerie left with 210 ethambutol, 168 rifampicin, 42 streptomycin injections, and 630 paediatric thiazina each. Then as a special bonus offer, a handful of chloroquine and paracetamol (in case they should get malaria), a tub of Whitfield's ointment (in case of fungal infections), some iron tablets (as they were admittedly a bit anaemic) and vitamin tablets (as really how could they be sure of good nutrition with the country overrun with rebels). We also gave Pa Ndanema a bag full of guaze swabs so he could keep dressing his stump. That little lot would be worth a fortune on the black market.

It was after five o'clock when Betty and I emerged from our cave to the bright whitewashed walls of a silent hospital.

"Poor Serabush," sighed Betty.

"It's so sad." I was actually leaving Serabu, probably to return home forever. Was I sad or relieved? I didn't really know - all I could think of was that awful journey to Freetown, which was bound to be littered with military checkpoints to slow it down even more. For a moment I envied Betty staying. After thirty-five hours with no sleep and the most stressful day of my life, I just wanted my bed. Then I thought of the rebels. "I'm sorry Betty."

"Aw fo do," she sighed. My stomach rumbled loudly. "Oh, Dr Gay, you get for chop!"

"Even Pa George' plassas will taste good tod..." I stopped, realising my blithe assumption that Pa George would make lunch was plain ridiculous. All the other staff had long gone, so why should he stay?

"You will be gladdi to sleep at Mokanje tonight, Dr. Gay."

"Mokanje?" What was Betty on about? Bernadette was going to drive us to Freetown in the truck in less than an hour.

"Mr. McGrane don come with the security men this afternoon. He say you can stay at Mokanje."

"Really?" Electricity, air-conditioning, a pool, chocolate, SLEEP!

"Tom and the sisters want to go direct to Freetown, but Mr. McGrane don insist you stay. Moses will take you at six."

"Well perhaps someone could give me a lift to Freetown

280

tomorrow." I mused, feeling just a little less tired. There was always some ex-patriate going to the big city from Mokanje. "What about you?"

"We must wait for Ben." Betty's smile faded.

"Have you heard from him?"

"No, he must still be near Kailahun, but the Catholic mission has gone, so there is no radio."

"Oh, Betty." What else could I say?

"Aw fo do." Betty folded her arms round herself. "We go see at the convent in one hour, Dr. Gay."

Wandering back to my house with goats roaming where once there were nurses and patients, my legs felt quite wobbly with hunger. I nearly cried when I spotted Pa George sitting, chin in hands, on my doorstep.

"Oh, Pa George, you stayed!"

"You no chop yet, Dr. Gay."

"I'm sorry to keep you from your family Pa George. You should have come to find me."

"You too bweezy. Chop bin ready four hours."

"Sorry."

"Hmmph." Pa George went to get my lunch that had been keeping warm on the embers of the three-stone-fire. I grabbed a plate, spoon and ladle from the kitchen and followed him eagerly.

"Aw fo do," said Pa George, stopping short of the fire.

"Aw fo do?" I asked. "Oh." The pan had been pulled off the stones and lay on its side in the dying embers with its lid lying two feet away.

The goats had eaten my lunch.

30. Running Away!

MT left Serabu Hospital with tears flowing down her grey cheeks. I wanted to hug her, but stood shuffling my feet instead. What could I say? Ultimately my posting in Sierra Leone had just been an interlude. I would resume my job, my life, my family and my friends, but Serabu had been Sister Ignatius' whole world and it had just collapsed.

"Er, goodbye." I limply raised my arm, but the old lady's eyes were fixed ahead. Next to MT sat Bernadette, dressed in veil and habit for ease of passage through the checkpoints. Tom sat in the back of the truck with six of his students.

"Good-bye, Gail," Bernadette waved. "Sleep well at the McGrane's tonight, and we'll see you at the Venue on Saturday night."

Oh to sleep… "Good-bye, safe journey." I managed a proper wave this time. Tom and his students all waved frantically from the back.

"God bless, Gail," said Bernadette. "Good-bye Betty. Look after that young man of yours now."

"I will Sister Bernadette. We go see back. Look, Hindolu is waving."

"God bless him." Bernadette smiled at the baby, then turned the key in the ignition.

Only then did MT turn to face me. "Look after my hospital for me, Gail. Please."

And the sisters who had devoted their lives to Serabu were gone. What a sad contrast to the throngs of laughing and waving people that bade farewell to Jean and his family only days previously. But what did Ignatius mean?

Before I could think further on her words, Moses pulled up in the Landrover. It was piled high with bags and rolled up belongings and filled with nurses and students hoping to get some transport from Mokanje to their homes across the country. Moses managed to strap my rucksacks on top of the mountain of luggage already bearing down on the vehicle, then opened the front door.

"We go see back, Dr. Gay," Betty hugged me before I climbed into the best seat.

"Very soon," I lied, squeezing her tight. The likelihood was that our Field Director would bundle me on the first flight home, leaving me free to continue my old life as if nothing had ever happened. Betty would soon be a figment of my memory. Ashamed, I released my grip and Betty clicked the door shut behind me.

The Landrover strained into motion as Hindolu took his first steps holding frantically on to Betty's thumb. Betty waved, her face lit with her beautiful smile, and Hindolu copied his mummy, letting go of her thumb to wave his own little hand, and landed promptly on his bottom in the dust.

Hanging out of the Landrover window, I waved frantically at the two giggling figures we had left dwarfed beneath the large white convent building and whispered "Oh God, keep them safe."

Ten miles out of Serabu I sat numbly in the front seat, secretly hoping that VSO would indeed order us all home. I had had enough. I did not want to witness any more suffering, nor take any more responsibility. I could board the plane, shaking my head and blaming the Field Director for overreacting, without having to feel guilty myself. Once in Gatwick, I would stock up at the nearest shop on chocolate and cheese and take it home to eat in bed. A bed that needed a cosy thick duvet rather than a mosquito net. A bed with a lamp beside it that would light up at the flick of a switch, and a socket that would power a cassette player that could blare out loud pop music. I could lie back, safe in the knowledge that nobody would come knocking at my door telling me that it was my job to stop someone from bleeding to death, or to kick a hospital full of patients out onto the street.

Vacantly looking out of the windscreen I thought of Chicken Tikka. Pa George had taken her. Well, I suppose he was as good a person as any to enjoy chicken stew. Suddenly, I realised I was crying - not for the death of poor Zainab for the want of some blood, or the end of the hospital that had saved so many lives, or the fate of my friends left to face the rebels, but for a stupid hen. Oh Gail!

Wiping away the tears, I saw that we were approaching a lone bent figure, hobbling on one leg and a single crutch, chasing the evening haze as it met the horizon. It was Pa Ndanema, carrying two plastic bags filled with dressings and tablets, clearly oblivious to the straining engine behind him.

"Kushe, Pa!" I called out of the window. Pa Ndanema snapped out of his reverie and straightened his shoulders.

"Kushe, Dr. Gay."

"How di body?" I asked him.

"I tell God tenki."

"You only get one crutch, Pa?"

"That crutch don break," he snorted.

"Well, you have done very well. Nearly ten miles, notto so Moses?"

"Ten miles, Dr. Gay."

"You better join us Pa," I offered, shuffling over, pushing Fatmata, who sat with me at the front, into Moses's lap.

"Dr. Gay, place not there," moaned Moses, trying to find his gear stick under Fatmata's thigh. Fatmata pulled her lappa protectively tighter round her waist and gave Moses the evil eye.

"I'll walk," came Dauda's voice from the back. "It's only twenty miles," he added virtuously.

"If Dauda walks, there will be space for two patients," teased Fatmata, "And Dauda will lose his belly." Dauda was the least fit Salonean male I knew.

"Nobody need walk. Shove over Dauda." I pushed him playfully, and squeezed myself into the back like an extra elephant in a mini amidst shouts, giggles, arms and legs. Moses sighed and helped Pa Ndanema through the passenger door, feeding his remaining crutch into the melee behind. The old man sat like Lord Muck himself in the prime seat, surveying the dusty road ahead with a gummy grin. Fatmata handed him an orange to suck.

Between juicy slurps of gum on pulp, Pa Ndanema alternately thanked us and complained about his crutch.

"I'm sorry Pa, but I doubt Sesay made them with long haul journeys in mind."

On our way once more, the nurses were joking about like their old selves, despite the long uncertain journeys that lay ahead of them all. The brave old Pa had lifted everybody's mood. I had done what had to be done, and was now a mere thirty minutes away from twenty-four hour electricity. Electricity meant air conditioning to clear up my prickly heat and fridges that could keep things from melting. Things like chocolate. It was a Swiss owned company after all. Surely there was at least one chocolate bar that someone could rustle up if I asked nicely? In fact, what was the rush to hurry back to Freetown, to be suspended in limbo again at the sweaty VSO resthouse, stuffed with evacuated volunteers whilst our Field Director decided what to do with us? Perhaps I could stay at Mokanje for a few extra days?

"Moses," I started, leaning forward. He grunted acknowledgement. This was Moses' third trip to Mokanje as a ferry service that day, after a morning calming down the rabble of staff clamouring for their wages and organising them into orderly queues to receive their precious packages. "Did you hear what Mr. McGrane said about my staying at Mokanje?"

"Mr. McGrane wants you to stay. He say you can get your very own house."

"My own house? Why would I need a whole house for one night?"

"If you go, they get only Dr. Momoh, Dr. Gay," answered Moses. "The house don empty. A very big house, Dr. Gay."

"Moses, what are you saying?"

"Freetown is too far, Dr. Gay. We gladdi if you stay at Mokanje."

"We? Who's we?"

"Oh Patrick, Tiange and Dauda. And MT."

So that's what she meant. "And where was I during this discussion?" I asked.

"You were bweezy. Sister Bernadette and Betty said you were too much tired. They said it was fine for you to stay in Mokanje this night, but that you get for go back to see them VSO people in Freetown."

"I see. What did the others say?"

"The staff don aks me to aks you to stay."

"But you haven't, Moses. We're nearly at Mokanje. Why haven't you asked me to stay?"

"You look too much tired, Dr. Gay." I looked at Moses' kindly face. It was drawn with fatigue and anxiety.

"We are all tired," I said through the lump in my throat, grateful that Moses had not actually asked the question. I steered the conversation away from myself. "I hear you will stay at the convent with your family."

"Yes. Sister Bernadette don give me the keys."

"To the convent?"

"To theatre, to pharmacy, to Admin...."

"That will be an enormous bunch of keys, Moses."

"When the rebels come to thief Serabush they look for me first to get the keys," he joked.

"Oh Moses, if the rebels come they won't bother with keys." I cringed as soon as the words were out. God, it was all very well for me, being driven off to safety. Fortunately Moses was as sanguine as ever.

"Aw fo do. The convent has plenty of rooms to hide in."

"What you need Gail, is a stiff gin and some fatherly solace." Paul McGrane had suggested late that evening after Anne-Marie, his beautiful French wife, had led my weary body from the Landrover first to a hot bath, then to a laden dinner table. Thus revived, a gin did sound good, so I followed Paul down to the bar in search of comfort.

Who was I kidding? Six priests sat at the bar, evidently several hours into a good session:

"Shouldn't have closed the hospital."

"A Sister's duty is to stay with her people."

"Father Pete knew his duty."

"You cannot be after running away and abandoning your mission."

"Sister Hillary would never have left...."

"Hillary should never have left in the first place, never been the same since."

"....running away."

"We were told to leave!" I exploded from behind them. "Ignatius was utterly devastated."

"Ah. It's Dr. Gail, returned from the mouth of the enemy." Father Gregory, the priests' regional head, turned round. "No dear, the sisters were strongly advised to leave," he corrected me.

"Oh come on!"

"No commitment," he said, taking another mouthful of beer. So what had they been doing all afternoon? Sitting here, drinking beer, boasting about how they would have braved it?

"So where is this army of rebels storming down the road?" sniffed Father Brendan, Mokanje's own priest. "You'd better sit down, Gail, while we sort this mess out."

"I don't know. Nobody knows," I protested. "The sisters were just obeying orders."

"Running away," muttered a voice from my left.

"Casting shame on the Catholic church," another voice added.

"Oh but we're not criticising you, dear." A hand patted my thigh. "You have bravely decided to stay here, only an hour away from the hospital...." I raised an eyebrow. Who said I was staying?

"Yes, at least Gail is still here," agreed Brendan. "She can go back tomorrow and see Outpatients, and perhaps get this hospital reopened in the next few days. What a farce."

"Wait a minute!" I interjected. "The High Commissioner ordered me out too!"

Go back tomorrow! My plans for the next twenty-four hours went more along the lines of bed, pool, arrange lift to Freetown, dinner, bed. I took a large slug of G and T. I paused. Perhaps I should have refused their drink on principal, but decided I was no longer big on principals and slugged down the rest.

"But you only left because the Sisters were leaving, I'm sure," Brendan continued.

Where did this heroic assessment come from? The others were the ones who had been willing to stick it out, despite their orders, whereas I had been glad to pack and run. Another gin and tonic appeared and it too vanished easily down my oesophagus.

"It broke the sister's hearts," I reiterated. "But they followed their orders, believing it to be in the best interests of staff and patients. We deserve your support, not your criticism."

"As I said, nobody's criticising you, Gail," Gregory assured me. "Your decision to stay when the others have fled is admirable."

"Yes, all is not lost while we still have a doctor, and Pete of course. We'll soon get Serabu back on its feet."

"But I'm going home!" I wanted to yell at them, but the words never came. Paul came to my rescue.

"Brendan, all of you, be realistic! Gail's just a young girl for heaven's sake, you can't expect her to return to risky territory alone, with or without permission. Even if she could, she can't run a hospital without funds."

"Hear, hear," I thought, but then Paul revealed his own plans for my future.

"What we'll do is employ her here at Mokanje clinic. Full rates of course Gail, not just a paltry VSO allowance."

"But I don't want to be a Mines' employee!" I exclaimed, self-righteously. Good Lord! What would Klaus and Lindsey have to say about that? Selling out to an evil multinational company, who stole the country's resources and reduced the landscape to dust.

"Steady on," laughed Paul. "I don't want you to abandon your principles, but listen. We are the only place that Serabu's patients can come to now. What if we agree to fund treatment for all who come, not just the Mines' employees?"

"But Serabu isn't dead yet!" Who was he to write off my hospital?

"No, so in the meantime I promise our security guards will give twenty-four hour protection from rebels or looters."

"Thank you," I added, suddenly remembering my middle class manners. The man was genuinely trying to help. "The sisters will appreciate that."

"Well Serabu does lie between us and the rebels, I'm not being entirely altruistic."

"So we make a good outpost." I raised an eyebrow.

"You know how heavily we rely on Serabu, Gail," Paul sighed. "We want you to reopen."

"Hmmm."

"But if it doesn't, why not continue Serabu's work here?"

Paul had argued me out of my excuse to go home. The problem with proclaiming principles was that then people expected you to stick to them. Bloody hell! I put my spectacles on the bar next to a third G and T and screwed my knuckles into the ridge of my eyebrows.

How had it all landed on my doorstep? Just because Jean's contract had happened to end and Fran had just happened to be in Freetown. I sighed. Jean had his family to think of and Fran had his wife. All I had was a touch of unrequited love. I picked up my drink - so nice after Star beer - and peered out from the bar to the pool, the surface ruffled by a little breeze, twinkling in the moonlight.

"Having Gail work here sounds like a grand idea now," said Brendan.

"Mighty," agreed Gregory.

"And you're just the person for the job, Gail," simpered Brendan. "You've got a mighty reputation you know. We'd hate to lose you."

"You can stay in the ex-Managing Director's house," Paul pressed on. "There's a gas oven, hot showers, air-conditioning of course, fridge, coffee percolator..."

"Chocolate?" I perked up.

Paul laughed. "Yes of course. An unlimited supply of Swiss chocolate."

"Well…"

"Think about it." Paul stood up and patted my back. "I'll see you back at the house."

Paul left me surrounded by his priestly accomplices, intent on claiming my soul with their conspiracy of luxury and ego stroking. Of course, that was exactly the way to go about it. I needed to change the subject.

"Father Pete isn't very well. He's had a little stroke."

"Oh dear. I didn't know that. Did you Brendan?"

"I did not. It makes his stance more heroic altogether." There was a rumble of support and nodding heads. I silently cursed myself for providing them with further ammunition to back up their original argument.

"He'll be all right, of course?" asked Gregory.

"Well..." I started, "his blood pressure is far too high. I'm really not happy leaving him so isolated in potential rebel territory."

"You'll be here to look after him though, Dr. Gail. And God and our prayers of course."

"That's not what I meant," I persisted. "Sitting alone worrying about rebels will shoot his blood pressure off the scale. If someone could stay with him for moral support, it would really help."

"We all have our own work and parishes to look after," came the excuse.

"I'm sorry, there is much to do here."

"When he has a full blown stroke, then will you help?" I tried some emotional blackmail of my own.

"Oh dear, oh dear," said Brendan. "We must pray that such a terrible thing does not happen but our own people are after needing our support and prayers at this difficult time."

Well none of them seemed to be too busy today. Only Brendan was actually based at Mokanje - the rest were just up for an afternoon visiting the bar from postings well removed from the rebels.

"Oh I see. My returning to Serabu would solve the problem of course." My sarcasm was completely lost at some point between my slightly slurred words and their self-righteous eardrums.

paused for another slurp of gin and this traitorous act gave the opening for my glass to be refilled and the priests to slide back into their Irish-charmer routine. Before I knew it, I was being led back to my air-conditioned room with its crisply laundered sheets, my head in the clouds, my brain mush and my signature on the dotted line.

31. Queen Without a Throne

The chocolate fairy had come in the night. I was sitting, tucked up in my duvet, tearing open the second bar of creamy Lindt when Anne-Marie appeared with fresh coffee and croissants. "Bon appetite."

"Hmm, Anne-Marie…" I put the chocolate temporarily aside and stuffed in a croissant instead.

"Gail, I must warn you, everybody is talking about Serabu today. There is a little bad feeling that the hospital has closed."

"Have those bloody priests been talking?"

"I don't know, but the staff, they think the evacuation was premature. It is easy to say now we know the rebels did not come." Anne-Marie rubbed my shoulders.

"Not yet. Anyway, it's none of their business. Oh, these croissants are heaven. Are there any more?"

"You are very welcome, but it will be lunch in one hour."

After lunch, I decided to indulge in all the luxury the Mines' Expatriate Compound had on offer and go for a swim. I dug my costume out of my hastily packed rucksack and skipped down the veranda steps. The McGrane's houseboy called after me. "Quick quick, run Dr. Gay. Dem rebels de come."

"Hmmph!" I turned my back on him and marched down to the pool. Seconds later a ten-year-old ambushed me from behind a tree, pointing his finger-rifle.

"Look, dem rebels. Bang bang."

"Ah! You little…" I jumped and was about to practise my Krio expletives, but I held my tongue. My giggling attacker looked just like Nurse. What had happened to the lad and his little sister? But before I could dwell on how Nurse would survive without volunteers to steal eggs from, two expatriate wives drinking coffee on their shady balcony interrupted my thoughts.

"It's the brave Dr. Gail from Serabu Hospital, off to the pool!"

"Don't worry rebels probably can't swim, you'll be safe there."

"Kushe," I replied through gritted teeth and walked a little faster.

No normal person would venture under the sun mid-afternoon, so the pool offered sanctuary from snide remarks. However, within ten minutes my skin was parboiled and I was doubled over from a well-deserved stitch, so I retreated onto my lounger beneath a palm tree. I pulled out Thomas Hardy and tipped into recline. This was the life!

Ten minutes later, I cast the book aside. "Tess you silly cow! Just tell Angel you love him and save us all a lot of trouble." I stretched to gaze at the lush green underbelly of the palm tree. Now what? Here I was, a cowardly intruder in Heaven, my hospital held in limbo and my love interest, uninterested. Hmmph. I was worse than Tess, lying around waiting for fate to squash me – it was time to take positive action. Serabu's fate wasn't really in my hands, but who said Klaus wasn't interested? I had never asked.

"Right then, Dr. Gail, find Klaus and tell him how you feel."

Hmmm. It shouldn't be so difficult, I was now closer to Moyamba than I had been in Serabu, and hadn't Klaus said they often bought supplies from the Mines? There was probably even a direct radio link! The boy had a motorbike, so all I had to do was invite him over.

Perked up by the simple plan, I dived back in the pool and swam an invigorating few lengths. A confident new woman, I was climbing up the steps when Paul appeared from under the palm trees by the empty bar.

"Gin, doc?" offered Paul. "For courage to fight those rebels."

"Not you too!" I spluttered. "This whole damned compound has been haranguing me. It's all very well for you lot, locked behind these walls with security men on the gates."

"I'm sorry. We've only just realised how comforting it was to know that Serabu was there for us if we got sick and now...well, we really want you to stay."

"You could all try being kind to me and my Serabu friends."

"We're not doing very well, are we?" Paul sat on the lounger. "Actually, I came to apologise for pressing you so hard last night. Anne-Marie says I'm an insensitive bastard."

"Well then," I sniffed. "A gin would be very nice."

"Good. Why don't you stay, as our guest only? You probably need a couple of weeks break before making any big decisions."

"Perhaps. Any chance of sending a message to CARE in Moyamba?"

"Moyamba? Why?"

"A friend."

"Ah." Paul smiled. "If we radio him, then you'll stay?"

"Okay," I shrugged. Yes, yes, yes!

So with that, I moved into the ex-Managing Director's house, complete with flower entwined veranda, gold trimmed bathroom and fully stocked pantry and freezer. The CARE worker on radio duty told me Klaus was out in the villages and wasn't expected back for a few days, so I settled down to my new found opulence and waited.

By day, I drank coffee with the wives, swam and played tennis. There was even a squash court. Come on Klaus get in touch. By night, I was plied with gin at the bar. Anne-Marie took me on quietly as an addition to her three children, feeding me meals and chocolate whilst her five-year-old allowed me first lick of the cake-baking spoon and her baby gurgled as happily on my knee as he did on anyone else's. It was luxury. It was bliss. It was boring.

On the sixth night there was a knock at the door. A waif stood, motorcycle helmet in hand, scabs covering his face, forearms legs, and presumably all the other bits hidden by shorts and teeshirt.

"Klaus!" I squealed, throwing my arms around him. "Have you got AIDS or something?"

"Thanks, doc, now I really feel better." He hugged back. "Hiding from the rebels in style, I see."

"Don't you bloody start! You told me to leave."

"Yes, and you didn't pay me the slightest bit of attention," he smiled. "Anyway, I was worried about you. I'm glad you're safe."

"How sweet!" My spine tingled. There it was again. He was worried about me!

"Will you allow a mere mechanic across your hallowed doorstep?"

"Do come in to my humble abode." I bowed and flung open the patio doors. "I'd better feed you some real food."

"Yes please. Hey, not bad." Klaus looked round my palace and threw his arms open to the cool air. "Mmmm. Air conditioning. Goodbye eczema! Oh, before I forget, I'm just back from Freetown. I've got a letter for you."

"Great!"

'Kushe Gail,
I'm so sorry about Serabu, are you okay? It's been chaos here. First the Canadians whisk Louise away, leaving us with only two doctors. The sisters weren't leaving, so Sheilagh and I decided to stay. Then Sheilagh fell in a pothole and broke her arm. She didn't fancy the chicken treatment, so she's gone back to

298

Ireland to have it plated. So that leaves me. There was
supposed to be a new volunteer turning up, but I don't
suppose anybody will be coming now. And then
Segbwema Hospital closed, so I've got all their
patients and, worse still, I've got nowhere to send my
surgical cases. Help! So if you're looking for another
job, come and teach me some surgery. Wouldn't that
be weird, you and me working together after all? Got
to fly, there are still hundreds in Outpatients.

Love Fiona'

Poor Fiona. I'd have to find a way up to Panguma to help out.

",,,and to think all of this is only an hour from Moyamba,"
Klaus was saying.

"What? Only an hour?" My mind started buzzing. Suddenly
Paul McGrane's job offer sounded very attractive indeed. After all,
it was a way of being available to my Scrabu patients, wasn't it?
Perhaps I could even negotiate the use of a vehicle into my contract.
Hell, I would even learn to ride a motorbike. In fact, Klaus could
teach me himself. This was my big chance. I would smother him in
luxury, take him for a swim in the pool, offer him a hot bath, drown
him in gin (or beer, if he insisted), fatten him up with Western fare
and then when he was mellow, I would oh so subtly slide in some
comment about undying love.

Gail, Gail, Gail. What about Fiona? And to think I always
hated those girls who abandon their friends for the sake of a man.

"Not a bad life," sighed Klaus. We were floating on our backs,
side by side in the moonlight. So far, the 'plan' was going really
well.

"Yes. I've adapted rapidly to my refugee status."

"You and our esteemed leader."

"Huh? The Field Director, where's he gone?"

"Home," said Klaus.

"Home home?"

"He's gone on holiday!"

"But we're in the middle of a rebel invasion!" I spluttered.

"Yep, he's back in old smokey watching EastEnders. He dropped into VSO in London, and they were all over him. They thought we'd all been evacuated," Klaus laughed. "Now he's stuck in London coz the Foreign Office won't let him return to Salone until things settle down."

"So how's Nick managing alone?"

"He's thanking the higher powers for Sam."

"I'll bet. Any news on Fatoma?"

"No 'fraid not, but you won't recognise the office."

"Good for Sam."

"Yep, it was obviously crying out for a woman's touch. So what's for dinner, Doc?"

"Well, now. It's a surprise!" I smiled. Now what was the most delicious thing I could rustle up with my pantry full of ingredients? It would have to include cheese, of course, with chocolate for afters......

"Dr. Gay?" Sia, an impressively obese nurse from the clinic, suddenly obscured my view of the stars. I choked on a mouthful of water, flipped onto my front and swam to the side.

"What?"

"We get one patient for you."

No, no! Not tonight! I wasn't bored tonight. "What's wrong with Dr. Momoh?" I spluttered. So much for my big evening. So much for being a guest of the Mines. "Can't Dr. Momoh sort it out?" I repeated when Sia refused to reply. She folded her arms. "Sia?"

"Dr. Momoh say he need surgery."

"And does he?"

"Lamin very sick."

"But you've only got a treatment room at the clinic! I know you're well stocked for drugs and dressings and things, but surely you don't keep any theatre equipment?"

"We get a couch in that treatment room," shrugged Sia "And two theatre packs-self."

"Okay." I hauled myself dripping from the pool. "Okay." I turned sadly to Klaus. "Sorry-oh."

"Oh don't worry about me, I'm quite happy."

I rattled my keys and dropped them down on a lounger. "Look in the fridge and pantry for something to eat."

"No problem." Klaus flipped back onto his back and sculled down the pool. "I'll get dinner on, Doc."

"Thanks," I smiled. Housetrained too! I dried myself off and pulled my dress over my swimsuit. "Let's go then, Sia."

Dr. Momoh had vanished, but he was right about Lamin. He would need surgery and very soon.

Tears were streaming down Lamin's face as I touched the exquisitely tender grapefruit in his groin. It was a strangulated hernia, so called because it throttles loops of bowel until they die and rot, killing the patient shortly thereafter. Strangulated hernias were tricky enough with top surgeons in the best of conditions, but here? And more to the point, without Tiange?

Our theatre for the evening was like any treatment room you might find in a GP's surgery, perfect for dressings, lancing boils and suturing small cuts, but a tad cosy for major abdominal surgery. Sia had sent a security guard from the front gate to find reinforcements and an hour later we had two more nurses, one from Dr. Momoh's clinic and AJ!

"What are you doing here, AJ?"

"My cousin works at the Mines. Person not there in Serabu to buy poyo. I get new job," he grinned. "Mines clinic cleaner!"

The two Mines' nurses hadn't been in an operating theatre since they were students under Sister Hillary, so that left the new clinic cleaner as the most experienced scrub nurse. Urgh!

AJ sorted out the theatre pack and I eyed up the instruments cautiously. "Well I think that's probably all we need." Oh Tiange, where are you? "Right Sia, you're the anaesthetist."

"Dr. Gay I no able!" she protested.

"Who else shall I ask, Sia? Mr. McGrane?"

"Oh but Dr. Gay..."

"Aw fo do, Sia. I'll put the spinal in, you just monitor the patient," I reassured her. "What are you looking out for?"

"Sister Hillary say the blood pressure get for go down. Maybe by too much because Lamin don dehydrate already. I go give plenty of fluid in the drip and check his blood pressure every five minutes. He awake so I get for talk to him."

"Perfect," I congratulated her. Gosh, Serabu had a bloody good nursing school. It would be criminal to lose it. "Okay, let's do it."

I put the spinal in then scrubbed with some proper surgical scrubbing fluid under real running water and pulled on crisp new rubber gloves fresh from the packet. Unfortunately they were size eights. They may have fitted Dr. Momoh, but on me they flapped around like outsize Marigolds.

At least Lamin was thin and the hernia loosened a little as his muscles relaxed under the spinal anaesthetic. Being careful not to nick the excess glove, I made my incision and cut the ring of tissue that was starving the herniated bowel of oxygen.

So here it was. My second ever bowel resection and anastomosis, but this time it wasn't Mr. Bewes's sheep's intestines, it was the real thing. Breathing deeply, I took a clamp from AJ.

"We've done it, Dr. Gay," AJ exclaimed half an hour later. "Better than Sister Hillary-self!"

Wow. The best thing anyone had ever said to me. Look, look, Mr. Bewes, the dead bowel has been removed and I have rejoined the ends with a fully patent anatomosis. No leaks!

"I couldn't have done it without you AJ," I said. Well I couldn't.

"You na fine surgeon, Dr. Gay!" The first year student slapped me on the back.

"AJ!" I chastised. "Sterility! We've still got to close."

"Sorry-oh Dr. Gay," giggled AJ. "I don forget. I go change my gloves."

"Fortunately there's no shortage here, but why such huge ones, Sia?"

"It's Dr. Momoh's size."

"So what do you wear for dressings or delivering babies?"

"The same gloves."

"Size eights?" The babies are lucky not to be suffocated. "Does Dr. Momoh ever take blood, or suture wounds, or lance boils?"

"We do all that."

"Does Dr. Momoh ever actually need gloves?"

"He's the doctor."

Rather than asking Sia if that was a yes or a no, I bit my lip and got on with repairing the hernia, leaving the bowel safely back in the abdominal cavity.

"Don don. Thank you team!"

It was nearly midnight when I left the tiny operating theatre. Lamin had to get through the next few days, but the early signs were good. Elated, I hurried back to my luxury quarters. What with another life saved and the miraculous appearance of Klaus, there was no way anyone could persuade me to go back to boring old Britain now.

32. Emergency Operation - Please Bring Welding Equipment

Cheesy tomatoey smells greeted me as I opened the back door. Hmmm, Klaus, what for chop tonight? Gentle snoring came from the spare bedroom, so I peeked in, just enough to glimpse a foot sticking out from the duvet. I refrained from tickling his toes as it had, I supposed, long gone midnight. But his lasagne was excellent, if a little crunchy round the edges. My big confession would have to wait until breakfast.

And so it was that my undying love was garbled out over a bowl of cornflakes.

"You'll get over it," was all Klaus had to say about that. "Wow, I can't believe I'm eating real Cornflakes!"

"Oh, okay," I said and slurped my coffee loudly.

"Oh Gail. Look at you."

"Hoi, what do you mean?" I glared at him. "I get body?"

"Yes, lucky you. I wish I got body. My insides have vanished down the latrine and I'm shedding my outsides like a snake. There's nothing left of my body."

"You think I'm fat," I sulked.

"Nah. Voluptous."

"Oh yeah? What's your problem, then? Scared of big strong girls?"

"Too right!" Klaus laughed. "And you're the biggest and strongest of the lot."

"Hmmph!"

"How could I cope with you? You're always so decisive, so cheerful and so bloody healthy!"

"What?" Was he off his head? Rejected because I was cheerful and decisive?

"Aw fo do."

Aw fo do? Bloody hell! Aw fo do! So that was that. My grand passion. Fortunately there was still a bar of chocolate left in the fridge. I had been saving it for Klaus, but munched it down on the way to see Lamin.

Lamin wasn't great either. His temperature was up, his pulse rapid and his breathing shallow. Not too surprising really, after rotten bowel had festered inside him for days. I knew strangulated hernias had a huge mortality rate, even when real surgeons operated on them with the help of real anaesthetists and scrub nurses in real hospitals, but I wanted a miracle to cheer me up. "Cheer you up Gail," said the little voice on my shoulder. "What about Lamin? He's the one in trouble here. Do you only ever think of yourself?"

Yes.

Klaus had left a little note when I returned:

'Kushe, Mad Doc,
Sorry, had to get back to work, but how about that trip up to see Fiona? We could have that game of squash and go up first thing Saturday.
Love
Klaus
Xxxxx'

"Hmmph, don't bother with the kisses, mate," I thought, scrunching the paper. Now if our roles had been reversed, I was sure Fiona would have come flying up to help me, at least until there was firm news on her own hospital. The VSO Field Office would have a fit, as Panguma was still in forbidden territory, but Fiona would follow her conscience. But that was Fiona. Unfortunately Klaus had been right about me that very first week in Sierra Leone – I was not Heroic Doctor material.

I knew what I was. I was jealous of Fiona for soldiering on

through adversity whilst we had so blatantly abandoned ship, I was scared of the rebels and I was scared of all that hard work. Besides, where would I put my hands on a six-hour journey on the back of Klaus' motorbike? I'd have to cling on to him else I'd fall off. No. I was humiliated enough already. I would stay here at the Mines, where there wasn't too much work and plenty of food, drink and chocolate. How many deadly sins did that make? Pride, cowardice, greed, lust... Oh, who cared? I would radio CARE to tell Klaus not to bother.

"Sorry Fiona."

Deciding I might as well compound my misery with alcohol, I went down to the bar. It was scarcely eleven, but what the hell.

Father Brendan was already there, drinking Star Beer.

"Hello, Brendan, you're indulging early," I sniped. At least I was not expected to be virtuous. I ordered a lemonade in a loud voice, just for spite. I would have that gin and tonic later.

"Hello, Gail. I'm after getting some bad news," he said. I wasn't sure I wanted to hear his bad news.

"Oh?" I asked.

"Gregory says Serabu's closing for good. It's official."

"Oh," I repeated. "Oh."

"I'm sorry."

"So that's that, is it?" I asked bleakly.

"I'm afraid so. Pete is going home next week."

"Really?"

"Yes. We decided he had better start his sabbatical a few weeks early and see his doctor back home. Pete is no use to anyone if he dies of a stroke."

"Well I'm delighted that you've all changed your tune, but I'm surprised he agreed."

"Gregory wasn't after giving him a choice. Besides there's hardly anyone left in Serabu now." Brendan paused for a mouthful of beer. "Pete's coming back in September, so he is. The church will not close."

"Hmmph." I was pleased that Pete would return, for the sake of the people of Serabu, but heathen that I was, I resented that the church would get funding at the expense of my hospital. "What about the others?"

"They took poor Ignatius back to Ireland, Tom and Fran will have been sent back to the States, and Bernadette's been redeployed to Freetown."

"But Paul sent some men out to Sumbuya yesterday," I protested. "All clear on the south-eastern front, they said."

"So I hear," agreed Brendan. "But 'tis all about money, Gail. Catholic mission funding policy isn't about free handouts any more. They feel the Saloneans have been passively accepting aid for too long now."

"But that's not true!" I howled. "Our staff are terrific. Admittedly our patients can't always pay their bills, but they just don't have the money. It's not their fault that their economy is in freefall."

"Jaysus, Gail, it's not my decision!" Brendan threw his hands up. "But you must admit Serabu's been on a downward slope ever since Hillary left."

"No it hasn't! Our attendances have gone up by nearly half!"

"For a few months perhaps. But now you're closed," he added brutally.

"That's not fair. We were told to close!"

"Life's not fair." Brendan took a slug of his beer. "Sierra Leone must be after teaching you that?" He was right. Life was bloody unfair.

"Make that a gin and tonic please," I told the barman.

So here I was, Dr. Gail Haddock, chocoholic, sort-of-surgeon, with no man and no hospital. And I couldn't even call myself a big strong girl any more. Big strong girls would always help friends in need. Big strong girls weren't wimps.

So after several gin and tonics with Brendan, I returned to my three-bedroomed house and packed my things. I'd scrounge a lift to Freetown in the morning and get Nick to put me on the first flight home.

"Gail?" Anne-Marie called from the patio doors. "You are there?"

"In here Anne-Marie."

"Brendan told me about Serabu. I am very sorry." Anne-Marie paused and looked at my things spread out on the bed. "Eh bien. You are leaving?"

"I'm sorry, " I sobbed. Anne-Marie rocked me in her arms.

"Do not be sorry. You have tried very hard for your hospital." She was assuming all my tears were for Serabu, when in reality they were for myself. I considered telling this kind woman about my thwarted love life, but it seemed all too pathetic in comparison to the end of Salone's best hospital, the region's lifeline for thirty years.

"You and Paul have been so good to me, it's just that....."

"Shhh. Shhh," Anne-Marie interrupted. "I will tell Paul that you are going, then we will say no more about it."

"Thank you. Sorry," I sniffed. Better they thought me a principled doctor, mourning her hospital than a frustrated spinster sulking because she could not attract her man.

"You will come for a big dinner tonight, yes?"

"Yes." I blew my nose.

Food could be relied upon to soothe most of my ills and Anne-Marie's dinner gave sufficient fortification for me to assess Lamin's post-operative progress before bed. I crept into the clinic with the same dread that a borderline student opens exam results…. and left skipping with joy.

A+! Lamin had farted. Yes! Yes! Yes!

I could go home now, content in the knowledge that although I hadn't saved Serabu Hospital, I had saved lives. And those other goals? Well, any weight lost under Pa George had been replaced by Anne-Marie, and you know about my love life. As for my soul, well it was still up for grabs. I was still the same single, selfish, only child with no real commitments or beliefs, but at least I had seen some of the best of what human nature had to offer. Meanwhile I was going to have a damned good night's sleep, free from worries or responsibilities.

My plans for a long lie in were interrupted by a seven o'clock knock at the door.

"Coming," I called, wrapping a lappa round me.

"Kushe, Pa. What's the problem?" I yawned.

"I get radio message for you." The Mines' watchman handed me a piece of paper. For all the Mines' financial resources, the paper still looked like it had been torn from a school jotter:

Laygby has started pains. We get emergency operation but the theatre is sealed with arc weld. Please bring welding machine and small generator for electric purpose.

Moses.

"Oh God! Laygby!" In my self-absorption, I had completely forgotten about Laygby. How could I? It could be fatal if she laboured for even a short time.

310

"I'm coming."

Pulling on my clothes, I dashed up to the main Mines' compound and barged into the radio room. Men arriving for their day's duty looked at me in amazement. Alhaji, Moses' cousin, sat headphoned on his barstool by the radio.

"Kushe, Dr. Gay." He swung round to greet me.

"Alhaji, kushe. Can I speak to Serabu."

"No problem." Alhaji twiddled a few knobs and shouted into the mike. I danced from foot to foot. Oh why oh why, had I forgotten Laygby? Serabu was all welded up. Who knew how long it would take to break in? And were there any staff there to help me? Perhaps Moses could bring her to the clinic in the Landrover and I could do the Caesarean in the treatment room. But there had hardly been room for three of us with a very thin Lamin, never mind for a baby too and an extra nurse to look after it. Still, we'd just have to manage.

"Sorry-oh, Dr. Gay. I no get any reply," said Alhaji after ten minutes of cruising the airwaves. "That message this morning was too much faint. Moses say diesel don don and they no able charge the radio."

"Damn." That meant no diesel for the Landrover to bring Laygby either. I'd have to take that welder to Serabu. At least I was in the right place. Mining Companies had all that sort of stuff, didn't they?

"Um, excuse me. Can you help?" I asked the first chap I met. "I need some welding equipment to do an emergency operation at Serabu."

"You no get scalpel Dr. Gay," he laughed. "See Mr. Kallon."

"Excuse me, Mr. Kallon. Do you have welding equipment? I need to do an operation?"

"You get for talk to Mr. Conteh."

"Mr. Conteh, I need the welding equipment to do an operation at Serabu. Can you help?"

Finally Paul McGrane appeared. "What's all the commotion, Gail?"

"I need someone to unweld theatre so I can do an emergency Caesarean on one of our Nurses."

"I don't believe you," guffawed Paul, then saw my face. "Okay, let's go to Serabu."

The goats had seized the initiative from the rebels and were occupying the hospital grounds. They lay contented in the shade of the empty wards, undisturbed by our truck's engine as we pulled up outside Outpatients. It was so quiet. No voices raised to argue over bills, nor babies crying as Latif pricked their fingers to check for malaria, nor was Nurse Sankoh trying to sell oranges and groundnuts to those waiting patiently in snaking queues. There was just the gentle snoring of the two Mines' security men, stretched out on the long wooden benches that were usually filled with patients.

"Kushe, gentlemen," said Paul. "I can see who we have to thank for keeping Serabu free from rebels."

"No rebels, Mr. Paul." Mr. Yambasu, the first, sprang up with a military salute. The second smiled sweetly, buttoning up his trousers over his paunch and squeezing his belt into its very last notch.

"I am most relieved," Paul replied.

"Dr. Gay, you don come!" Betty came flying out of nowhere and hugged me over and over, laughing and crying. "You are here, you are here! We thought you don go home!"

"Betty what a welcome!" I gasped, all the air hugged out of me. "How's Hindolu?"

"He is very fine. He can walk!"

"Great! And Laygby?" I asked anxiously.

"She is labouring too much. We have prepared her for theatre. Tiange is with her."

"Tiange is still here?"

"She came back yesterday."

"Any others to help us?"

"Peter never left. He don arrange shifts to guard the hospital and the village."

"Our very own vigilante!" I clapped. "So with you and Peter and Tiange, we're in business. Is the generator working?"

"Diesel, don don," apologised Betty.

"Aw fo do, " I sighed. "At least it's daylight. Let's go."

"Oh Dr. Gay, I gladdi for see you," gasped Laygby. The ward was empty but for her - it was weirder than a single passenger on a poda-poda.

"Kushe, how di body, Laygby?" I took my friend's hand.

"I tell God tenki," she smiled weakly in reply. "Tenki-ya, Dr. Gay. Plenti tenki." I squeezed her hand, embarrassed to receive such gratitude from one I had abandoned. Her contractions were very strong now, and her weakened womb wall would not hold for much longer.

"Kushe Dr. Gay," beamed Tiange. "We are ready. Mr. Yambusa get for open dem theatre doors just now."

A small crowd of the remaining staff and their families had gathered outside theatre to watch the grand opening. Mr. Yambusa sizzled his way down the doors and flung them open. He strode into the theatre like John Wayne into a saloon bar. Peter and Patrick Kpukoma carried Laygby, the star of the show, in on the stretcher behind him.

With Laygby installed centre stage, Peter slipped in an effortless spinal whilst we scrubbed to start the performance.

The theatre cast was triple the usual quorum for an operation. Everyone who had remained or returned to Serabu, men and women alike, were in on the act. It was all Betty could do to keep the dusty, oil-streaked Mr. Yambusa out of Theatre.

We celebrated our reunion with the best show in the business in the best theatre in the country. I pulled a fine new man into the world and handed all nine pounds of him to a delighted Laygby. His furious cry was only matched in volume by the cheers of the audience.

"Serabush is back!" proclaimed Tiange triumphantly.

How could I tell her that Serabu's death warrant had already been signed?

I turned my attention to tying off Laygby's fallopian tubes and started to pummel the staff with questions. I wanted to avoid having to tell them the grim news about their hospital.

"What happened to that bobo, Nurse?"

"Nurse and Maternity live with us, Dr. Gay," said Patrick. "Ma Kpukoma missed Geraldine and Matthieu too much."

"You are very kind, Patrick."

"Notto so Dr. Gay. Maternity is a beautiful girl and Nurse is a fine worker. My wife teaches him to die gara cloth. We were blessed with only one daughter and no son. Now we get three pickins."

"I'm so pleased," I smiled. Trust Nurse to land on his feet. God helps those who help themselves.

"So no rebels?"

"Two rounds of gunfire no more," said Peter.

"Gunfire? How awful!" I exclaimed, taking a length of suture from Tiange to sew up the first layer of Laygby's abdominal wall.

"No problem, Dr. Gay," explained Tiange. "Only the soldiers who try shoot a pig."

"I didn't know you had wild boar round here?"

"No no, Dr. Gay. One of Patrick's pigs."

"Are you telling me it took four soldiers two rounds of ammunition to kill an ordinary domestic pig?"

"They don miss!" laughed Peter. "Too much poyo."

"No wonder you set up your own vigilantes, Peter. But how about the hospital? Did any patients come?"

"A few," said Betty. "Patrick and I don treat some outpatients".

And the Catholic mission said there wasn't enough commitment from the local people? Why wasn't there someone here today, to see with their own eyes our staff's commitment and motivation? But our funders were in a land far away, trying to do their best with only so much money to distribute. MT had been right all along, Serabu's only way forward was self-sufficiency, charging reasonable fees and scrimping and saving. We couldn't stake our future on crumbs from the Western World's table, as there were other hospitals and schools and missions in other countries, all with their own stories to tell, all competing for those crumbs and their own survival.

Well, our staff had proved they would fight for survival, so I would fight too.

I was their Medical Superintendant, and I was going to set myself just one goal: Get my hospital back! Oh and the little matter of the unresolved squash match.

33. The Return Of The Prodigal Daughter

Friday evening: Mokanje squash courts

I beat him, I beat him, I beat him! HA!

I must say Klaus was very sporting about it and I, well I hardly gloated at all! We shared a companionable beer at the bar, then a hot chocolate at my place, then went to our respective beds. I fell asleep contented. The Medical Superintendent of Serabu Hospital did not need a mere man. She had friends to visit and hospitals to open.

After six nerve-racking hours surfing Salonean potholes on Klaus' refurbished Honda, we finally arrived at Panguma Hospital. Where Serabu was the heavy rough that, at the best of times, could only be kept under control by a scythe, Panguma was all fairways and greens. But the bustle of patients and nurses running back and forth was reassuringly familiar.

Naturally Fiona was out saving lives. So we knocked on the convent door instead. A nun greeted us.

"Hello, I'm a friend of Fiona's, Gail Had..."

"It's Dr. Gail!" she squealed and five more sisters suddenly appeared at her shoulder.

"Dr. Gail! Oh sweet Jesus, our prayers are answered."

"Thank the Lord."

"He is smiling on Panguma Hospital today."

"Thank the Lord."

"A new doctor," the last said, crossing herself.

"Isn't it nice to be wanted?" whispered Klaus behind me. Telling him to fok-off didn't seem appropriate to the company, so I just smiled graciously.

In the morning, the sisters had Klaus repairing their Landrover whilst Fiona took me on her rounds. She floated from overcrowded ward to overcrowded ward and patient to patient with the same sweet smile that put every frightened child and old man at ease. It was gratifying to see a doctor in action, running a hospital in full working order, assisted by smartly uniformed nurses. The only drawback was the queues and queues of patients waiting to be seen.

"Good heavens, Harrods sale and Wimbledon finals eat your hearts out. Is it always like this?" I asked when I had finally persuaded her to stop for a coffee and a banana.

"Panguma has a bigger catchment area than Serabu, so we're never short of outpatients. But it's been worse since the rebels closed Segbwema."

"Gosh, poor you." The sight of all that work piling up was giving me palpitations. Only two patients, Lamin and Laygby, had interrupted my life of luxury in the past ten days. "What about Segbwema's doctors? Can't you nab them?"

"Their last doctor's in Freetown trying to get Segbwema reopened for refugees."

"Well then, Fiona, it looks like we might end up working together after all."

"Funny how things turn out," she laughed. "But you'll get Serabu back. The rebels have gone and our sisters won't stop talking about your break-in with the welder."

"How do they know about that?"

"Catholic mission radio."

"Oh yes. Moses radioed Bernadette, to reassure her about Laygby."

"Well he obviously didn't spare the details. Quite a PR coup."

"Possibly. Officially Serabu is don don, but I've written to Sister Hillary to ask for a reprieve. Have you heard of Hillary?"

"Who hasn't? But will she have the power? The sisters are so beholden to their superiors."

"I don't know. From what I've heard, if Hillary wants it, it happens. Trouble is Jean says Hillary secretly believes Serabu's become a white elephant. It's pretty inaccessible since all the roads and railways have crumbled. But how will you cope with all this work if on the offchance I did succeed? You can't go on at this rate."

"I've got a terrific staff. Our nurses are all Serabu trained, you'll be pleased to know."

"Really? We're the best you know." I fluffed up my feathers

"Meanwhile we've got TB ward to see." Fiona stood up purposefully.

"Kushe, kushe, Dr. Gay. How de body?"

"Good Lord, it's Pa Ndanema! And Bockerie! What are you two rogues doing here?"

"We've come to finish our treatment. Dr Fiona tells us only one more week to go."

"How did you get here?"

"We de walka," Pa Ndanema shrugged.

"You walked! A hundred and fifty miles! On one leg!"

"No other hospital is open."

"No. Probably not. Are you behaving yourselves?"

"Oh Dr. Gay, we have been very good. Notto so Dr. Fiona?"

"Very good," she agreed.

"We get charity feeding," boasted Bockerie.

"All the TB patients get charity feeding," explained Fiona.

"I rest my case. No wonder you don't have any problems with them."

Panguma was beginning to sound like a good place to work. Fiona vanished again that evening.

"Let me help," I offered. I didn't really want to be left with

Klaus all evening and her workload was making me feel guilty.

"Don't worry, I'll put you to it tomorrow. There's a couple of beers in the fridge."

"Really, cold beers?" exclaimed Klaus.

"Twenty four hour electricity here you know," boasted Fiona. Panguma was looking better by the minute. "Well, be good you two."

I gaped at her. Had I hinted anything to her in my letters about Klaus? I didn't think so, but she was pretty perceptive. "Meaning?"

Klaus was sniggering. I kicked the bastard under the table.

"Well, you know. You'd make a good couple," she said cheerfully.

"He won't have me," I snapped.

"Why ever not?" joked Fiona. "Look, I really better go. We go see back."

A timely knock at the door rescued me from prolonged embarrassment. "Dr. Gay?"

"What?" I opened Fiona's door.

"Dr. Fiona say you get for do Caesarean," puffed the nurse.

"Sorry Gail, but I've never done a Section," said Fiona as we stood in Panguma's little used theatre.

"Okay, let's go. I've got quite good at them now."

"I thought so. I'm going to have to start aren't I, with no Segwema?"

"God, Fiona, if I can do it, you'll have no trouble. Come on."

I assisted Fiona while she completed the first Caesarean Section at Panguma Hospital for five years.

"Who needs Segbwema?" I said while Fiona jiggled baby Dr-Fiona back on the ward.

"Me! I couldn't have done it without you," she retorted, but there was a note of triumph in her voice. As anticipated, she was a natural.

Next day Fiona did her rounds, I made a start at Outpatients and Klaus serviced the generator. We all met back at Fiona's for lunch.

"Guess what?" Fiona burst in the room as Klaus and I tucked in to our platefuls of plassas.

"What?" we chorused

"There's a new doctor arriving tomorrow!"

"Really?" I exclaimed.

"That's great!" said Klaus.

"Yes, isn't it. He sent a message last month, but it never arrived."

"Panguma's grass might be better than Serabush, but your communication's are the same!" I said. "So you won't want me anymore?"

"You're joking, there's plenty of work for all of us."

Dr. Eelco Krijn arrived the next day, a thirty-five year-old tousle-headed Dutchman fired with schoolboy enthusiasm. He was Jean reincarnated, before the flesh had fallen off his bones and MT's purse strings had strangled his grand ideas. But food was more plentiful in Panguma and its funding more generous than Serabu's. Even the broken legged chickens were fatter. Eelco would do well.

That evening we helped him unpack caseloads of medical and surgical books, various bits of equipment, syringes, needles and rubber gloves, plus seeds for carrots, onions and flowers and a teddy bear.

"For Zita." Elco straightened the lapels on the bear's stripy waistcoat. "Karin's bringing her next month. Look, here they are."

He pulled out a photo frame, and sat his beautiful smiling wife and dimple-cheeked toddler with her dad's curly hair and endearing grin, in the middle of the dining room table.

"Wow! You're one lucky guy, mate," sighed Klaus.

"I know," blushed Eelco.

"Isn't she just adorable," enthused Fiona, with a hitherto undisplayed surge of maternalism. Hells bells, that gorgeous little girl even made me feel broody.

"Ah, but I have forgotten something." He pulled a letter from the side pocket of his rucksack. "Somebody left this for you at the VSO office."

The letter was from Bernadette, asking me to return to Freetown to discuss their decision on Serabu. I frowned.

"Bad news?" asked Klaus.

"I don't know." I showed him the letter.

"Well you'd better get down there ASAP. I'll take you on the Honda tomorrow."

"All the way to Freetown?" I exclaimed. "Would you really, Klaus?"

"Anything for you, Mad Doc. The sooner you get down there, the sooner you can get that hospital up and running again."

"Yes. I know you can do it Gail," beamed Elco. For a moment, I almost believed them.

"Here we are madam, the Freetown convent," announced my pal Klaus.

"Aren't you coming in?" I asked once I'd freed my head from its overheated goldfish bowl.

"Nah. Better get back to CARE to do some work, I suppose."

"Sweet Jesus, it's Gail already!" Bernadette burst through the convent's mesh door to greet me.

"We heard all about the welding equipment; oh, you're a mighty woman!"

"It's lovely to see you." I hugged her.

"So how's Laygby? And the baby? A little boy wasn't it?"

"Yes. A grand fellow." I smiled at the precious memory. "They're both just fine."

"I'm being very rude now. Enough questions. Come inside and sit down." Bernadette took my hand. "And your young man?" She held out her other hand to Klaus whilst I cringed at her terminology. Klaus was unperturbed.

"Thanks sister, but Preston's expecting me at CARE," he smiled and put his helmet back on. "See you, Gail."

"We go see back," I called as he kicked his motorbike back into action. "Thanks Klaus."

Three revs of his engine and he was gone.

"What a nice young man. Tea?" Bernadette lifted a teapot on the tray that sat in permanent readiness for visitors. "I think it's still hot."

"Thank you." I flopped into the flowery patterned armchair in the airy sitting room and lifted the gold-rimmed china teacup off its saucer. "Well? Father Brendan said Serabu is closed." I came straight to the point.

"Oh, these are terrible times." Bernadette averted her eyes and toyed with her plain white cup.

"Well? Is it true?" I pressed.

"My superiors rely on funding from the Catholic Mission you know." She looked up at me. "Yes, yes. It's true, Gail. They've been threatening us with closure for years."

"And the rebels gave them the perfect excuse. Was that why we were told to close the hospital?"

"Oh no! Oh, please believe me that was genuine concern over the safety of staff and patients." Bernadette looked horrified.

"It's just....I mean....oh, I really don't know."

"Bernadette, I'm sorry. I didn't mean it." I touched her arm. "But do the superiors know how marvellous the staff have been? What with Peter's vigilantes protecting the hospital, Betty and Patrick treating Outpatients and all those who came to help save Laygby. We deserve another chance."

"We do, we do," agreed Bernadette. "I wrote to Hillary when we closed, pleading for a reprieve. She's back in Ireland you know."

"Yes, so Brendan said. So even Sister Hillary couldn't persuade the superiors?"

"Hillary feels she cannot argue too strongly for Serabu."

"Whyever not?"

"She says it would lack humility to argue too forcefully for her own hospital."

"Lack humility! Good God, what constraints you nuns have to work with," I exclaimed. "Whoops. Sorry. But if Hillary isn't even on our side..."

"Of course she's on our side, but she feels that if Serabu is to have any future, we must be able to fight our own battles. She's going to be too busy with all the refugees in Bo to come back and be our doctor."

"Don't I count as a doctor!" I protested.

"Of course, but Hillary assumed you had gone home with all the others. She did suggest that Serabu could open its doors for refugees in the short term until we build up our numbers again."

"But refugees won't make us any money."

"My dear Gail, you're beginning to sound like Ignatius."

"I'm sorry, but I thought that money was the problem."

"Yes indeed," agreed Bernadette. "But the Catholic Mission has special funds for refugees. It's a cause people will donate to."

"Ah. The politics of charity," I sighed. "Still, you're right. We might as well play whatever game we can win."

"You are learning," Bernadette smiled wryly. "But if we can tell them we have a doctor who is willing to stay after all...."

"Of course."

"Good. Meanwhile I have asked a mighty fellow to fight in our corner. He is flying out to Ireland tomorrow to turn all his charms on for the superiors."

"Oh yes?"

"He's coming to visit us very soon with another grand fellow," Bernadette announced. "They are both dying to see you."

With that we could hear tyres, brakes, slammed doors and laughter outside. The door burst open.

"Well now, would I be hearing the musical voice of our very own Dr. Gail?"

"Alan!" I was too busy throwing my arms round the old rogue to notice a thin pale figure hobble in on crutches behind him.

"Hey girl, where's the hugs for me?"

"Fran! What happened? You look awful. Did the rebels get you?"

"Gee thanks."

"Brendan said you'd gone home."

"Who's Brendan?" asked Fran. "Are you trying to get rid of me?"

"No. It's great to see you." I hugged him again. "But you look like you need to be tucked up in bed at home convalescing with that beautiful wife of yours. Seriously, what happened?"

"Nothing as exciting as you and your rebels, I'm afraid," moaned Fran. "A sting ray."

"A sting ray?" I repeated.

"You know, one of those big fish with wings and teeth," Alan prompted helpfully.

"Yes and believe me, this boy had my name written all over it." He pointed to a two centimetre diameter hole punched in his foot, with a sinister red line of infection tracking up his leg.

"Fran, that looks a mess!"

"Hey, it's heaps better. I stood on the sonofabitch the first day that we were down at the Venue having farewell drinks with Jean and Francoise."

"Ouch!" I sympathised.

" Still, what about you? We didn't hear about Sumbuya until I went to report in to the American Embassy. Naturally they slapped an immediate ban on leaving Freetown."

"Fran, if you hobbled in on crutches looking the way you do now you're lucky they didn't slap you on the first plane home."

"Well, we couldn't abandon you in your hour of need." Fran looked sheepish. "Jean felt real bad that he left you when he did."

"But he had a family to think of, for heavens sake..."

"That's what I said, but then our embassy was real pissed with Tom for working in a banned area with no permit, so they threw him out. The guys made me promise to hang around to check you were okay."

"Your knight on shining crutches," Alan winked.

"Oh poor Fran. Trapped in Freetown. And what about you Alan? I hear you're going back to Ireland to have a word with the powers that be."

"Tomorrow. I'll be back though. I thought a personal account of Serabush would help: its rising attendances, the lives saved, the increasing staff morale, and the heroic young lady doctor..." Alan sighed melodramatically.

"Alan!" I punched him in the arm.

"Worth a try," he shrugged.

"And I promise to come back with Sharon if we get the go ahead from Ireland," said Fran. "I'd hate to miss any more excitement."

"....so apart from the soldiers manfully trying to shoot a twenty stone pig it's all peace and quiet," I concluded my tales to a very harassed looking Nick at the Venue, who had just arrived from a late finish at the field office. "And so we're trying to get the hospital reopened."

"Serabu may well be a haven of peace and tranquillity but you're not allowed back," Nick said, thrusting his forefinger into my chest wall.

"What's up? Where's our cool, carefree Nick?"

"Aaagh." Nick put his head briefly in his hands then looked up, flicking back his designer fringe. "With the Field Director in Britain, thank God I've still got Sam."

"How is she?" I interrupted, eager for news, "Any word from Fatoma?"

"No, not yet."

"Poor Sam." I shook my head.

"I ought to send you home," said Nick irritably. "You would be one less person for me to worry about."

"I don't want to go home!"

"Sister Bernadette told me you were hiding from us at Mokanje. I even heard a rumour that you and Klaus had eloped to Panguma. Is that true?"

"Shouldn't listen to rumour, Nick."

"Pah! Panguma is more dangerous than Serabu." Nick gave a gallic shrug. "And Klaus? I thought he at least was sensible."

"Mokanje isn't off limits though, is it? Even the wives and children are still there."

"You are thinking of defecting from VSO to work for the Mines?" Nick looked up from his beer. Working for the evil Mines did not fit into Nick's code of ethics at all.

"Then I'll go back to Serabu."

"This is the blackmail! And if it's thumbs down for Serabu?"

"Then I'll work at Panguma, but Alan won't let them close

Serabu."

"Jaysus! Don't be putting any pressure on now," Alan complained, sounding unsure of himself for the first time since I had met him.

Bernadette put Alan on the plane next day, and Fran on the plane four days later. I spent the next six days waiting: mornings at the Crown Cafe and afternoons at the Venue. On the seventh day, a Saturday morning, I wandered into the Crown. There was Lindsey, in her Saturday morning seat, sitting with an older lady.

"Dr. Gail. Over here!" the lady called. Lindsey was smiling.

"Er, hi. Hi Lindsey," my eyes begged an introduction to her mystery companion.

"This is your greatest fan, Gail."

"Oh?" I smiled tentatively. My biggest fan? Surely Lindsey's granny hadn't come over on holiday in the middle of a rebel invasion. I looked at the petite lady dressed in gara that Alan would have killed for.

"Hello, pleased to meet you, Mrs. er..."

"The mighty Dr. Gail. We meet at last. I'm Hillary."

"Sorry?" Lindsey's granny wasn't called Hillary, was she? No. Good Lord it was her! "Sister Hillary?"

"Hillary, please."

"The Sister Hillary. The great Sister Hillary?"

"Jaysus, will you sit down. What will you have? Coffee?" I nodded dumbly at the iron angel. "So, have you heard the news?" she asked. I shook my head. "Serabu is to reopen."

My eyes widened.

"Partly thanks to you running around with welding equipment. Alan told us the story, with great flourish altogether. He had tears running down our faces."

"Did he sing too?" I found my voice.

"Of course. But everything depends on you. Bernadette has

328

to stay in Freetown for at least six weeks. She'll need to clear some red tape and run our convent here, so you must be willing to go back on your own. Well?"

"What? Yes. Yes of course. Can't you come?"

"I'm afraid not. We have many refugees of our own in Bo."

"Of course," I nodded.

"Serabu has a year's grace for refugee, then we'll review it."

"Okay."

"I am really glad to finally meet you, Gail. You're a mighty girl."

"You're very sweet Sister Hil..."

"Just Hillary. I'm quite jealous of you, you know. For twenty five years I ran that hospital. Every patient that walked through the door I assessed and treated. Then I would go back to that dreadful big convent with only Ignatius for company," she flashed me a knowing smile. "It was very lonely. I was separate, you see, from real life. I was not human, I was.... I was...."

"The legendary Sister Hillary!" I added.

"Hmmm. You, Gail... you... however..."

"I am full of human weakness," I suggested.

"No, no. Well, yes, of course you are, like the rest of us, but you play football with the villagers! I couldn't do that!"

"I only touched the ball four times!"

"But you were on the field with everyone. Don't you see? Serabu has no future unless the people run it themselves. There are so few sisters left these days, and even if there were, a hierarchy is no way to run a hospital in someone else's country. You volunteers can facilitate the hand-over. Why can't Tiange do the Caesareans and Betty and Patrick run Outpatients? You see what I'm saying? I did it all wrong."

"Oh, no!" I protested.

"Yes. I was a ...a graven image." Hillary gave a wry smile.

"But, now I think Serabu really can have a future. The Saloneans have proved it to themselves."

"Let's drink to Serabu Hospital." Lindsey stood up.

"To Serabush!" Hillary lifted her coffee cup. "Pity this isn't something a bit stronger."

"Aw fo du," I giggled at my heroine, who was getting marvellously less angelic by the minute. "Serabush!"

The rains were due again. The storm clouds hovered in ambush above the streets of Freetown. The sauna's thermostat was jammed and the doors were locked. Hillary, Bernadette and I drew up contingency plans A to Z to put before the VSO Field Director, then headed out to confront him on Monday morning.

The Field Director sat back at his desk under his broken fan, with sweat patches creeping out from under his arms. He wasn't a bad man really. We knew he had a heart of gold where the Saloneans were concerned, but when it came to we volunteers, he was just in the wrong job. The heavy atmosphere dampened the little energy he had ever possessed, leaving him uninterested in battle. He shrugged agreement to our every detail. We didn't even need to mention his little holiday to force his hand.

That evening, I tried to radio Serabu from Santano House, but the battery must have been on the blink again, so the best I could do was inform Alhaji at Mokanje. He promised to send news of my triumphant return with the changeover of security guards. Three days later I met a kindly Mines' engineer at the Venue (not uncoincidentally – we VSOs could all spot a potential lift from a hundred paces) who offered to take me back to Mokanje.

"See ya, Gail." Lindsey hugged me before I got my lift. "Perhaps Klaus will bring me up for a visit next month."

"Klaus would take you anywhere you wanted, Lindsey."

"Meaning?" Lindsey put her hands on her hips.

"Nothing. It'd be great to see you. I'll need all the company I can get."

"Are you sure you'll be alright?" said Bernadette. "A young girl like you alone, even without rebels?"

"No problem. Peter and his vigilantes will look after me."

"I'm sure they will, but there are so few staff left..."

"I'll be fine and you said Fran was determined to return soon."

"But he has a wife...."

"Don't worry sister, Klaus will keep an eye on her," smiled Lindsey. I shot her a glance. But something told me she was right. He probably would.

Moses had left the hospital truck in the McGrane's drive, polished out of all recognition and with a tank full of Mines' diesel. Since I was to be the only expatriate in Serabu, Bernadette said I should have my own transport. For emergencies. After nine months of scrounged lifts and poda-podas, I was as excited as I had been on being given my first bicycle by my parents. Anne-Marie fed me a big breakfast and then produced the keys. Just wait till I told Klaus.

Unfortunately I was about as adept at driving it as I had been the first time on that bicycle. This time I did not have my Dad puffing behind, hanging reassuringly onto the back of the seat. There were several false starts as I tried to remember what to do with a clutch, but finally I was hiccoughing out of the Mines' compound.

Heading down the road, watching the speedometer hit thirty miles an hour, I yelped with glee. This was it. I was going back, the last remaining poomui, the conquering heroine, returning to her mission to save the world (or at least a couple of patients). With four bars of Swiss chocolate, a jar of jam, a pound of cheese and a jigsaw puzzle given to me by the McGrane's seven-year-old, I was ready for anything.

Coming down the hill into Serabu, I had to turn on my lights as the skies were clogging up with black cloud. By the time I jumped out of the truck outside the convent, God was emptying buckets of water over the hospital compound.

My drumming fists on the convent doors blended with the hammering rain. Either Moses and family were out or they just couldn't hear me. I parked the truck in its shelter and stayed at the wheel, watching the rain splash into the dust and gradually dissolve it into puddles.

Forty minutes passed and nobody came to meet me. Admittedly they didn't know exactly what day I was coming, but I had still rather hoped for fanfares and fireworks. What I got instead was a cascade of water, rushing off the corrugated roof of the lean-to garage. Even the goats had taken shelter. Only the jungle grass was thriving, drinking up the rain and seeming to grow even higher before my very eyes. Panguma's neatly clipped lawns seemed a long way away.

My enthusiasm of the past few days washed away with the rain into the ditch outside Medical Ward.

"Well, Dr. Gail, you'll sit here forever if you wait for a lull in the rain." I threw open the truck door, jumped down into a puddle and heaved my rucksack on my back. The rain bounced off my glasses and my feet slid in their flip flops as water streamed over the parched ground that led to my house. The path was now lined with shoulder high grass that damply fingered my neck as I made my way home.

Home!

Why hadn't I flown home when I'd had the offer, the several offers, from the Field Director? I could have gone with Susan, or Tim, or Jean and Tom, or Fran. What had made me so keen to come back? To show off to Klaus, Fiona and Lindsey's granny? To prove that I was equal to Hillary's challenge? Why couldn't I make my mind up about anything? And Klaus had rejected me for being too sure of myself! Why had nobody come to meet me and tell me how marvellous I was for returning? Hmmph.

This was not the grand reopening I had imagined. Aw fo do. I sniffed, tears of self-pity starting to mingle with the raindrops on my face. What was I doing, trudging through an empty hospital after nine months in Sierra Leone? I had offered to take the baby, and now here it was screaming for food, needing new clothes and lots of love that I was just too tired to give.

Nine months in Africa. Hmmph. Surely I should now be a more rounded and mature person with a firm grasp on the meaning of life. No chance. Whims rather than morals had formed the basis of every decision I had made; *Tess of the d'Urbervilles* remained unfinished and I hadn't even lost weight!

Gail! Honestly! Never mind death, disease, malnutrition or civil war, all this silly spoilt Western woman was worrying about was that she get body. Come on! Yes, I was fat. Yes I get body! A big healthy body. Just what Salonean men liked. I started walking more quickly, squaring my shoulders against the rain, closing my eyes briefly to enjoy the cool water against my face. I had been in the perfect place all along, a place where the big strong girl was queen. Ha!

Suddenly I was outside my house, facing a bedraggled figure sitting on my doorstep. There was something moving by his side. A chicken! It was Pa George and Chicken Tikka! My reception party.

"Kushe! Kushe Pa George." I squealed with delight. He looked up.

"What for chop today?"

"Plassas."

I quite fancied a nice plate of plassas.

Epilogue

On 12th March 1994 the sisters and volunteers evacuated Panguma Hospital. Their Landrover was ambushed by rebels, who shot and killed Eelco, Karin, three year old Zita and Father Felim McAllister, an Irish priest who had worked at Panguma for twenty-five years. Dr. Anne Greening, Fiona's successor from New Zealand, survived, holding Eelco until he died. Her back broken, she was later rescued by soldiers and taken to Sister Hillary in Bo.

This book was written in their memory and for the people of Sierra Leone who are now in the midst of a full-blown civil war. The rebels burnt Serabu Hospital to the ground in 1995.

Charles Taylor is still in power in Liberia, supplying Foday Sankoh's rebels with ammunition to destroy and mutilate the local people of what was once a happy peaceful country.

The rebels attacked the Mines in 1995, capturing the Managing Director and six other expatriates, plus ten Salonean staff. They were held hostage for over three months, along with two VSO volunteers who had been kidnapped weeks earlier. Foday Sankoh thus put an end to the mining and fuelled his propaganda machine.

Robin Cook rewarded Mr. Sankoh's services to Sierra Leone following the 1999 Lome Peace Agreement - senior government minister responsible for mineral resources (ie: the gold and diamonds!)

Not surprisingly things got worse - more limbs were hacked off, and Liberia's diamond exports increased substantially, before Mr. Sankoh finally found his way into prison. The rebels may no longer have an effective leader, but they retain control of the diamonds.

12,000 UN peacekeepers remain in Salone, propped up by

800 British troops. Perhaps they have achieved some stability, for as this book goes to print, democratic elections are planned for 2001, the 40th Anniversary of Salonean independence.

Betty writes regularly and I know that she and her family are safe in Freetown, as are Tiange, Peter and Dauda. She tells me that people are gradually moving back to Serabu to rebuild their farms, but that Pa Kpukoma was killed and Sesay joined the rebels. I have no news of Pa George or my other Salonean friends.

On a happier note, I spent a further eventful eighteen months in Sierra Leone. I returned to York, became a fully-fledged GP and married a handsome man. Nat sang beautifully at our wedding. Klaus, Fiona, Lindsey and six other VSOs also celebrated our happy day. I am now the mother of two beautiful little boys.

Alan never became a priest, preferring to work with people rather than preach at them. He finished a theology and philosophy degree and now works with the homeless in Dublin.

Fiona married her childhood sweetheart, and is now a GP mum to a two year old girl that can count to ten in three languages and identify male and female chaffinches.

Klaus has built up a very successful motorcycle business in Fife (single women take note - a very eligible bachelor!)

Tom lives in an eco-house with his doctor wife in the middle of a remote forest in the States, whilst Jean and family went on to work in Namibia.

Fran did return to Sierra Leone, only to be pulled out six months later by the American Embassy during the coup of 1992. He now works as a real life George Clooney in a Virginia ER with Sharon and their young family.

Paul McGrane is growing grapes in France.

Sam and Fatoma were finally reunited, and are now married,

regardless of the opinion of any British High Commissioner.

Even Father Brendan got married.

And as for Sister Hillary, she left Sierra Leone in 1995 when all the sisters where pulled out, leaving no Holy Rosary sisters in Sierra Leone for the first time in 103 years. After 42 years in Sierra Leone she went to Cameroon to work in primary health, where she stayed for three years. She then returned to Ireland to 'make a nuisance of herself' with the Irish government, persuading them to adopt a more leniant approach to Salonean refugees and increase their aid donations. She has also written her own book on her years in Salone.

Despite the atrocities in Sierra Leone that I can scarcely bear to read about, my experiences have taught me to believe in the power of the human spirit, even in the most appalling circumstances. One day I shall return to Sierra Leone with my boys.

Highlights For 2001

Jasmine And Arnica

Author: Nicola Naylor

Editor: Hazel Orme

ISBN:1903070104

RRP:£16.99

With the benefit of hindsight any extreme venture can be classed as either lunacy or bravery. The idea of a blind woman travelling alone around India certainly fits into one or other of these categories.

As a child Nicola dreamed of a life of travel, a glittering career as a journalist, and the glamorous lifestyle of a foreign correspondent. She shone at school, excelled at university and after leaving the BBC to take up a place at Journalism College, was well on the way to realising her dream.

Less than a year into the course her world collapsed, a congenital illness had left her completely blind. She was institutionalised, forced into a mould, and churned back out into society complete with guide dog, housing and the weight of endless constraints imposed by her disability. The next seven years were spent fluctuating between anger and despair, as she came to terms with a lifetime of denial.

Massage and aromatherapy classes started as an excuse for getting out of the house and exercising her dog, but she recognised that it offered her real direction and set up her own soft tissue massage clinic. But despite professional success she was still trapped in a safe circumscribed world. She needed to break out, and in pursuit of an almost forgotten childhood dream – she made plans to travel alone around India under the guise of learning about essential oils and alternative healing.

'Jasmine And Arnica' chronicles the seminal journey that allowed Nicola to restart her life, rediscover her love of writing, and most importantly to push back the stifling restraints that had once threatened to suffocate her.

Nicola now lives in London where she runs a successful clinic and has just had a baby girl called Poppy.

Riding With Ghosts: South Of The Border

Author: Gwen Maka   ISBN: 1903070090

Editor: Gordon Medcalf   RRP: £7.99 $14.95

This is the second part of forty something Gwen Maka's epic trans-continental cycle ride. Her first book *Riding with Ghosts* covered the first 4,000 miles, from Seattle to Mexico. The second leg goes through Mexico to Central America – Guatemala, El Salvador, Honduras and Nicaragua – down to San Jose in Costa Rica, not far short of Panama.

Everyone she consulted, and most of those she met on the way, assured her that for a single cyclist, let alone a woman, this mission was absolutely impossible. But readers of Gwen's first book will know that impossible is not a word in her vocabulary.

Gwen's vivid account of her adventures reflects her Her intense feeling for nature and for history's magic – and tragic – traces brings both geography and history alive.

As she heads south, the ghosts of Custer and Geronimo begin to fade and are replaced by the shadowy figures of Columbus, Cortes and Montezuma, Pancho Villa and Zapata, and the adventurer William Walker, who gain colour and definition as they ride with her through this most vivid of regions.

Triumph Around The World

Author: Robbie Marshall   ISBN: 1903070082

Editor: Joss Guttery   RRP: £7.99 $14.95

At 45 Robbie Marshall had it all, or so it seemed. He'd been married, had two children, and built up a successful advertising agency.

So what on earth made him risk it all for a great British motorcycle and life on the road.

Over the course of this double or nothing adventure he would come face to face with his own ignorance, enormous danger and wracking lonliness hand in hand with some of the best that human nature has to offer. All this and more comes his way, in a bid for knowledge and exploration of our fantastic planet.

But what price did he pay for this freedom and did life on the road provide the longed for dividends?

Cry From The Highest Mountain

Author: Tess Burrows   ISBN: 1903070120

Editor: Joss Guttery   RRP: £7.99 $14.95

"This is an enthralling journey of courage and endurance"
Joanna Lumley

Their goal was to climb to the point furthest from the centre of the Earth some 2,150 meters higher than the summit of Everest.

Their mission was to promote Earth Peace by highlighting Tibet and His Holiness the Dalai Lama's ideals of peace, harmony and justice as an arrow of light for the new millennium.

But for Tess it became a struggle of body and mind as, in the ultimate act of symbolism, she was compelled to climb to the highest point within herself.

"I am pleased to offer my prayers to 'Climb For Tibet' and all that it touches"
His Holiness the Dalai Lama

Travellers Tales From Heaven and Hell ... Part 3

Author: Various   ISBN: 1903070112

Editor: Dan Hiscocks   RRP: £6.99

People are not automatons, 'should', 'must' and 'ought' have to be the most overused words in the modern vocabulary, and they have their place. But so do you- the individual.

You have the right to feel and experience highs and lows within your own social context - what you find hellish may be heavenly for somebody less privileged but that does not devalue the extent of your emotion in any way. Often, modern life does not give us the space to really feel - for many, travel provides this space and fufills a real need.

Heaven And Hell is a unique chance for you, to share your most outrageous, disastrous or fantastic travel moments with the rest of the world, for the winner there is a free flight to a destination of your choice into the bargain.

Already in your local bookshop

Jungle Janes
Author: Peter Burden

ISBN: 1903070058

RRP:£7.99

At a dinner party two bored army wives challenged
their host Major Ken Hames that anything he could
train men to do, they could do. In response he devised
an expedition for 12 middle aged women - A month
long trek through the Primary Malaysian jungle.

We go beyond the battles with scorpions, snakes,
spiders, giant hornets and further than the harrowing
12 hour treks to question whether the expedition was
simply a battle of the sexes, or did it turn into
something far more interesting?

Based on the documentary made by Anglia Television Ltd.

Travels With My Daughter
Author: Niema Ash

ISBN:190307004X

RRP:£7.99

"You could say I had an unconventional upbringing. At the age of four I
was sharing my bedroom with Bob Dylan, and by the time I was fifteen I
had been taken out of school to go travelling and was smoking joints with
my mother".

This honest and often humorous account describes
how Niema copes with:

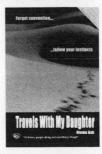

> The desire to travel conflicting with the ties of
> motherhood.
> Finding the confidence to believe in herself and
> her instincts.
> Being a single mum in the sixties while mixing
> with some of the most talented poets and
> musicians of our time, including Bob Dylan,
> Leonard Cohen, Irving Layton, Seamus Heaney and Joni Mitchell.
> Developing a unique mother and daughter bond which many only
> dream about.

This book will touch a hidden nerve in everyone who reads it as it turns a
world of convention and protocol upside-down!

Desert Governess

Author: Phyllis Ellis
Editor: Gordon Medcalf

ISBN: 1903070015
R.R.P: £7.99

In 1997 badly in need of a new start in life, Phyllis answered an advertisement: *English Governess wanted for Prince and Princesses of Saudi Arabian Royal Family.* She soon found herself whisked off to the desert to look after the children of HRH Prince Muqrin bin Abdul Aziz al Saud, the King's brother. In this frank personal memoir Phyllis describes her sometimes risky reactions to her secluded, alien lifestyle in a heavily guarded marble palace, allowed out only when chaperoned, veiled and clad from head to foot in black.

Both as a Governess and as a modern western woman she constantly ran up against frustrating prohibitions and unexpected moral codes, only a few of which she could work her way around – usually in the interests of her young royal charges.

Discovery Road

Authors: Tim Garratt & Andy Brown
Editor: Dan Hiscocks

ISBN: 0953057534
R.R.P: £7.99

Their mission and dream was to cycle around the southern hemisphere of the planet, with just two conditions. Firstly the journey must be completed within 12 months, and secondly, the cycling duo would have no support team or backup vehicle, just their determination, friendship and pedal power.

"Readers will surely find themselves reassessing their lives and be inspired to reach out and follow their own dreams."

Sir Ranulph Fiennes, Explorer

Fever Trees of Borneo

Author: Mark Eveleigh

Editor: Gordon Medcalf

ISBN: 095357569

R.R.P: £7.99

This is the story of how two Englishmen crossed the remotest heights of central Borneo, using trails no western eye had seen before, in search of the legendary 'Wild Men of Borneo'. On the way they encounter shipwreck, malaria, amoebic dysentery, near starvation, leeches, exhaustion, enforced alcohol abuse and barbecued mouse-deer foetus.

"Mark has the kind of itchy feet which will take more than a bucket of Johnson's baby talc to cure… he has not only stared death in the face, he has poked him in the ribs and insulted his mother."

Observer

Frigid Women

Authors: Sue & Victoria Riches

Editor: Gordon Medcalf

ISBN:0953057526

R.R.P:£7.99

In 1997 a group of twenty women set out to become the world's first all female expedition to the North Pole. Mother and daughter, Sue and Victoria Riches were amongst them. Follow the expedition's adventures in this true life epic of their struggle to reach one of Earth's most inhospitable places, suffering both physical and mental hardships in order to reach their goal, to make their dream come true.

"This story is a fantastic celebration of adventure, friendship, courage and love. Enjoy it all you would be adventurers and dream on."

Dawn French

Riding with Ghosts

Author: Gwen Maka

Editor: Gordon Medcalf

ISBN: 1903070007

R.R.P: £7.99

This is the frank, often outrageous account of a forty-something Englishwoman's epic 4,000 mile cycle ride from Seattle to Mexico, via the snow covered Rocky Mountains. She travels the length and breadth of the American West, mostly alone and camping in the wild. She runs appalling risks and copes in a gutsy, hilarious way with exhaustion, climatic extremes, dangerous animals, eccentrics, lechers and a permanently saddle-sore bum.

We share too her deep involvement with the West's pioneering past, and with the strong, often tragic traces history has left lingering on the land.

Slow Winter

Author: Alex Hickman

Editor: Gordon Medcalf

ISBN: 0953057585

R.R.P: £7.99

Haunted by his late father's thirst for adventure Alex persuaded his local paper that it needed a Balkan correspondent. Talking his way into besieged Sarajevo, he watched as the city's fragile cease fire fell apart. A series of chance encounters took him to Albania and a bizarre appointment to the government. Thrown into an alliance with the country's colourful dissident leader, he found himself occupying a ringside seat as corruption and scandal spilled the country into chaos.

This is a moving story of one man's search for his father's legacy among the mountains and ruin of Europe's oldest, and most mysterious corner.

The Jungle Beat – fighting terrorists in Malaya

Author: Roy Follows

Editor: Dan Hiscocks

ISBN: 0953057577

R.R.P: £7.99

This book describes, in his own words, the experiences of a British officer in the Malayan Police during the extended Emergency of the 1950's. It is the story of a ruthless battle for survival against an environment and an enemy which were equally deadly. It ranks with the toughest and grimmest of the latter-day SAS adventures.

" It tells the story with no holds barred: war as war is. A compelling reminder of deep jungle operations."

General Sir Peter de la Billière

Touching Tibet

Author: Niema Ash

Editor: Dan Hiscocks

ISBN:0953057550

R.R.P:£7.99

After the Chinese invasion of 1950, Tibet remained closed to travellers until 1984. When the borders were briefly re-opened, Niema Ash was one of the few people fortunate enough to visit the country before the Chinese re-imposed their restrictions in 1987. *Touching Tibet* is a vivid, compassionate, poignant but often amusing account of a little known ancient civilisation and a unique and threatened culture.

"Excellent - Niema Ash really understands the situation facing Tibet and conveys it with remarkable perception."

Tenzin Choegyal (brother of The Dalai Lama)

Tea for Two...with no cups

Author: Polly Benge

Editor: Dan Hiscocks

ISBN: 0953057593

R.R.P: £7.99

Four months before her 30th birthday Polly finds herself in a quandary. Fed up with dancing a swan or woodland nymph every night, failing to impress Barry Manilow with her singing abilities and falling in love with a New Zealander with a rapidly expiring visa, she needs to come up with some answers quickly. She decides the only way to do this is by embarking on a 'love test'. With a yet uncalloused bottom she joins Tim and Lee on a bicycle ride from Kathmandu to Assam in the hope of finding some answers.

"This colourful paperback is tailor made to give armchair adventurers hope. If Polly, who secretly packs her eye repair gel, can manage a few months on the road, so can anyone!"   On Your Bike Magazine

"infectious"   The Daily Telegraph

Heaven & Hell

An eclectic collection of anecdotal travel stories – the best from thousands of entries to an annual competition. See website for details.

"…an inspirational experience. I couldn't wait to leave the country and encounter the next inevitable disaster."   *The Independent*

Travellers' Tales from Heaven & Hell

Author: Various   ISBN: 0953057518
Editor: Dan Hiscocks   R.R.P: £6.99

More Travellers' Tales from Heaven & Hell

Author: Various   ISBN: 1903070023
Editor: Dan Hiscocks   R.R.P: £6.99

A Trail of Visions

Guide books tell you where to go, what to do and how to do it. A Trail of Visions shows and tells you how it feels.

"A Trail of Visions tells with clarity what it is like to follow a trail, both the places you see and the people you meet."

Independent on Sunday

"The illustrated guide."   The Times

Route 1: India, Sri Lanka, Thailand, Sumatra

Photographer / Author: Vicki Couchman
Editor: Dan Hiscocks ISBN: 1871349338
R.R.P: £14.99

Route 2: Peru, Bolivia, Ecuador, Columbia

Photographer / Author: Vicki Couchman
Editor: Dan Hiscocks ISBN: 093505750X
R.R.P: £16.99

TravellersEye Club Membership

Each month we receive hundreds of enquiries from people who've read our books or entered our competitions. All of these people have one thing in common: an aching to achieve something extraordinary, outside the bounds of our everyday lives. Not everyone can undertake the more extreme challenges, but we all value learning about other people's experiences.

Membership is free because we want to unite people of similar interests. Via our website, members will be able to liase with each other about everything from the kit they've taken, to the places they've been to and the things they've done. Our authors will also be available to answer any of your questions if you're planning a trip or if you simply have a question about their books.

As well as regularly up-dating members with news about our forth-coming titles, we will also offer you the following benefits:

Free entry to author talks / signings
Direct author correspondence
Discounts off new and past titles
Free entry to TravellersEye events
Discounts on a variety of travel products and services

To register your membership, simply write or email us telling us your name and address (postal and email). See address at the front of this book.

About TravellersEye

I believe the more you put into life, the more you get out of it. However, at times I have been disillusioned and felt like giving up on a goal because I have been made to feel that an ordinary person like me could never achieve my dreams.

The world is absolutely huge and out there for the taking. There has never been more opportunity for people like you and me to have dreams and fulfil them.

I have met many people who have achieved extraordinary things and these people have helped inspire and motivate me to try and live my life to the fullest.

TravellersEye publishes books about people who have done just this and we hope that their stories will encourage other people to live their dream.

When setting up TravellersEye I was given two pieces of advice. The first was that there are only two things I ever need to know: You are never going to know everything and neither is anyone else. The second was that there are only two things I ever need to do in life: Never give up and don't forget rule one.

Nelson Mandela said in his presidential acceptance speech: "Our deepest fear is not that we are inadequate. Our deepest fear is that we are powerful beyond our measure... as we let our own light shine, we unconsciously give other people permission to do the same."

We want people to shine their light and share it with others in the hope that it may encourage them to do the same.

Dan Hiscocks
Managing Director of TravellersEye